An
INSPECTOR
calls

D1421943

An INSPECTOR calls

Ofsted and its effect on school standards

EDITED BY
Cedric Cullingford

KOGAN PAGE

First published in 1999

Kogan Page Limited
120 Pentonville Road
London N1 9JN

British Library Cataloguing in Publication Data

A CIP record for this book is available from the British Library.

ISBN 0 7494 3053 2

Typeset by Jean Cussons Typesetting, Diss, Norfolk
Printed and bound by Clays Ltd, St Ives plc

Contents

List of Contributors

Robin Alexander is Professor of Education and Director of the Centre for Research in Elementary and Primary Education at the University of Warwick.

Dr Pat Broadhead is Professor of Education at the University of York.

Dr Pat Cuckle is Senior Researcher at the School of Education, University of Leeds.

Cedric Cullingford is Professor of Education at the University of Huddersfield.

Dr Sandra Daniels is a senior lecturer in the Department of Mathematics and Computing at the University of Huddersfield.

Dr Derek Glover has been Research Fellow at Keele and Nottingham Trent Universities.

Dr Carol Taylor Fitz-Gibbon is Professor of Education at the University of Durham and Director of the Curriculum, Evaluation and Management Centre.

Dr Vivienne Griffiths is Director of PGCE at the University of Sussex Institute of Education.

Dr Angela Jacklin is Primary PGCE Co-ordinator at the University of Sussex Institute of Education.

W Norton Grubb holds the David Gardner Chair in Higher Education at the University of California, Berkeley.

David Hustler is Professor of Education at Manchester Metropolitan University.

Maurice Kogan is Professor Emeritus of Government and Director of the Centre for the Evaluation of Public Policy and Practice, Brunel University.

Sue Law is Professor of Education at the Nottingham Trent University.

Margaret Maden is Professor of Education at Keele University.

Nicola J Stephenson-Forster is the Research Associate leading the MidYIS team at the Curriculum, Evaluation and Management Centre, University of Durham.

Dr Gerran Thomas is in the Department of Education at the University of Wales, Aberysthwyth.

Sir David Winkley was formerly Head of the Grove School and is the founder of the National Primary Centre.

List of Tables

List of Figures

Preface

The Office for Standards in Education, always known as Ofsted, has continually attracted controversy, ever since it replaced earlier agencies of inspection. Its role and particularly that of the Chief Inspector has been kept in the public eye continually and assiduously by the mass media. There are those who conclude that Ofsted has actively sought publicity by fostering controversies.

This book is not about the media attention or the personality aspects of Ofsted. It is about the effects of inspection in schools, on the people in them and on standards. Long after the controversies have faded away the material in this book will remain valuable. When the opinions of select committees and unions are forgotten the evidence that this book presents will be salient, because the underlying issues of accountability and control will always be with us.

The strength of the contributions in this book is that they are empirical. Every effort has been made to get at the facts, as neutrally as possible. Whatever the personal conclusion drawn, or whatever distaste one might feel about the conduct of the inspections regime, the concern is to present objective evidence. The approach taken is to make as fair a summary as possible about all aspects of inspection. While some of the impacts on Ofsted are very personal and emotional, inspection is also judged in its own terms, by whether there is evidence of raising standards. While the chapters vary in stance they are all centred on the need to present data that is valid and reliable, whether through case studies, through qualitative analysis or through quantitative research.

Despite all the publicity surrounding Ofsted, I was surprised at the amount of empirical work that has been taking place on the whole subject of inspection. I am grateful to the contributors for producing material that raises many questions about the culture of education, the status and professionalism in teachers and the impact of inspection on pupils. I am also grateful to Mary Russell and Sue Smith for their help.

Introduction: some issues of inspection

Cedric Cullingford

The inspection of schools and other agencies seems like a fairly recent phenomenon, but the issues that it addresses are ancient. They are matters of power and control, of personal and public accountability. They invoke complex questions about the nature of evidence, and the effects of change. There have always been questions about judgements, the significance of ancedote and personal opinion, and the effects of these on other people. Judgements are always made, privately if not always publicly. What is relatively recent is not only the ever-growing manifestation of inspection, as demonstrated in so many more public 'watchdogs', nor the rise of state education and other systems, but the separation of the public from the private (Elias, 1978). The concept of 'accountability' raises all kinds of questions.

The context of the most recent developments in public inspections is, therefore, very important. The systems and the way they operate can be too easily taken for granted, and the bureaucracies of inspection, growing even faster than Parkinson's Law could envisage, can too easily be accepted as opportunities to carve out lucrative careers. While no one would question the need for some kind of accountability, it should be noted that it takes many forms and has many kinds of side effects. It is linked, as studies of other public systems like the National Health Service (NHS) demonstrate, to notions of managerialism and outcomes of the type that can easily be measured.

In the judgements made about the performance of schools, about which are 'good' and which 'bad' there have always been political manipulations (Silver, 1994). This is inevitable since what is being observed is so complex that there is bound to be an element of choice in what is seen as significant. Inspection itself is not such a new concept. Her Majesty's Inspectors (HMIs) had a right to enter schools and report on what they found. What is new is the use of inspection as a public and official exposure of any failing; failing, that is, against those criteria that are laid down by the inspectors. As we will see throughout the book, the views about values, about what really matters and what is successful could not be more varied.

The key word that encapsulates the official view of the education system, and the need for the present system of inspection is the government's mantra about 'targets'. All inspection systems, from the anecdotal to those, as in the former East Germany, which involve a significant percentage of the whole population, depend on knowing what evidence is being sought. The larger and more inclusive the system the more control is exerted on what people must demonstrate in order to be successful, or survive. One of the most characteristic features of the present inspection regime is the attempt to match what is observed against clear externally agreed criteria. The targets are 'closed', in so far as there should be no subjective judgement made in seeing if they are met. What counts is what is observable. There are questions to be asked both about whether such objectivity is possible and about whether what can be measured in that kind of way is worth measuring. The intention, however, is clear.

While the particular stress on 'targets' is comparatively new, it arises from a growing concern with the measurement of 'competencies' (Mackenzie, Mitchell and Oliver, 1995). Control always depends on being able to observe. The holy grail of all inspection is a check–list that provides clear answers; has something been achieved or not? Thus actions are easier to measure than understandings, demonstrating the ability to remember a fact easier to measure than thinking skills (Quinn, 1997). Competencies become the more important for lending themselves to measurement. This can have inadvertent results. One is that those higher–order abilities that are traditionally treasured are no longer deemed important, since nothing that cannot be measured easily can be taken into account. Another is that if people are asked to set targets that cannot be demonstrated there will be a tendency to create targets that will guarantee success. In several interesting examples in the United States, the stress on the importance of meeting targets was such that the targets kept being lowered, until standards were falling so rapidly that what had seemed such a good idea in promoting standards through accountability was quickly abandoned (Vold and Homisham, 1989). We await to see what happens here.

The setting of targets and the measurement of competencies are the direct results of external controls. Power lies not in the hands of those who are delivering the education system but in the inspectors. The political beliefs which promote inspection rest on the assumption that external forces can make real differences, that external political will is all that matters. This is in itself a notion that has been tested all over the world at various times (Dalin *et al*, 1994). In many countries, especially developing ones, the drive to raise standards has been seen as an absolute necessity. The will-power is strong. But the research results have also been strong, and consistent. There are certain factors which raise standards and others which do not. One, to which we will return, is the relationship between simple mechanistic means and the acceptance of complexity. But to summarize the others, those factors that impede improvement are constant outside interference, and detailed external control and inspection. Factors which help improve standards include teachers' feelings of ownership and responsibility over change, and the sense of the school as a centre of change, changes which happen over time rather than at once.

These are the conclusions of a series of research studies. The problem with research is not so much the research itself but the way it will be used, or ignored. The relationship of research to policy is always an interesting question. There are many examples of research evidence that are valid and reliable, and universally agreed and verified but are then countermanded by policy. There are also many examples of policy decisions being taken based on no evidence or poor evidence. While this is not the place to give examples, the question of evidence in relation to policy decisions must constantly be raised in terms of Ofsted inspections. There is a tendency to dismiss any negative findings as biased or defensive. The reason that such dismissals are not questioned points to some deeply entrenched political stances about education, and the education system, as well as an antipathy to evidence itself.

One motivation among many for dismissing evidence is the fear of what is complex. To make changes is always a political motivation, if one can be held personally responsible for it, providing it is successful. Real effects are, on the other hand, far more complex. This can be said of the whole 'industry' that surrounds school effectiveness. The motivation is to find out how to raise standards, how to find what works in *all* schools, and how such measures can be uniformly imposed. The problem is that while there is general agreement about what factors make a difference (Rutter *et al*, 1979; Mortimore *et al*, 1988) these appear to be rather more complicated than external measures would desire. The personality of the head-teacher in relation to others, the ethos of the school, the motivations of staff, and the belief in the possibilities of students, are all too lubricious concepts in the minds of the inspectors. The result is that the real functions of the school are reduced to what, in the minds of inspectors, seems like a measurable quantity: the performance of the staff. The irony is that the recognition of the significance of persons makes them the targets themselves.

When one looks at the systems of inspection and the motivations of inspection, it is clear that it is not the pupils who are being inspected but the teachers. The pupils count in so far as they are the 'products'. But the standard assessment tests (SATs) are measures of the efficiency of the system. Inspections are based on what is observable. What goes on inside the pupils' heads, and what happens to them in their own lives, is irrelevant. What is observable is supposed to be what is measured.

Ofsted inspections attempt to be as objective as possible. But even they have untoward or unexpected consequences. Before we approach their affects on teachers and pupils, let us consider their effects on schools. The impending inspection, or the notice of an inspection, has in itself an effect on schools. The head-teacher who is trying to make changes can use an Ofsted inspection as an excuse to implement new policies. Those who feel weak might find the additional burden too much to bear, even before it is imposed. The whole teaching strategy might change because of the need for documentation. One cynical researcher suggested that Ofsted should be more like the TV detector vans; the very threat of its presence is supposed to make a difference.

If there are inadvertent effects of Ofsted inspections, they are not easily measured in Ofsted's own terms. All who observe what goes on in schools before, during and after inspections have tales to tell. These are easily dismissed as anecdotes, but how many separate cases are needed to accumulate valid evidence? There are many instances of the reactions of teachers to inspections that suggest some grave doubts. Let us take but three examples.

Example 1

In this first example the small rural school has a new head who finds things difficult. The Ofsted inspectors point this out and put the school on special measures. Some parents withdraw their pupils as the local authority appears not to be acting. The school is then closed; which was not the original intention.

Example 2

Or, from a distinguished secondary school: the Ofsted inspection of the school, in terms of pupil achievement and school performance was an absolute 'disaster'.

Example 3

And from a primary school: 'a flawed process carried out by a blinkered team'.

There are many more such examples in this book but the question that is raised here is the extent to which they are allowable as evidence? What are the real effects of Ofsted on schools, laying aside for one moment its own terms of reference? What are the inadvertent consequences of such a policy? Are the rising numbers of truancies and exclusions pure coincidence?

One effect of Ofsted inspections is well documented, and probably endorsed by the organization itself. That is on the stress levels of teachers. We are constantly confronted by phrases such as 'stressful and punitive'. The policing of 'naming and shaming' is deliberate. As one anonymous person put it – 'A few deaths are a price well worth paying'. There are many questions about the ethics of such a policy, let alone its efficiency. But even without such extreme outcomes the language used to describe the experience of Ofsted inspections is consistent and telling: 'confusion, anomie, anxiety, dehumanisation, weakened commitment, loss of values' (Jeffrey and Woods, 1996).

That the emotional effects are strong, that there are elements of fear and that the impending inspection takes up all the attention, is clear. The question remains whether this is a necessary, if unfortunate, side-effect to the raising of standards, or whether this is, in fact, a sign of a system malfunctioning.

The purpose of inspection is to be able to measure, against set criteria, the exact levels of performance. The more simple the formulae, indeed the more simply quantifiable, the better. This raises, of course, the question of different perceptions of education. The sense of a holistic, humanistic vision of teachers is set against a technocratic approach. In several chapters in the book these conflicts of value, and the question of whether what happens in the educational process can be summed up by numbers, make their appearance. These are the signs of clashes of culture.

We are concerned with empirical evidence. The question remains what that evidence consists of; that which can be scientifically quantified, which means having to manipulate complex data, or that which is more long term, more difficult to measure and sometimes inadvertent. This is not the type of evidence with which Ofsted is now concerned. But let us be eccentric. Let us take the pupils into account. They are after all the ostensible if not the actual reason for inspections. What do they make of all these inspections? What effects do the latter have on their own performances? This is one territory that is rarely explored.

To find out about the effects of inspection on pupils is difficult since they make assumptions about and react to the school system as a whole. Their awareness of the context of the school in the inspection system of clear. They detect teachers changing behaviour and they realize the constraints teachers are under. There are, however, two side-effects which are cause for concern. One is the ever-increasing pressure on them to do well at exams and tests. The emphasis on getting good grades is not, of course, new but the awareness of the pressure, and the consequent rejection of such pressure by some, is growing (Cullingford, 1997). More worrying still is the evidence that is starting to emerge for the reasons for disaffection with school. In a survey of secondary schools a series of interviews were carried out with those approaching GCSEs, prompted by evidence of a lack of motivation. What appears to be emerging is that this lack of application is not because the teachers are not cajoling and urging on their students. On the contrary, the evidence is consistent. The teachers are 'hammering home' the need to work hard and do well. But the pupils are dismissing this not as a sign of the teachers' interest in them but as a fear of being inspected and not coming up with the right results. Pupils suspect the motivation of teachers who are dominated by personal fear and, therefore, pure self-interest. Ofsted inspections might not only deprofessionalize teachers but undermine the pupils' confidence in them.

After all, seeing teachers lose their nerve, play safe, change standards, and certainly in some way change their attitude and behaviour is bound to be detected by pupils. They cannot remain unaware of what goes on in schools, and even if they are not taken into the confidence of the system, they observe it closely (Cullingford, 1991). The effects of what they see are difficult to measure but it should be acknowledged that what teachers feel and think are a matter of close scrutiny. Ofsted inspectors could argue that what pupils detect is the fault of the teachers, but it should at least be allowed that the constraints on the professionalism of teachers could be inhibited by inspection.

Parents also question some of the new 'values' in the education system (Cullingford, 1996). They witness the change on teachers and they see the passing on of anxiety to their children. Again, these consequences might be deemed to be just and necessary outcomes of a greater measure of accountability and control. After all. these expressions of the imposition of standards are carried out partly in the name of the parents themselves, to make sure that their children are performing adequately in competition with others, as well as the education system competing successfully against other nations.

One fact must be accepted, and that is that in any system that employs thousands of people there is no act, or inspection, or policy, that can have exactly the outcome that is desired, either instantly or in the long term. This is a source of despair for some, and a source of comfort to others. All would agree that the intention of any system should be to improve standards. That much is easy, until you define a 'standard', let alone what 'improvement' consists of. Those who are engaged in empirical research, in observing how society operates, have every sympathy with the frustration of those who want to make things happen instantly. Unfortunately, the understanding is not reciprocated. What, therefore, actually happens remains often uninformed by thought, or evidence.

Those who are caught up in a system of forcing change, of making things happen, have a clear idea that there are measures that can be isolated. One sense of an isolated measure is that of the school as if all that happened within its walls were unaffected by the outside world. The fact that, as these chapters demonstrate, there is a relationship between the performance of schools, the Ofsted inspections and their socio-economic circumstances is something that inspectors find too uncomfortable to deal with. The correlation does not fit into the inspection system. It also challenges deeper issues. As one unpublished survey concluded, 'disparities in achievements are shown to relate to socio-economic factors, clearly indicating that deprivation plays a major role in determining results'.

Can inspections change society as well as record what is happening? The emphasis of the system is that it should.

There are many questions that underlie some of the more public and superficial examinations of the inspection system but Ofsted does declare that its inspections raise standards. The purpose of the book is not only to raise the types of issue briefly mentioned here but to look at the process in its own terms. Forgetting all the other measures, does Ofsted work within its own remit? The research that is reported here is as neutral and objective as possible. To repeat the preface we are after the empirical, as a matter of faith, whatever the outcomes. If the conclusion is reached that Ofsted inspections raise standards that is heartily to be welcomed for that would justify what we are doing to our children and future generations and would suggest the best ways forward in developing educational services. Let us see what the evidence is.

REFERENCES

Cullingford, C (1991) *The Inner World on the School*, Cassell, London.

Cullingford, C (1996) *Parents, Education and the State*, Ashgate, Aldershot.

Cullingford, C (1997) *Assessment versus Evaluation*, Cassell, London.

Dalin, P, Ayono, T, Blazen, A, Didava, D, Jahon, M, Matthew, B, Rojas, M and Rojas, C. (1994) *How Schools Improve: An International Report*, Cassell, London.

Elias, N (1978) *The Civilizing Process*, Vol 1: *State Formation and Civilization*, Blackwell, Oxford.

Elias, N (1982) *The History of Manners: State Formation and Civilization*, Vol 2, Blackwell, Oxford.

Jeffrey, B and Woods, P (1996) Feeling deprofessionalized: the social construction of emotions during an Ofsted inspection, *Cambridge Journal of Education*, **26**, pp 325–43.

Mackenzie, P, Mitchell, P and Oliver, P (eds) (1995) *Competence and Accountability in Education*, Ashgate, Aldershot.

Mortimore, P, Sommons, P, Stoll, L, Lewis, D and Ecob, R (1988) *School Matters: The Junior Years*, Open Books, London.

Quinn, V (1997) *Critical Thinking in Young Minds*, David Fulton, London.

Rutter, M, Maugham, B, Mortimore, P and Ouston, J (1979) *Fifteen Thousand Hours*, Open Books, London.

Silver, H (1994) *Good Schools, Effective Schools: Judgements and their Histories*, Cassell, London.

Vold, E and Nomisham, D (1989) Teacher appraisal, in *The Primary Teacher*, Cullingford, C (ed), Cassell, London.

Chapter One

*An evaluation of evaluators: the Ofsted system of school inspection

Maurice Kogan and Margaret Maden

ORIGINS AND STATUS OF THE RESEARCH

Our evaluation of Ofsted was undertaken with the aid of a grant from the Joseph Rowntree Charitable Trust made to the Office for Standards in Inspection (Ofstin) for an independent review of the Office for Standards in Education (Ofsted) system of school inspection. On the face of it, this might have placed our project straight into the category of adversarial evaluation. But we concluded it within the ethic and methods of quite traditional academic research, and it is for others to consider how far our findings were affected by our own policy preferences. We were in any case required by our terms of reference to make recommendations, supported by the findings of the study.

The research design consisted of a literature search of primary and secondary sources; questionnaires to samples of schools; case studies conducted largely through interviews in schools; national level interviews with teacher, subject, local authority, governor, parent and inspector associations; and financial analyses.

---

*   This chapter is almost wholly based *The Ofsted System of School Inspection. An Independent Evaluation.* Published by the Centre for the Evaluation of Public Policy and Practice, Brunel University (from which available) and Helix Consulting Group, January 1999. The study was directed by Sandra Jones and the team consisted of Valerie Beale, Maurice Kogan and Margaret Maden.

SALIENCE OF THE ISSUES ARISING FROM OFSTED

The activities and impact of Ofsted are a matter of high public interest. An index of this is the multiple references either to Ofsted or to Her Majesty's Chief Inspector (HMCI) in the *Times Educational Supplement*. This is no doubt generated by the anxiety felt by the public at large on the question of standards achieved in schools, the prominence given to education and its standards by political leadership of both recent governments, and a vigorous policy of publication and publicity by Ofsted itself, including the particular stances taken by the HMCI on key educational issues of the day.

Ofsted dominates the thinking of most of those whom we have encountered in the schools, local authorities and professional associations. In this respect, both Ofsted and the political initiatives underpinning it have been highly successful although we critically examine the Ofsted claim that it will secure the improvement of schools through inspection.

Ofsted's significance extends beyond education. It is a prime, if extreme, example of the way in which the post-welfare state regulates its relations with the key professions, and with client groups. Its prominence could be described in terms of the ending of the corporatist bargain with a public profession in which the State conferred resources, trust and legitimacy on practitioners and institutions to work with their clients in an altruistic and expert manner. Instead, the substantive content of education and the ways in which it is mediated to its client groups are regulated by state prescription through the national curriculum and other mandatory devices, and enforced to a large extent by inspection.

The importance of Ofsted should also be construed in terms of the total range of evaluative activities which schools now encounter. District auditors, the Audit Commission, local education authorities and the Health and Safety Executive are among those who have the duty to form judgements on different aspects of school performance. Ofsted is part of a system that has grown up to investigate performance in the interest of explicit public policies.

THE POLICY CONTEXT IN ENGLAND

Inspection is a tool of Government and management, and its nature is affected by the policies that it is meant to advance and reinforce. The wide changes in the public services have been identified as constituting new public management (Pollitt, 1993) in which several elements comprise a shopping basket for those who wish to modernize the public sectors of Western industrialized societies. They include cost cutting, disaggregating traditional bureaucratic organizations into separate agencies; separating the purchaser and provider functions; introduction of market and quasi-market mechanisms; requiring staff to work to performance targets, indicators and output objectives; performance related pay (PRP); and emphasis on service quality, standard setting and customer responsiveness.

A subset of changes has been called 'the rise of the evaluative state' (Neave, 1988; Henkel 1991a). This has involved the replacement or, as in the case of education, the strengthening of central controls by evaluation systems which go alongside the *ex ante* avocation of objectives, targets and plans in place of the *ex post* self-evaluation administered by the professional leadership of the service.

Some of these changes fit what has affected education and other public services. In education it is central government above all that has taken on the task of inferring consumer wishes and installing them in its own policies. On the face of it the creation of a national inspectorate with unprecedented powers to evaluate all aspects of education runs counter to the declared intention to release energies by decentralization. In other European countries the starting points have been different from those in the United Kingdom; there have been moves away from old-fashioned prescription towards varying degrees of self-evaluation or freedom but with outcome measurements.

Now, however, England stands out as *sui generis* in its modes and objectives of school inspection. The degree of externality, prestructuring of criteria and power of the system are in accord with successive governments' declared intentions to raise educational standards and to extirpate those elements of the system that are identified as falling below nationally determined norms. The schools are thus evaluated through the agency of an institution of unprecedented power and resources, and on the basis of explicit assumptions of what constitutes school effectiveness and what will cause improvement. We next briefly discuss models of effectiveness within which we can locate Ofsted's assumptions.

THE RANGE OF MODELS OF SCHOOL EFFECTIVENESS AND IMPROVEMENT

It has been observed that 'in many ways our knowledge of what makes a good school greatly exceeds our knowledge of how to apply that knowledge in programmes of school improvement'. Increasingly, sophisticated and large amounts of school effectiveness research (especially in Europe, North America and Australia) do not appear to have been successfully transferred to the everyday business of how to make schools better, from whatever base or condition. Additionally Reynolds and Stoll (1996) observe that 'school improvement scholars rarely base their school improvement strategies upon the knowledge of school effectiveness researchers' ... there are 'two very distinctive intellectual traditions and histories'.

It is against this indeterminacy of knowledge that we have to place Ofsted's apparent certainties.

Some of the factors likely to impair the transfer of school effectiveness research findings to school improvement practice are the relatively static 'snapshot' nature of researchers' accounts and analyses of schools which often fail to include or express the dynamic nature of school change processes. There is also a frequent lack of school context, especially the organizational system of which the school is a component and from which exogenous support and/or constraints may operate. Additionally, there is often a failure to identify either priorities and sequences, or cause and effect, amongst the factors and characteristics associated with effective schools and there is a relative lack of significant-in-school variations such as sub-systems (eg, departments/subjects), classroom and teacher differences and the school's history and culture.

The extent to which such variables and dynamics are fully considered in the Ofsted four-yearly cycle of inspection is at least debatable, as is its effectiveness as one among several mechanisms established by Government to secure school improvement. Such mechanisms include an underlying assumption that competition between schools in an education marketplace will contribute to an overall raising of standards and that more information about schools (league tables and Ofsted inspection reports) will not simply increase the public accountability of schools but will also galvanize them into behaving in ways which bring about faster, more prescribed and standardized forms of improvement. Government legislated in these ways not because of school effectiveness research; instead, the rhetoric was primarily about the benefits of choice and competition in solving the alleged or actual shortcomings of state schools.

The evidence implies that an understanding of the dynamics of school effectiveness is not the only important base upon which educational policy can be built if the ultimate objective is to improve pupils' achievements. Speaking on behalf of the school effectiveness research community, David Reynolds (1998) has recently observed that 'we have been instrumental in creating a quite widespread popular view that schools do not just make a difference but that they make *all* the difference. This is wrong'.

The focal point of a substantial field of research is the child's achievement rather than that of the school. Accordingly these analyses identify those factors which need to be evaluated alongside and in relation to 'school effect'. These include school system and structure issues, as in Goldstein and Sammons' (1997) research on the 'value-added' effect of primary school on a child's GCSE results and Goldstein's analysis of the significant effects on academic performance of the number of primary schools a child attends. In a related field of investigation are the Scottish studies of how a non-selective system and the social composition of schools make a difference to pupil attainment levels.

More recent Scottish work has linked the raising of pupils' achievement over the past three decades less to school effectiveness (and, therefore, differences between schools) than to larger structural issues. It is suggested that the five major contributory factors to better educational outcomes are:

1. the second generation effect of better educated parents (referred to as 'rising educational capital');
2. comprehensive secondary education (allowing the tapping into educational talent previously excluded from a full range of opportunities);
3. demographic decline of socially disadvantaged groups;
4. successful demonstration that educational demand can be stimulated via appropriate policy drives;
5. curricular reforms and assessment systems.

These findings are a salutory reminder that understanding the dynamics of school effectiveness is not the only important base upon which educational policy can be built if the ultimate objective is to improve pupils' achievements.

In the Netherlands, school effectiveness research has distinguished itself by being 'bottom up' and especially concerned with classroom practice and conditions. In this sense, the English and US tradition has been more 'whole school' and, perhaps, more managerialist. The latter emphasis is reflected in Ofsted's (1995) *Framework for the Inspection of Schools,* with a rather reductionist approach to related lines of enquiry, which stress the importance of a collegial ethos in schools or concepts such as the 'intelligent school' and 'goodness' in relation to school characteristics.

Among the effectiveness is Michael Fullan's (1992) in Ontario, especially in relation to the Halton School improvement project, which emphasizes the central place of the teacher in any improvement project. Teacher rather than school is his critical focus: 'change efforts have to have a focus and, above all, must have meaning for teachers, as it is they who have the chief responsibility to implement changes and make them work'.

MacBeath *et al*'s (1996) work demonstrates a distinctive Scottish approach to school improvement which is reflected in the policies of the Scottish Office Education and Industry Department (SOEID). The emphasis placed on a school self-review process is known as the SOEID 'How Good is our School?' procedure. This includes peer review as well as external monitoring elements, and builds on and articulates those research findings which focus on teachers and classrooms and on the need to enlist teachers' commitment and trust.

A related issue on the improvement side of the school effectiveness improvement nexus is the relative rarity of structural reform as a means of bringing about better student outcomes. In an unpublished Ofsted report on three quite different school improvement programmes in the United States, the two most effective appeared to be those which were holistic and integrated at a systems level, rather than exclusively – or mainly – school-centred. Thus the 'naming and shaming' (of failing schools and teachers) strategy in New York City appeared to make things worse rather than better.

However, the Kentucky State reforms highlighted the need for peda-gogic change in schools, but also ensured that other infrastructure reforms were instituted. Schools and teachers were supported by massively improved professional development programmes and by social projects, including a multi-agency *Barriers to Learning* strategy aimed at tackling rural poverty, adult illiteracy, ill-health and poor housing. The need for out-of-school youth projects, through which drug and alcohol abuse programmes and supplementary educational opportunities are provided, has also been acted on. New curricular entitlements and structured assessment systems have been developed, with teachers properly involved and trained. Maximum class sizes and a minimum 15 per cent increase in teachers' salaries were introduced, conditionally on school level improvements.

This reform package was enacted in 1990, initially as a six-year programme, but intended as a 20-year strategy. Early results include significant improvement in high school graduation rates and reading scores among younger pupils. Perhaps as – or more – important is the independent evaluation which notes the 'changing and more positive culture, attitudes and assumptions within the Kentucky schools visited'. Also, a widespread acknowledgement that 'school improvement is long term and demands continuous effort'.

Thus the range of school effectiveness research and school improvement strategies is considerably broader than the Ofsted inspection system either encompasses or seeks to represent. Ofsted is a key player in the reforms introduced in England since 1988 and its role and contribution to rising standards of pupil achievement need to be placed and evaluated in this wider context.

We now turn to the ways in which different forms of inspection are directed to achieving improvement and accountability.

THE RANGE OF INSPECTORATES

Inspectorates both within education and in the whole range of public services have varied both over time and among themselves. In England and Wales, HM Inspectorate (HMI) until 1898 acted as stern enforcer of the system of payment by results, introduced by Lingen in 1862, whereby a proportion of teachers salaries depended on the results of an annual examination of pupils held by them. From then on, the system became increasingly permissive and although some elements of enforcement remained in HMI's role, for example, their recommendations could lead to the deregistration of independent schools, they inspected schools largely on intuitive and connoisseurial criteria and regarded themselves mostly as professional colleagues whose role was to advise local authorities, teachers and schools rather than enforce national standards.

Within government, inspectorates vary in power and function. The Social Services Inspectorate has moved in much the same way as HMI from a largely colleague advisory body to one brought in to identify default. HM Inspectorate of Constabulary has the duty to certify to the competence of police forces and central grants may depend on their certification, as is also the case with the Fire Service Inspectorate. Other kinds of inspectorates are represented by the Health and Safety Executive and the Factory Inspectorate which have powers and duties to enforce statutory requirements.

The local authority inspectorate and advisory services share some of the ambiguity implicit in the former role of HMI. In local education authorities (LEAs) there have been both adviser and advisory teacher services but often the two roles are combined in one when the task is to help the schools meet educational problems and advance their own development. At the same time, however, the inspectors or advisers (in the past, the term has been used indiscriminately) may also exercise a quasi-managerial role and form judgements on the performance and needs of schools. Some inspectorates have had a decisive voice in the appointment and promotion of teachers. Since the creation of Ofsted, many local authority inspectors, but not all, have moved from the classic inspectorial role, which is to form judgements for the purposes of control or management, and into an advisory role where schools, so far from having to receive their services, may have the freedom to buy or not to buy them.

There is, therefore, a wide range of authority exercised by inspectorial and advisory services. Ofsted and the general trend of national legislation have clarified the difference between a national inspectorate armed with strong powers to inspect on the basis of nationally determined criteria and deliver judgements that have explicit and sometimes drastic consequences, and local advisory services which now operate on the basis of a mix of statutory and discretionary functions. The latter, under 'fair funding' arrangements, include advisory and consultancy services which schools may purchase, while the former are expressed in the LEA's Education Development Plan (EDP) which is primarily concerned with school improvement and which has to be approved by the Department for

Education and Employment's (DfEE's) Standards and Effectiveness Unit (SEU).

The role of inspectorates must also be considered alongside the changing fortunes of evaluation in general in education. In the 1970s, the first attempts at systematic evaluation were undertaken by the creation of the Assessment of Performance Unit and the assumption that national standards would be identified by the light sampling of schools. Some authorities, for example, the Inner London Education Authority, introduced schemes of systematic self-evaluation for schools which would serve as the prime data upon which local evaluation would be based. Currently, ministers seem to be moving towards acknowledging that a marriage between self-evaluation and external inspection will be desirable.

Some consideration is being given by the main professional associations to alternatives to a national system of inspection, acting on national criteria, and leading to definite consequences for schools and teachers. If Ofsted inspection has enabled the system to make judgements about the standards reached, then it could be justifiably argued that there should be separate exercises by a national body conducting statistical samples which will be capable of producing authoritative aggregates of school improvement data. Some authorities have used the judgements made by Ofsted as part of the system in which local authorities can offer advice on development. And some of the national teacher and local authority associations would, instead of Ofsted, promote a system based on self-evaluation but externally moderated by a national inspectorate.

Within this range of inspectorates, the position held by Ofsted is clear. It is a statutorily based inspection system, creating its own criteria and procedures, all related to the objectives of public policy set down by the ministers and incorporated in legislation, making summative judgements on the performance of teachers and schools, and capable of prescribing the consequences of poor performance. It has the authority to make judgements that affect the future of schools and teachers, and to punish or reward through the publication of reports. In reaching judgements, which may be based upon professional knowledge, it does not take in the judgements of other professionals such as would be provided by self-evaluation.

Key findings

Our key findings were in three parts:

1. the accounts given by schools of how they experienced the Ofsted inspection process, the outcomes and impact of inspection (both imputed and ascribed by the key players in schools);

2. the reflections and evaluations of the Ofsted system by schools some time after the event;
3. the costs of the Ofsted system at national, LEA and school level.

At the outset it is important to note that none of the head-teachers, teachers and governors or national representatives interviewed (or surveyed) were fundamentally opposed to the principle that professional educators should be accountable or that the work of schools should be inspected.

Preparing for inspection

The main findings relating to the preparation for and process of inspection showed that despite the issues and concerns highlighted by the study, an important achievement of the Ofsted system of school inspection is that it has promoted acceptance of a 'culture of inspection'. However, these concerns were consistently raised:

- The period of build-up to inspection is too long, even within the revised arrangements, and leads to unnecessary 'anticipatory dread'.
- Preparation for inspection, despite efforts to the contrary, interferes with normal school development work. The emphasis during the preparatory period tends to be upon Ofsted-related paperwork and the physical presentation of the school.

The inspection experience

- The relationship between the inspectors and the school is crucial to the way in which the inspection process is experienced: these relationships vary between different stakeholder groups.
- In the main, head-teachers characterize these relationships as professional and oriented towards management issues, especially with the registered inspector.
- Teachers report the most variation and inconsistencies in their relationships with inspectors. The perceived credibility and professionalism of the members of the team (including their qualifications and experience) represents their central concern, and the manner in which the inspection is conducted.
- With the exception of feedback to teachers about their teaching performance, the feedback given by inspectors, both formal and informal, verbal and written, is seen as generally fair, valid and of good standard.

The inspection aftermath: input and take-up

With few exceptions, there was little found or presented in the final reports that the schools were not already aware of and working towards remedying within their own school development plans.

Example 1

Following Ofsted inspection,
25% of schools had changed their management structure
58% of schools had changed their teaching styles and curricular organization
20% of schools had experienced more staff retirements
24% of schools had experienced more staff absence linked to stress etc.

Changes in staff were also attributed to the inspection and some retirements, resignations and absence through stress and ill health, are a cause for concern.

Example 2

Average staff attendance of between 96% and 100% had been recorded in 69% of schools in the three-month period before notification of an impending Ofsted inspection. This rose to 84% during the inspection week itself and fell to 50% in the three months following inspection.

Over two-thirds of schools felt that they were more focused and rigorous in school development activities, such as target setting, curriculum development, pupil assessment and class observations, as a result of the inspection.

Example 3

More target setting and pupil assessment were attributed to Ofsted inspection in 40% of schools, the same or less in the remainder.
Less teacher appraisal in over 56% of schools
21% of schools reported more staff development mainly as a result of Ofsted inspection (76% the same, 2% less).

Additionally, there were changes reported in some pupil behaviours and performance outcomes:

Example 4

Under 10% of improved pupil attendance was linked to the impact of an Ofsted inspection, but more in secondary than in primary schools.

Over 41% of reduced pupil exclusions was attributed to Ofsted inspection in 16–20% of schools.

Example 5

Two-thirds of schools attributed no impact on SAT/GCSE scores as a result of Ofsted inspection, although there was a significant impact (improvement) on maths at 14, Key Stage 3.

Stakeholder perception and evaluations
Example 6

Overall impact of Ofsted on educational quality, standards and financial management was judged to be greatest by parents, least by heads, with governors in between. (In 70–88% schools heads believed there was no improvement caused in these).
Governors rather than teachers or head-teachers were more likely to ascribe performance improvements to the inspection.

With regard to later reflections on the experience of an Ofsted inspection:

Governors and parents were more strongly accepting of the validity of the inspection findings. However, the usefulness of the summary report for parents is in doubt and very few parents ask to see the full report.

Example 7

Half the headteachers and almost 60% of school governors rated Ofsted inspection as very good/good on, overall accuracy – identification of key issues – objectivity but heads, in particular, gave much lower ratings to, fairness of teacher assessment – usefulness of action plan/future school development.

With respect to outcomes and impacts on schools, whether acknowledged by them or imputed, the key findings included the following:

● Schools were relatively sceptical about the impact of the inspection findings on school processes or performance, believing that, although Ofsted may have accelerated them, most changes would have happened in any case.
● However, a range of organizational changes resulting from the inspection findings was reported, most particularly in relation to teaching style and curriculum issues but also in management structures.

- But when survey respondents were asked to specify changes which have taken place which could be attributed to the inspection it was clear that the Ofsted process of inspection is judged to have had a positive impact in only a minority of schools with 21.1% head-teachers, 24.9% governors and 25.9% parents believing that it has had an impact on the quality of education and fewer (18.5% head-teachers, 20.8% governors) believing that educational standard had been improved.
- However, the impact of inspection on failing schools is acknowledged but the benefits for better schools are less certain. Many suggest that the Ofsted framework assists school improvement perhaps more than the inspection itself.

Stakeholder conclusions

This analytic account concluded with respondents' evaluations of the validity and fairness of the system as a whole (including whether or not it represented good value for money) and any preferred approaches to and models of school inspection.

The main *benefits* identified were:

- The process of self-examination which leads up to the inspection week.
- The value of external perspectives on the work and running of schools.
- The increase in mutual support among staff generated by external inspection and a related recognition of improvements in self-esteem which flow from public affirmation of the work of staff, schools and pupils within schools.
- The fact that the same framework and process can be applied to all schools.
- The development of greater clarity about roles and responsibilities particularly among governors.
- The clear framework which promotes improved management systems and structures and which can be used as a valuable aid to self-development.
- The systematic form of the inspection process which can result in greater rigour in self-evaluation procedures.
- Parents saw the main strength of the system as leading to improvements within their own child(ren)'s school.
- Governors (though not school staff) were more likely to see the inspection process as a catalyst for change.

- While most governors did feel that school accountability had been improved as a result of the Ofsted system this was a view shared by virtually no head-teachers or teachers in the study.

The main *disadvantages* associated with the Ofsted arrangements were that:

- The system is seen as punitive and fault finding and generates a climate of fear which leads to stress and anxiety among staff;
- although parents are more likely to see benefits of the system, they also recognize the adverse impacts on staff – especially in the period leading up to inspection – and are concerned on the impact this may have on their children;
- the summative, judgemental outcomes are not effective in promoting reflective professional development within schools;
- the system is intolerant of alternative approaches to school improvement and effectiveness.

Despite the inadequacies of the previous HMI system, informants, with the exception of the parents, were agreed about the expertise that HMIs had accumulated. Partly in relation to such observations, there was agreement that a reflective continuing dialogue is a more effective way of promoting school improvement. The current large pool of 'journeymen' inspectors competing for contracts works against this expertise.

On the question of Ofsted's role in identifying ineffectual teachers there was also a great deal of consensus among head-teachers, teachers and governors that the current arrangements would not contribute to the reduction in the number of ineffectual teachers.

Moving funds to a better system.

A variety of suggestions for a revised system of school inspection were proferred. The main suggestions were that:

- inspection should be more developmental in its mode of operation with strong elements of self-evaluation and peer review;
- it should involve a professional reflective dialogue between professionals, all of whom should be ascribed equal status;
- the system should be tied to professional staff development and rigorous staff appraisal;
- there is a key role for LEAs in a revised system.

Value for money?

The final component of our key findings relate to the costs of the system; for schools, LEAs and for Ofsted itself.

For schools, the costings include those incurred during the preparation for and follow-up to inspection as well as special arrangements during the inspection itself. It is important to judge, with the help of head-teachers and others, the point at which the activities and expenditure incurred are beyond those which could reasonably be expected in relation to normal school improvement/development and self-review. This includes identifying opportunity costs, expenditure and activities which might or would have taken place if the Ofsted inspection was not occurring.

For LEAs, costs include additional and/or special intervention activities before, during and after an inspection such as, eg mini-inspections, audits or practice runs before an inspection. It would also take account of the provision of additional supply staff, special professional development events and additional advice and/or consultancy.

At the level of Ofsted itself, the following component needs to be quantified and costed in order that the full costs at this level can be calculated:

- average fees paid to contractors (registered inspectors and their team) for a range of school types, sizes etc;
- the additional contracting costs such as processing the contract, operational costs incurred by Ofsted in establishing the specifications per school for competitive bids, evaluating the bids, drawing up and managing the contracts etc;
- training, briefing and information costs for the pool of actual and potential inspectors;
- HMI and other quality, management and development (QMD) costs incurred in relation to monitoring inspection standards and in action required in the case of schools with serious weaknesses and in need of special measures;
- the costs of maintaining a database and research activity to include data input, analysis and research costs associated with school inspections;
- the appropriate share of organizational costs to include overheads. Within these would be legal, capital expenditure and depreciation, publications and public relations costs.

In the following analysis, the study was able to assemble data at the school level even though most schools are not accustomed to conducting this kind of costing. In the main, these data have been collated from the questionnaires to head-teachers, with some supplementary data from the governor survey.

At the LEA level it has been possible to extrapolate costs from known adviser/officer day rates and Service Level Agreement (SLA) data, but it is also a matter of regret that no LEA has been identified where this kind of costing exercise has already been carried out. The data have also been augmented by reported (and costed) LEA involvement at school level before, during and after inspection.

At the level of OFSTED, the Annual Reports for 1993/94, 1995/6, and 1996/7 and the Corporate Plans for 1997/8 and 1999/2000 have been examined as well as the DfEE Department Reports for March 1996, 1997 and 1998 and Appropriation Accounts 1996/7. In addition, the relevant DfEE Divisional Manager and Director of Strategic Planning and Resources at Ofsted have been interviewed.

Through extrapolating these data sources and undertaking some financial modelling, we were able to conclude that the following costings were well founded (see Table 1.1).

Table 1.1 *Full cost of an Ofsted inspection for a median-size primary school*

	£	% of total cost
Ofsted costs	13,500	52
School costs (2% of ASB)	11,520	44
Other (including LEA)	1,000	4
Total	26,020[a]	

Note[a] This is equivalent to 4.5% of the annual school budget.

For a secondary school with 850 pupils on roll, each yielding £2,400, it is possible to assume an annual school budget (ASB) of around £2 million. If, as advised by Ofsted, this warrants 45 inspector days and a daily rate of £230 is assumed, then the full costs would be as shown in Table 1.2.

Table 1.2 *Full cost of an Ofsted inspection for a secondary school*

	£	% of cost
Ofsted costs	24,293	37
School costs (2% of ASB)	40,000	60
Other (including LEA)	1,600	3
Total	65,493[a]	

Note[a] This represents 3.3% of the annual school budget.

We believe that this kind of analysis should have already taken place. To the best of our knowledge no similar analysis has been attempted. This is a task that we would have expected to engage the attention of such a body as the National Audit Office. It is difficult to think of another public or private body of Ofsted's size and importance that is so free of rigorous financial accounting. Whether for purposes of normal public accounting or for providing an informed basis for value for money appraisals, such analyses should be conducted on a regular basis.

POLICY AND PRACTICE IMPLICATIONS

Criteria for evaluation

Our study was based on empirical research. Drawing policy and practice implications from our findings involves moving from the reporting of evidence to essentially value-laden propositions which, however, preferably spring from the evidence and at minimum do not conflict with it. Policy analysis may begin with propositions that are less empirically based than based on what seems self-evidently right to the analysts. Of this logical status are the criteria that our team concluded should be observed in any system of public evaluation. But they also, in our view, respond closely to criticisms of Ofsted made by our main research samples.

In our view, evaluation must give a credible and technically competent account to the stakeholders by those being evaluated of what is being provided. In addition evaluations should be performed in such a way as to avoid:

- causing unnecessary hurt to the evaluated, although some hurt cannot be avoided;
- imposing particular values or practices on the evaluated in such a way as to reduce their self-sufficiency and the development of practice created out of their knowledge and experience. In particular, the assertion of values and practices simply to justify the modes of evaluation adopted by the evaluators would be dysfunctional and unprofessional;
- creating undue dependency of the evaluated on the evaluators;
- imposing unreasonable cash, time opportunity costs or other resource costs on the evaluated.

Evaluation should be compatible not only with the appropriate rendering of accountability, but also with the effective development of the activities being evaluated; and avoid making inappropriate claims as to the contribution that it makes to school improvement. Its methods and objectives should be under constant external review, and its impacts not taken for granted.

Policy suggestions

With our findings and these criteria in mind, we offered suggestions on actions and issues that might be taken up by different parts of the education system.

National Government

In supporting Ofsted's ways of working, the national authorities have implicitly endorsed a particular model of school improvement. This assumes that there are ascertainable standards against which educational performance can be judged in scalar fashion, by particular forms of observation. A further assumption is that the publication of the grades achieved by schools, and the awarded of inspection grades to teachers, will of itself enhance standards and help extirpate poor performance.

A substantial proportion of heads and teachers, and the national professional associations, do not share that view. The arguments and evidence produced, both from ours and other studies, show that it is hazardous to assume any connection between Ofsted inspection and improved performance. While all our informants, at school, local authority and national authority level, believe it essential to have a system of external inspection, many are unhappy about the extent to which it assumes that performance can be judged on a calibrated and tested set of criteria, and on a limited exposure of inspectors to that which they are inspecting.

Most teachers and national organizations are uneasy about an evaluative process which they feel to be purgative rather than developmental. All the current arguments, now apparently supported by ministers, flow in the direction of installing the capacity of the schools to evaluate themselves. It is also accepted widely that their self-judgements should be subjected to rigorous meta-evaluation and the evidence now provided by a full range of quantitative indicators.

Government should, therefore, acknowledge that 'cold' inspection has limited utility as a component of a change model and that it will be acceptable only if placed alongside other and more interactive forms of evaluation and school development measures. We favour the use of self-evaluation but its operational implications are not fully worked out. We return to this point later. A further conclusion would be that inspection and associated evaluative and developmental activities should not be set in concrete but assumed to be capable of continuous improvement and review and evaluation by independent analysts.

The international literature on school improvement emphasizes the need to focus on a wide range of factors which affect pupil achievement. Current English policy, however, concentrates on ways of affecting school management and assessing the performance of teachers. The two sets of considerations should be brought into better balance, with school and teacher development given greater emphasis.

Ofsted

The fact that all groups accept the need for external inspection is a credit to the way in which Ofsted has changed the culture of evaluation in education. It has forced the issue on to the political and professional agenda. It has already made strenuous efforts to monitor its own reliability, and it has also proposed changes (Ofsted, 1998a) that will relieve at least some schools of the heavy burdens imposed by full dress inspections.

Ofsted may feel that the judgements made of its work by schools, which are shared only to a limited extent by parents and governors, are unjust, or based on misunderstanding, or self-interest. But schools and local authorities have to reckon with an unparalleled level of inspection precisely because they were alleged to have lost the confidence of their clients. Client judgements might thus with equal equity be applied to Ofsted. The opinions of those affected by inspection are evidence that must be treated seriously. Opinions may be contestable, but just as the unreal market, based on sentiment rather than on economic fundamentals, affects real values on the stock exchange and the functioning of enterprises so perceptions of Ofsted affect its legitimacy and effectiveness.

The alternative to analysing impacts by listening to those affected by them would be to attempt to make some definite connections between Ofsted activities and changes in school performance. Such global estimates must be shallow, as would be to relate the advances in reading comprehension in the 1960s and 1970s to the alleged spread of progressive primary education of that period. As Cullingford, Daniels and Brown (1998) have demonstrated, even on the basis of a rigorous analysis of school performance statistics, the Ofsted case appears unproven.

The criticisms of Ofsted must be compared with the virtual absence of complaints about district auditors and the Audit Commission, SSI or other public service inspectorates known as rigorous in their approaches. The general critique concerns the whole set of assumptions about what will make for effective education. It is one contribution only to school improvement. It cannot be proved to be more effective than would be externally moderated self-evaluation by schools, associated with developmental follow-up and support by such bodies as LEAs.

Other criticisms concern the ways of working of the inspections. It seems unlikely that problems of credibility will ever be solved while inspection is in the hands of over 14 000 registered, team and lay inspectors in contracting teams, some of whom appear to display the journeyman characteristics of jobbing builders. Inspection must incorporate not only dispassionate judgement but also extensive knowledge of what is being inspected. That requires access to, and not competition with, colleague groups over continuous periods. The system of parcelling out to available contractors, who might start with little previous knowledge and never stay in action long enough to acquire it, is dysfunctional, and the unworthy inheritance of an immature and raw ideological commitment of politicians now off the scene.

The schools

We identify the schools as being in danger of potential dependency on Ofsted as the source of models of change and development and of standard setting in the schools. Too many schools engage Ofsted passively. Dependency is sometimes manifest in the somewhat desperate hope of feedback from inspectors. Some teachers feel they have done well to keep up their guard in what should be instead a robust, developmental encounter with fellow professionals.

Thus, too strong an inspectorate can lead to infantilism in what should be a confident and self-sufficient profession. It should be for the profession to take the lead in these matters and for inspectors to use the professionally set standards as their starting criteria.

In fostering greater professional self-sufficiency, the best hope will be the development of self-evaluation. This will require schools to build up modes of self-critique that are convincingly capable of being linked to both external inspection and the desktop data now to analyse outcomes and the factors that affect them. In addition, a return to teacher appraisal and self-appraisal would be beneficial, as would the growth of evidence-based practice and peer review, all of which would enhance confidence and professionalism. If schools can grip this key professional task they stand some chance of shifting the current trend to the creation of an inspector-led system.

It follows from our findings that schools could do more, perhaps in conjunction with their professional associations, to evaluate the effects of reforms including the work of Ofsted. They find it difficult at present to estimate the costs to them of inspections. This may imply a general failure to cost effectively the different activities in which they are engaged.

School dissatisfaction with Ofsted raises questions of the extent to which schools are able to affect educational policy at large. It also raises questions about the public control of Ofsted. The model adopted for the highly respected Audit Commission, whose Comptroller is accountable to independent commissioners, is worth considering.

It is noteworthy that parents and governors do not share, in anything like the same degree, teachers' discontent with Ofsted. It is important that reasons for this discrepancy of judgement are considered by schools if they are to secure changes in the system.

Local authorities

Our evidence supports that of other studies in noting the felt need of primary schools, in particular, for support by local authorities both generally and in the face of the challenges presented by Ofsted. Recent 'fair funding' policies have given local authorities even less leeway for helping schools to improve. It restricts them largely to working to action plans, follow-up of inspections and other work restricted implementing particular national policies school improvement.

Effective LEAs should be helping schools deal with the challenge of self-evaluation and advising them how to monitor themselves, decide targets and plans on the basis of the self- and external evaluations. They could be accredited by HMI for assisting schools take up the skills required by self-evaluation.

Parent and governor associations

It is not surprising that many governor and parents' bodies feel that they benefit from Ofsted which brings them judgements and information about schools not hitherto available to them. It is important, however, that governors note our evidence about the strain and doubts engendered by Ofsted while taking account of inspection findings.

Teacher associations

The associations vary in their judgements about Ofsted but almost all share the general belief that a shift towards a system with a large component of self-evaluation will be desirable. Their function *vis-à-vis* Ofsted might be:

- The teaching profession seems to lack a clear mandate in terms of its duties and powers, and its claims to expertise in relation to such bodies as Ofsted. The associations could take the lead in establishing such a mandate.
- They could, perhaps working together, monitor the impacts of Ofsted.
- They should press for the training of all teachers in methods of self-evaluation and peer review, perhaps by advancing the case with the Teacher Training Agency (TTA).
- They should guard against the dangers of an inspector-led and centrally dominated system and the dependency they might create in what should be a confident profession.

Whether the current proposals for a 'modernized' teaching profession (DfEE, 1998) or for a General Teaching Council will assist in this also has to be considered.

Self-evaluation

Self-evaluation would have to be capable of allowing for the variety of school styles and values and the development of new ways of working, perhaps deriving from such initiatives as the TTA's sponsoring of schools-based research.

However, these inwardnesses must be capable of being subjected to external evaluation which will incorporate the generic qualities demanded by local authority and national educational policies. To get this right will require technically competent and creative development. To some extent the internal and external exercises will produce incommensurate statements, and common ground must be sought which will make it possible to publicly attest to standards.

Many proposals have been made and some have produced details of what self-evaluation might entail. We quote, as an example, the National Association of Head Teachers (NAHT) scheme which contains proposals similar to those being made by other associations. Their points include:

- schools to be fully involved in the inspection process;
- schools to look closely at their own provision, resourcing and outcomes enabling them to set targets based on their previous achievements;
- staff training for self-evaluation;
- the inspection team to meet school staff at an early stage to discuss aims, objectives and evaluation outcomes. This would attempt to trace progress in the school.

Data should include examination results, assessment scores, financial data, school development plan and other internal documents. Discussion would put these in the following context:

- a national framework for inspection to which the process would have to conform;
- full discussion with staff during and after the inspection;
- LEAs would need to support and provide external moderation of self-evaluation. It has been suggested by other associations that LEAs should be accredited by HMI for this task;
- the cycle of formal or external inspection should be longer.

Such a plan matches many of our criteria for an inspection system that can meet the need to respect individual schools' style, problems and achievements while attending to the legitimate demands for public accountability. Some such shift from inspectors to the profession is called for, but the system must be technically competent as well as responsive and account-able. That will involve careful development of appropriate procedures.

A further proposal that has been made is that there should be peer review across schools and teachers, which would not only provide a bridge between self- and external evaluation, but also strengthen professionalism.

Ofsted's (1998b) proposals for self-evaluation make a noteworthy effort to ensure connection between external inspection and self-evaluation. They analyse what might be common features, such as a focus on the standard achieved by pupils, and point the way to common criteria for each. Ofsted's framework is offered as a basis for both forms of evaluation.

The extent to which that might channel other potential formats needs consideration. It is clear, at any rate, that a self-evaluation movement is again under way after a somewhat fallow period. It could help mitigate some of the aspects of the existing system.

CONCLUSION

Our underlying premise in approaching this evaluation has been that schools are an essential public service and that to be part of the public domain should be a matter of social and individual self-esteem. Inspection and evaluation can enhance professionalism; our criticisms contained in this report turn on the extent to which Ofsted is contributing to that goal.

REFERENCES

Centre for the Evaluation of Public Policy and Practice (1999) *The Ofsted System of School Inspection: An Independent Evaluation*, CEPPP, Brunel University and Helix Consulting Group

Clarke, C (1998) Speech on evaluation made at NUT Seminar, London, 3 November

Croxford, L (1996) *The Effectiveness of Grampian Secondary Schools*, University of Edinburgh Centre for Educational Sociology

Cullingford, C, Daniels, S and Brown, J (1998), 'The effects of Ofsted inspection on school performance', University of Huddersfield

DfEE (1998) Green Paper. *Teachers; Meeting the Challenge of Change*

Fullan, M (1992) *Successful School Improvement*, Open University Press, Milton Keynes

Goldstein, H and Sammons, P (1997) The influence of junior and secondary schools on sixteen-year-olds' examination performance, *School Effectiveness and School Improvement*, **8**.

Henkel, M (1991a) *Government, Evaluation and Change*, Jessica Kingsley

Henkel, M (1991b) The New 'Evaluative State', *Public Administration*, **69**.

MacBeath, J, Boyd, B, Rand, J and Bell, S (1996) Schools speak for themselves, National Union of Teachers, London

Neave, G (1988) On the cultivation of quality, efficiency and enterprise: an overview of recent trends in higher education in Western Europe, 1986–1988, *European Journal of Education*, **23**.

Ofsted (1995a) *Framework for the Inspection of Schools*

Ofsted (1995b) *School Assessment and School Improvement in the United States: Three Case Studies*, Ofsted, London

Ofsted Corporate Plan (1997) Table 2 HMSO, London

Ofsted (1998a) *Proposals for a Differentiated System of School Inspection* Ofsted

Ofsted (1998b) *School Evaluation Matters*, HMSO, London

Patterson, L. University of Edinburgh (1998) You take the higher road, *Times Educational Supplement*, 9 October

Pollit, C (1993) *Managerialism and the Public Services*, Allen and Unwin

Reynolds, D (1992) in *School Effectiveness*, eds D Reynolds and P Cuttance, Cassell, London

Reynolds, D (1995) The effective school: an inaugural lecture, *School Effectiveness*, **9**

Reynolds, D (1998) Speech to International School Effectiveness and Improvement Conference, Manchester, England

Reynolds, D and Stoll, L (1996) Merging school effectiveness and school improvement: the knowledge base in *Making Good Schools*, D Reynolds eds *et al*, Routledge

An examination of Ofsted*

David Winkley

THE INSPECTION PROCESS

At the heart of Ofsted lies the assessment of a 20-minute delivery by a teacher in a class of children likely to number in the region of 30. This lesson is classified against a reference manual on a seven-point scale. The accumulation of numerical data arising from the observation of numerous lessons in a school is presumed to give one key indication of the quality of the school as a whole.

The question that arises is whether this act of interpretation is reliable, and if so in what sense, bearing in mind that its reliability or otherwise depends upon the view you take of the interpretative process itself. In what sense is the data drawn from lesson observation truly empirical? The argument we shall now pursue is that the seven-point scale analysis – the core data of an Ofsted inspection – is based on something more akin to a textual analysis than to a scientific experiment.

What kind of 'text' is a lesson? There are at least four obvious components:

- background – what has happened so far;
- teacher – skills and intentions;
- learner – attitudes, ability, response;
- transmission – the nature of the performance itself.

_____

* A version of this chapter was originally written for *Primary Practice (Journal of the National Primary Trust*, 1998)

These could in textual terms of, say, a play or a film, which a lesson surely resembles, be translated as script, production, actors and performance. Each of these is required to be assessed, and in the case of Ofsted, we must add to the critic's chart the response of the *audience*, ie the class of children.

It is worth reminding ourselves of the detailed responsibility of the critic. The critic – the inspector – is required to produce a critique based upon 20 minutes observation. This episode may be at the beginning, in the middle or at the end. The lesson itself is likely to be an episode from a sequence, ie one episode whose sections may span a number of weeks. The 'play' will be specialist, focused for the most part on a single subject area. It may, for example, be about music or history or maths or modern languages. These various subjects may have styles of their own, making use of specialist equipment and techniques. The 'play' will have a plot with programme notes given to the inspector-critic before it begins, and the actor (teacher) will have intentions in mind. Despite these plans and intentions, however, there will be a strong element of unpredictability because a very strong component in the assessment will be audience involvement and audience. This element is, of course, an additional and unique responsibility of the inspector-critic who must decide not only on the quality of the play but whether the 'play' is appropriate to the audience and how the 30 individuals responded. After 20 minutes an assessment must be made of these various components compounded into a single figure 1–7. We are, then, asking for an accurate assessment of the quality of this snippet in relation to its supposed, calculated or imagined impact on its diverse audience and then to consummate this variety of impressions in a number.

The question now arises as to how a critic might go about such a formidable task. There is, of course, a set of rules, a highway code of inspection, but as the philosopher Michael Oakeshott once said, 'There is no way you can learn to drive from reading the highway code', or as Ella Fiztergald put it, 'When you're talking about it, you ain't doing it'. Inspection, like criticism, is a skill, and requires experience and judgement. The business of encapsulating all judgements into a single magic number can, of course, be easy: anyone can get a vague impression based upon past experience and prejudice, make a snap decision, and assume the authority of knowledge. But let us presuppose that inspectors try to stay true to their formidable task. Because the play is moving, and because time is so limited, the mind must move quickly, and the practice of inspection like any other practice will require its reference points – like rocks to hold on to in a flowing current – merely to survive. And the kinds of reference points which the inspector will fall upon will inevitably be as follows:

1. Control is everything. If the audience is controlled by the teacher, and if the teacher is substantially in control of the presentation then there is a security in the performance to start.

2. Presentation, clarity and confidence follow. If the film is lively, and like any good performance gets the audience interested, attending and involved then a second parameter is established.
3. Then there is the matter of external evidence – impressions of the context in which the performance is taking place, the liveliness of the room (the scenery) the relevance of material – all this provides important clues as to the quality of the piece.
4. Finally there is the alertness, involvement, enthusiasm and performance of the audience in response to the stimulus on offer. If there is writing or speaking as part of the show (as it were) then that has to be appropriately adjudged under this section of the critical analysis.

All this, however, takes place in an atmosphere of high artificiality and stress. The critic has substantial powers to make or break the show. The inspector is not unlike the legendary feared newspaper critics, such as Richard Watts of the *New York Post*, who could make or break a show in a single piece. For the teacher the situation is much more dire than that. The teacher only has one show or set of shows, which is her life's work. The judgement is not merely a threat potentially to her career, but equally to her self-esteem. The judgement is by a single person of a single performance: there are no other witnesses, no other members of the critical press to offer different or demurring judgements. The judgement of the inspector is absolute. Furthermore, there is no comeback, no discussion, no opportunity to engage in debate – and in that respect the criticism bears resemblance to press reports after a first performance. And finally the critic falls back on his number, rather as the *Radio Times* analyses films, or some sections of the press grade theatre performances, on a 1 to 5 scale.

Yet for the teacher this assessment has two other problems. One is that, as in a real play, there is a risky element of dependency on external factors such as size of class, helpfulness of other staff, quality of support of curriculum coordinators, general school discipline, level of equipment, social class of the audience and so on. The same performance can vary from one day to another, one audience to another. The other is that for the teacher the experience sets up massive defences that change the nature of the play in the process. One teacher has described it as like someone marching uninvited into your home and going through your knicker drawers, marking up you and your family, slipping out as silently as they came in, leaving you with a number that you will know for the next four to six years as *your number*. That's all very well, you might say, but why not? Schools are, after all, publicly funded at great expense, and parents have a right to a view of how things are going, to which teachers might try to argue that the best of them have a personal commitment which goes way beyond being paid for the job – and it is this part of them that is most vulnerable, and hardest to define and confine to a number. We can certainly identify factors that are difficult to take account of, such as:

- the feelings of the participants (including the teacher herself);
- the ability of the teacher to work as part of a team;
- variability of past experiences of the audience;
- the varied abilities of the various members of the audience;
- background hazards, which might even include the weather;
- long-term commitments and contributions by the staff in the evolution of the show;
- the performance history of the show.

Some of this can be intuited, but the more it is intuited – intuition becomes part of the evaluative process – the more the judgement slips away from the checklist – the critical highway code – to something both more interesting and more hazardous – the inspector's own opinion.

Post-modernist critical theory takes the extreme and provocative view that all forms of interpretation are a problem: even in the simplest reading the text we read is in principle the text we have written for ourselves. It is well established in phenomenological research that the individual judgement is never quite separate from the set of factors to be adjudged. Phenomenology asserts that we cannot know for sure, and what is appropriate for us to study is our own procedures of perception. It is certainly the case that the complexity of a text, whether book, film, play or whatever, throws a challenge out that touches on the huge range of skills, preconceptions, interpretative styles and values of the individual critic. As we have argued, inspection is a form of textual analysis: we may now take one step further: that the quality of an Ofsted inspector's judgement is affected by the qualities of critical skills and intuitions, and these will certainly be located in an interpretative style and a set of principles. The notion that inspection is a scientific process is unconvincing. Inspection is by an individual of a kind of text, and that process is inherently both personal and variable. Its quality lies itself in its subtlety and skill, not in the efficacy of any manual. Good critics differ from bad ones not because they differ in what they try to do, or because they are working from a different set of basic references: by and large they are trying to understand and pass judgement on aspects of a text. The good critic differs from the bad one because of procedural skill and insight – and the kind of person he or she is dealing with. As Antony Powell puts it, 'in the dance every step is ultimately the corollary of the step before; the consequence of being the kind of person one chances to be'.

This leads us to the core of the Ofsted problem: that it pretends to be a depersonalized check-out-the-smartness-of-the-barracks kind of blueprint carried out according to a rule-based agenda – a checklist based on centrally conceived sets of values as to what constitutes a successful school. That's the theory. In practice, as an all textual interpretations, the theory is mediated through the minds of different inspectors. And with Ofsted inspections in action we see classic examples of evidence reconstructed against the background of the values of the inspectors themselves and perhaps most formatively, those of the registered inspector.

The fact is no critic examines a text in a value-free way: interpretation is by definition ridden with values, and there seem to be two broad features to consider here.

Attitudes may be subconscious, or articulated, but they permeate all approaches to interpretation: important matters are that:

- they may be positive or negative in orientation;
- they may be broadly sympathetic (to the individual teacher, the school etc.);
- they may be cautious or incautious, tentative or confident.

Here is one inspector writing:

> I have a grading principle that every lesson/teacher at the start of an observation is 100 per cent and then this usually reduces. Far too many Ofsted inspectors are afraid of giving a 1 or a 2 and this unbalances the system, especially one where the lower marks seem too popular with the bosses.

This approach reflects an attitude diametrically opposed to this one:

> We are essentially bidden to examine aspects of the operation which are not up to scratch. My own view is that there will be a very few high grades, as these are by definition likely to be exceptional.

These are examples of the rationalization of fundamentally different preconceptions. It is worth nothing that either can be moderated or enhanced by local events – the manner of the head, the 'feel' of the school. Such impressions will press upon the inspector to confirm or modify their 'natural' approach. To this we can add a broad concern either: (1) to be fair to the school, or; (2) to be true to the check-list schedule.

It sounds absurd, at first sight, to be so bleakly diametric: but the truth has to be faced that inspectors are reported by teachers as broadly positioning themselves clearly in one category or another, not exclusively, of course (both positions will figure in all inspections) but as a matter of emphasis. It is not difficult in all inspections to place the inspector and his team on an attitudinal spectrum.

Then there are the values of the inspector, which will guide the process of the interpretation. We identify here three important ones:

1. managerial;
2. numerical;
3. personal.

The assessor will have access to all three kinds of data but will value them in some kind of order.

Managerial will represent the quality of control, neatness, tidiness, efficiency, administrative order and quality data presentation.

Numerical will put particular emphasis on standard attainment tasks' (SAT) results, attendance figures, data collection, and all manner of figurative and numerical evidence.

Personal will be focused on more intuitive matters, the 'feel' of the class, enthusiasm, apparent evidence of motivation, and 'liking' or 'disliking' what is seen.

There will be an element of all three in the interpretative approach, but there will be different balances in the structures of values that any individual brings to the inspection. It is also true, of course, that teachers have values, and so do the schools inspected. Considerable problems arise when the pattern of values espoused by the inspector turns out to be different from those of the school.

How do such subtleties work out in practice? Here is a registered inspector of a positive persuasion writing about inspectors who espouse a check-list-driven approach to evaluation:

> What disturbs me is that people whose quality I know and respect and whose observation forms often write so glowingly of the right kind of criteria being matched, still end up putting Grade 4. And they won't be talked out of it at least until the quality of the teacher or school is manifest in their minds near the end of the week when in their own subject they may give a G3 or even a clarion G2. Often I re-grade during the end of the week. I doubt if most teams do.

Here is an example of an inspection team that made clear its position by remarking:

> I really don't think that Circle Time and all this stuff about developing feelings is relevant to junior aged children. It takes up unnecessary time that could be better deployed on the National Curriculum.

This school, which performed badly overall, none the less had SAT results well above the national average. The key emphasis of this team was on control and management.

In another case:

> a young teacher brought her children into the hall. The inspector interrupted the lesson with the observation that there was a child missing.

The teacher looked round, 'No there's not', she said. He insisted that there was. Both went back to the classroom to see, but there was not one missing. 'But the numbers on the register do not then represent the numbers in the class'. It turned out that there was a register error. The effect, inevitably, was to disorientate the lesson because the feelings of the teacher – now distraught – were so inevitably aroused. When this was pointed out to the inspector, he was mystified. He was not, after all, there to inspect feelings, and they did not on the whole matter very much.

Now it doesn't take much imagination to foresee how inspectorial values can clash with the school values:

X school values league tables but is dull. A team which values SAT results will be more likely to rate it highly than a team looking for (say) managerial wizardry or an exciting, motivating culture.

The school that will do well will invariably find that its own values match the values of the inspectorial team. A predisposition by the team to be positive will also help:

Mr X, I honestly don't know how you work here. This is the most difficult school I have encountered. There's no way we could fail this place. I couldn't work here.

This inspectorial team was aware of the feelings of a staff struggling to cope. It took into account issues that go well beyond the check–list. Another team with a different set of values might have taken a very different line. 'We could have gone on to special measures', said the teacher bluntly.

The paradox here is that any consortium of values between the team and school is in danger of leading either to an undercritical or an overcritical approach. Undercritical where the inspectorial team overvalues the very component that the school feels is overwhelmingly the most important. Overcritical where the team feels on the same value grounds as the school but the school seems to be evidently failing against its own set of principles or objectives. On the other hand the school is even more at risk when team and school values clearly do not converge.

It is only fair to add here that the Ofsted schedule is by no means unsophisticated on this issue. Indeed it is a feature of its progress since 1991 that it has continually tried to widen its focus in order to take account of the full value-laden range of textual evidence. That the inspector needs to examine raw numerical data and visually obvious material evidence (such as book marking) was always clear. It was both right and inevitable that 'management' would be inspected (though this is, of course, in itself a very complex phenomenon which cannot be simply 'observed'). There was all along a problem with the 'personal range of data'. An attempt was made by Stuart Sutherland, the first Chief Inspector of Schools, under the regime of John Patten, to tackle the formalization of 'personal' issues by incorporating them under the labels of 'spiritual', 'moral' and 'cultural'. In 1993 Sutherland distributed a bizarre questionnaire to all schools on these issues; inspectors now had a responsibility to inspect the spiritual lives of the pupils in school, as well as their 'moral' behaviour. The aim was to introduce 'interiority' into the inspection, acknowledging subjective factors in the check-list.

This sophistication and complication of the schedule, to make it ever more comprehensive and watertight, does not, however, invalidate the point that personal value structures will always contend with the inspectorial 'highway code'. Reading about what you have to do is not the same as the actual practice of what you thereby do. Moreover the ever-expanding inspection map creates new problems for inspectors through its very complexity. All practices of whatever kind reduce in order to survive, and inspection is no different. They require a first focus, a second, a third etc. There is a limit to how much you can hold in mind at any one time. The skilled practitioner moves the focus about, integrates and cross-references, working towards judgements – combining linear references with global impressions in extremely complex ways. The movement is from reduction to an ever-growing sense of complexity of different kinds of evidence leading back to reduction in the judgement phase. A complex schedule is just as likely to provide a platform for the exploration of personal values as it is to reinforce comprehensiveness. Paradoxically in practice the more comprehensive the schedule the more room the inspector has to manoeuvre. This explains why so many inspectors approve of the schedule and do not see it as a constraining or diminishing document.

The final point to add here is, of course, practicality. It is questionable whether the schedule can be truthfully carried out in its entirety *without* a significant fall-back on to rules of thumb or personal impressions, simply because of time constraints. Try assessing the quality of a film or play based on seeing a section of 20 minutes – one third, say – as well as taking into account not only the behaviour of an audience but their internationalization of the data on offer – without falling back on short-circuiting and value-laden impressionistic technique. It can't be done.

All the hazards of the interpretative act are, therefore, present in the inspection. The business of assessing and grading a lesson is essentially no different from the business of criticizing and assessing a piece of drama or a film, with a few complications thrown in – such as the problems of assessing the audience response.

Are we to suppose, therefore, that the outcomes are invalid, personal, hazardous, unpredictable, and ultimately meaningless? All critical judgement is open to question. But it would be wrong to suppose that the interpretative process is inevitably invalid in all circumstances. (Teachers might none the less familiarize themselves with the Derridan arguments for the invalidity and difficulties of all kinds of judgemental textual analysis.)

If we stick to our play/film analogy it seems perfectly reasonable to argue that in the broad spectrum between good and bad there will be some measure of general agreement. This will be much the strongest at the extreme ends. We can very likely agree that certain plays or films are – in their category – excellent or dreadful. It's the same with teaching. There isn't likely to be much controversy about the high quality performance and the hopeless one (where the audience is likely to be out of control or bored out of its mind). There may perhaps be an element of dispute in the case of a lesson, which is outstandingly well presented and prepared, given to a surly and uninterested audience of naughty children (see the compensatory approach taken by the sympathetic inspector above).

It is, however, in the movement between extremes – say the two- three- four-star film – that the problems arise. This would account for the high level of divergence of opinion between two independent assessors of lessons (40 per cent disagreement: Ofsted's own – unpublished – data). The complexities of text and of interpretation are such that there is likely to be a high level of variation between judgements of individual assessors between (say) 5 and 2. There will be some dispute given a many-facted verdict between 5 and 6 and between 1 and 2, though overall levels 6/7 and 1/2 will have the highest levels of agreement. The factors influencing judgement have already been described – a positive or negative predisposition, and a value position about various elements encompassed in the judgement. Preparedness to take risks will also make a difference. There is plenty of psychological evidence to show differences between individuals in the degree to which they 'spread' their judgements, cautiously or not. Passions and preferences enter into this: if I like cowboy films I may give them higher value than war films (which I dislike) though if I know a lot of cowboy films I may be very particular about grading them. My internal grading system for cowboy films may well be different, therefore, from my system of grading war firms. The same dilemmas apply to lesson assessment.

Overall, then, we are engaged in an act of self-deception if we think that an interpretative system refined into 7 (or even 5) categories is anything like watertight. It is, as currently constructed, an unreliable exercise at a number of levels. It was, it should be noted, Coleridge's view that dualities should only be distinguished, never divided, ie only treated as functions of each other, never as entities absolutely distinct from each other and independent of each other's existence. The business of lesson interpretation is then – like textual criticism – a matter of considerable sophistication, calling for high levels of understanding of the processes involved in making judgement.

Inspection is a practice of its own, demanding a high level of skills and self-understanding. Its outcomes are highly fallible, and teachers are vulnerable to the diversity of quality and insight of the teams as well as to the circumstances of the inspection itself. For, unlike most art forms, there is no going back, no repeating of the evidence. At least if you're the Royal Shakespeare Company you are repeating the play the next night to another audience which can make up its own mind. And the play is reviewed by more than one newspaper. The inspection, by contrast, is short, private, partial and open to controversy but the teacher has no comeback, no evidential data to question. Like the old style police unrecorded interview, it puts the teacher in the dock with little or no defence, which is not to say, of course, that a critique of performance is not important, or that critics don't have have a role – merely that we have undervalued the skills involved, the difficulties of implementation. And in so doing Ofsted has pretended that it is engaged in truth-defining empirical research by scientifically trained authenticated researchers when at its heart, the core of its rationale – the lesson assessment – it is doing nothing of the kind.

THE VIEW OF THE SCHOOLS

There is little doubt that teachers feel peculiarly vulnerable to the Ofsted process, and many feel personally damaged by it. The National Primary Centre (NPC) was commissioned by Channel 4 to assess the view of 200 recently inspected schools in detail, and the results were unexpected both in their balance and in the intensity and dislike – even fear – of the process. One school accidentally sent their HMI post-inspection evaluation sheet in with the questionnaire: the responses of the anonymous questionnaire (wholly negative) were the opposite of those sent to Ofsted (wholly positive). There is a genuine fear in schools that any public statement criticizing Ofsted will be logged and used punitively. There is a brief out in the field that Ofsted will use its powers to apply a second inspection to any school – at any time – should it choose. Second inspections have, after all, been imposed at very short intervals for no apparent reason, even on highly successful schools. It is understandable that schools feel nervous about openly criticizing a process that – as it turned out on our data – 95 per cent want to see changed.

The problem seems to lie not so much with the principle of external analysis and review as the nature of the process that Ofsted has adopted, and the spirit in which the organization at the centre carries it out. Most schools in the NPC review (60 per cent) thought that the inspection team itself was fair and professional in the way it carried out its brief – a credit to the difficult task Ofsted set itself to manage and quality control the plethora of *ad hoc* teams out in the fields. A credit, too, to the professionalism of the teams and of the registered inspectors, many of whom are developing considerable analytic skills. Even so 40 per cent of the schools had criticisms of the teams and their final judgements, even, curiously, in cases where schools had good or even outstanding reports. Forty per cent of schools thought that the inspection did not give a satisfactory picture of the school's strengths; and more surprisingly, 58 per cent thought that it did not give an adequate view of their *weaknesses*. In fact the vast majority of the schools ended up with positive reports, and the tiny number of schools on special measures – with occasional striking exceptions – were not defensive about their weaknesses. This makes the depth of criticism of the Ofsted process all the more striking.

The powers of Ofsted are, of course, formidable. Teachers and schools are exposed to an analysis of their performance based on the assembling of a vast array of numerical data that both depersonalizes the process and creates an opportunity to turn the numbers into complex data patterns to use as a comparative instrument and (at a national level) a research gold mine.

The act of inspection sets out like every good scientific enterprise to eliminate the corrupting or complicating elements of the personal and (as is frequently used as a term of abuse) 'the anecdotal'. I have already suggested that this assumption of a 'scientific-empirical' stance is vulnerable to close critical analysis, and that the core process of inspection is an interpretative act that is itself highly personal. But the reality is that the inspection is imposed upon a school in such a way that the views and feelings of the participants are formally excluded from the exercise.

Informally, of course, teams vary enormously as the questionnaire responses strongly indicate. Some teams take the opportunity to help and advise the school in confidential ways; some are highly sensitive to the feelings of the teachers. Others, however, maintain their quasi-scientific high road, in which feelings become irrelevant, and at worst, ignored. One inspector was described as taking a book off a child's desk in front of his nose without so much as 'do you mind ...' This is symptomatic of a mind-set that presses an individual to *objectivity* the circumstances of his or her actions. In this mind-set the child and the teacher become instruments to be surgically examined as though under anaesthetic. There is a sense in which they are irrelevant to the enterprise except as objects to be observed.

An extension of this positivist version of empiricism is the pressure to eliminate from the evidence *anything which cannot be seen*. In one school, drama is a strong feature and has for years produced highly imaginative, innovate productions, some of which attract national attention. Because they didn't happen at the time of the inspection and, therefore, *couldn't be immediately seen*, no reference to them features in the report.

The distinguishing aspect of the Ofsted process is to bypass the opinions of those who carry out the teaching which is being assessed. In order to reinforce the impression of dispassionate and objective enterprise the teachers are from the moment the inspection begins made to feel powerless. They are for the most part not expected to contribute in any personal way to the assessment they are about to undergo. This procedure has been described by Professor Henry Minzberg, as the 'glass ceiling phenomenon' whereby the supervisor (in this case the inspector) looks down on the worker through soundproof glass. The worker can be observed but cannot communicate. It is the powerlessness and depersonalized nature of this process that creates both the levels of stress and the potential abuse. This is particularly threatening in a situation – such as the teaching of young children – in which control itself is a high premium concern and *yet can never at any given time be guaranteed*.

If I am a doctor or a manager (say) I have a specifically identified task to do with a patient, or a set of clearly focused and documented activities. As a teacher I am dealing with a community of young individuals for whom I have multiple responsibilities. The circumstances of schools are such that there is a high level of unpredictability, ranging from the emotional state of the children in the class to the hazards of staff illness or the weather. Schools reported the example of the June week in 1997 when it rained continuously for four days. Schools which compared notes found a striking increase in the number of weak lessons on the fourth day accounted for by the stress on the children who had not been out to play at any time for four days running. Such risks – of which there are many – create profound unease.

The stress of the experience for the teachers, and perhaps especially for head-teachers, is exceptional – so exceptional, indeed, that it has to be asked whether it was ethically acceptable in a mature democratic society. Story after story unfolds of profound personal angst at the experience. Paranoia and self-doubt emerge. Personal damage is clearly in some cases profound. A number of commentators said it was the worst experience of their lives, and one said 'it may surprise you that this includes both my divorce and the death of my mother'. This was from a teacher judged 'outstanding' by the report. This teacher is planning to leave the profession. A number of commentators said there was no way they would go through the experience again. It was a real concern that 53 per cent of the 200 schools thought that they were actively set back by the inspection process, with a 43 per cent negative impact on staff morale. Only 16 per cent found the inspection a worthwhile experience. Typical remarks about the process were:

- The threat of Ofsted looming ahead dominated too much of our lives (in and out of school). The burden and stress on schools is out of proportion to the benefits. I don't feel I would want to go through the process again.
- The Ofsted inspection that my school was subjected to was hugely damaging for staff, children and governors alike – we all wanted a critical yet honest appraisal to carry the school forward – the team that inspected us did not have the expertise and background to do this.
- Ofsted inspections are a snapshot of a school which has spent an inordinate amount of time preparing. Staff are often highly stressed before the event and sometimes deflated and demoralized afterwards. Inspections should be of schools as they are.
- As the head of a relatively small primary school I found our recent Ofsted inspection to be a traumatic experience despite a supporting team and the fact that we received a very good report. The amount of pressure I was under as a teaching head was unbelievable. I now thoroughly resent Ofsted as I feel they have taken the pleasure out of the job I have enjoyed doing for the past 23 years.
- Although we had a super Ofsted team and a very positive final report the whole experience brought little benefit to our school and has in some ways set us back.

The only counter to this largely negative impact on the 'feelings' of the schools was the tendency for the inspection to draw the staff together, binding them against – as it were – a common enemy. This sometimes improved relationships, teamwork, with staff, parents, children and governors alike, though largely as a defensive strategy against an external threat.

One consequence of this is the tendency for the inspection to create a range of defensive strategies: the inspection becomes a challenge to the organization to 'sell itself'. This is the expected reaction of organizations under threat from outside powers, creating survival strategies. A striking example of this was the school which prepared for its inspection for three years, employing a registered inspector to check every lesson, every move, every document over a three-year period. A secretary was employed for 12 months to type and retype paperwork. Every lesson was prepared, rehearsed and checked. A battery of 'successful assemblies' was prepared along with priming of parents and children well ahead of schedule. The inspection team turned out to be sensitive and sensible – which helped – and they were exposed to a brilliant prepared operation in which every conceivable hitch was covered. The school became one of what in the field is described as 'Woodhead's 100'.

It is important to look closely at the reasons why such a system exists – unique in its inscrutability, size, power and ambition in any education inspection system in the Western world. It is, as a Swedish colleague said to me, 'A kind of educational policing based on the notion that a crime has been committed.'

Ofsted is based upon two theories driven by Conservative Governments and used to underpin policy throughout the 1980s. (1) the notion that schools are poor, performance is weak and many children are failing; (2) a particular view of what education is – namely a form of training developing competencies that can be measured in practical and meaningful ways, generating performance data against which progress – local and national – can be tested and compared.

These two strong theories provide the justification for a policing system which eliminates any requirement to trust or involve the teachers. It is highly centralized with a hands-on chief inspector with tight direction of the ideological base and transmissional arrangements. It provides a fusion of a central unity of purpose with a Jacobean denial of the need for mediating institutions such as local education authorities. In this respect it has the feel of a kind of educational Marxism in its belief that the State can manage, direct and control to a high level of detail.

An interesting comparison can be made between educational and economic issues in the modern State. Let us for a moment imagine the Department for Education and Employment (DfEE) was managing not education but the economy. We would then ask the question much more clearly of how much the current raft of policies spun through the 1980s has been a utopian project running flatly against enduring realities. The Conservatives quixotically banged the drum both for traditional values and market forces, as if the free market isn't the most powerful solvent of traditions that we have. As the Department of Education and Science (DES) grew ever larger and more formidable as a department in the late 1980s, so resources were held in check. Between 1979 and the early 1990s class sizes were held constant in State schools during a period of demographic reduction in the child population. This effectively amounted to a reduction of 50 000 teachers in the State sector during that period. In every other Western country (and most Far Eastern countries) as well as in the UK independent sector, class sizes continued steadily to improve over the same period (Szreter, 1998).

The counter to the message of no extra resources was to drive forward a raft of high profile relatively cost-free initiatives from the centre, which combined an orchestrated denigration of the system (poor performing, needs dramatically improving) with a focus on the weakness of teachers, the virtues of large classes (David Reynolds cites the 'Taiwan' model) and the requirements of a heavily Government-authenticated policing system (Ofsted). It is a matter of some amusement that Stuart Sutherland, Her Majesty's Chief Inspector (HMCI) who first developed and implemented the Ofsted programme for schools, is the very same Stuart Sutherland who then led a ferocious opposition to the quality assurance audit plan for inspection, when faced at Edinburgh University with the threat of very similar measures by QAA – the body charged with measuring and improving standards in higher education. This is a fascinating example of the gap that has developed between the professional workers on the ground and governmental 'perception' at the centre. So it was that education could be given an increasingly high political profile while at the same time the service was quietly defenestrated of funding.

Education policy in a Labour Government has in a different way provided a new platform for Government enterprise in a political world which has seen the demise of the grand ideological aspirations of the old socialism. Where there is no enemy there is no political dialectic worth its name; where there is no ambition the people grow bored. Governments are perhaps right to recognize right now that the political enemy is simply boredom by the public with serious political issues. So now education has fallen under the spotlight as a high profile front-line public concern that gives a bit of spice and momentum to progressive political aspirations.

For New Labour education is now the priority of all priorities. The core objective is an aspiration to provide *equality of entitlement*. David Blunkett's concern above all is to bring the failed and disenfranchized into the mainstream of educational opportunity. This highly desirable objective is a translation of what has been historically an *economic* objective for socialists and social democrats into the educational field. The old socialist concern for redistribution and equalizing economic politics has been replaced by a high profile campaign to raise standards for all in education. Labour, like the Conservatives, is compelled by economic facts of life to support the belief that an educational pupil revolution can be generated without a substantial reassessment of per capita funding. The HMCI has said that *'there is not a resource problem'*. Raising standards, therefore, does not need to cost – or at least not cost much. Mr Woodhead may be speaking here for the short-term pragmatics of a Labour Government, though not, I suspect, for its deeper beliefs and instincts, or long-term hopes.

Both Conservative and Labour Governments have been keen to exploit international league table comparisons to drive up standards but the truth is that in wealthy countries everywhere voter demand for improved education and health care is growing at a faster pace than the economy grows, implying that there will be increasing pressure on governments to increase spending in these areas as a proportion of GDP. Either taxes must increase to finance the extra spending or private expenditure must plug the gap.

Ofsted might be seen as small beer in this wider scenario, but it is interesting for all that as symptomatic of wider political and ideological movements and attitudes. And teachers are caught in the wash of the revolution – albeit someone else's revolution – in danger of being seen as the stick-in-the-muds, the whiners, the conservatives, old romantics defending the indefensible. The Old Left rearguard rises up like a ghost of the past at every National Union of Teachers' (NUT) conference and is matched by ghosts of the tub-thumping Old Right at the NASUWT. These stroppy and defensively negative refuseniks speak for the most part to an unconvinced audience of the vast majority of teachers; their representation is small and out of touch – uncool, serious, impassioned, unvisionary. *Daily Mail* readers, confronted by these spectres from the past, are thus reassured at how right government policies are.

Ofsted had achieved its influence by full use of its access to the panoply of government, its departmental and political clout, above all its access to large sources of funding. Since its inception Ofsted has cost approximately £1,113 million to the exchequer. Its budget for 1998 was £151 million. To this we must add the substantial costs to the schools themselves in administrative, teaching and advisory support time. An Ofsted inspection is a very expensive exercise seen from the perspective of schools, and one of its features has been a lack of formal financing auditing since its inception in 1991. On the other hand, from a political perspective, Ofsted provides a rationale, a programme, a series of eye-catching headings, speaking on behalf of that mysterious phenomenon the Rousseauist 'general will', at low cost relative to the whole educational budget. For governments set to raise the heat on education this low-cost high-profile exercise has been seen as good value.

An added bonus for Ofsted has been its direction in the confident hands of an HMCI able to span ancient and modern traditions of educational inspecting by drawing together under a single umbrella the claim of independence from government in the old HMI tradition with the modern business-like drive to politicize and make every possible use of media high profile, advice and opinion. A ceaseless flow of headlines is ensured through a panoply of annual addresses, lectures, reports and the like with full access to the government press machine and a large publishing budget. There are times when even the HCMI's most ardent admirers have perceived him to be beyond government control, a kind of Jeremaid freelancer supporting with considerable cool the scaffolding of a decade of educational policy, adaptable (as he is) to the upgrades, adjustments and new initiatives of changing government regimes. It is no surprise that the Prime Minister should want to retain so able an operator.

Mr Woodhead's many critics must bear in mind the possibility that he may be more right than wrong, and the stirring of complacency in the foothills – if that is what has happened – is a good thing, and that short-term frontal attack may be an expensive but necessary chastisement, like a smack for a recalcitrant child.

Some argue that there is little evidence that Ofsted has achieved very much except target a small percentage of weak schools overwhelmingly situated in areas of high social poverty. A harsher view – which I have heard – is that Ofsted's agenda has consisted of a low-cost attack on a profound inner city problem, creating a smokescreen to avoid facing the need for massive compensatory resources. It is an irony that Ofsted has found it hard to justify its performance through the kind of empirical evidence it itself tries to demand of its school inspection operation. There is little evidence that it has raised standards for the large mass of children. But it is equally arguable that this is not the main point of the exercise: revolutions and centralist initiatives do not necessarily require such hard data. They are more about changing cultures and responding to political imperatives than empirical evidence of short-term or local gains.

An inspection is perhaps like an MOT test – overpriced, certainly, and conceptually vulnerable with inflated aspirations – but contributing to a quality assurance debate that raises the level of public demand for higher standards and concerns itself with the underprivileged and short-changed youngsters who have to suffer an unacceptable poor-quality educational commodity. To change anything so large, practice-driven, so irresolutely unadaptable, as an education system is, if it can be done, something of an achievement. A Leninist approach encourages the revolution onwards and may in the long run be cost effective. The simplest, speediest and on the surface of things most cost-effective form of management is to say *this shall be done* and then ensure *it is actually done*. And if such a process results in improving schools generally, however painful the process, then the case, m'lud, surely speaks for itself. Some fanciful play with the evidence, the occasionally rhetorical features of the exercise, the impressionistic ethnography, the inevitable degree of unevenness, then fall into place as means justifying ends.

Ofsted, then, is an interesting exemplar of contemporary politics in action. It dismisses trust as an option. It expresses the muscle of a greatly enlarged and growing department of government. The DfEE (like the DES since the mid-1980s) now behaves in the manner of those much criticized LEAs of the mid-1970s with an almost cavalier expansion of departments and a plethora of initiatives based on relatively generous departmental funding. Above all it eliminates the need for a 'middle' – such mediating agencies, as the local authorities (whose power is evermore diminished, and who are themselves under the scrutiny of Ofsted) though it was an irony, too, that it is the despised local authority advisers who are, in fact, propping up the whole enterprise by taking on large numbers of Ofsted inspections. The system is paradoxically increasingly both more centralized and more decentralized. The key players at the centre are civil servants, quangos and heads of departments; at the periphery they are the head-teachers. At the centre heady confidence combines with rapid planning and plethoras of initiatives; at the periphery the recipients of the policies, who are expected to interpret and deliver them, feel evermore vulnerable and insecure.

There is inevitably a downside. The problem with such an oligarchical approach is its fragility. It proffers a view that we have reached the end of history in the sense that we – the government, the centre, – know what is right, know what we need to do, which is to storm the barricades with (eg) literacy and numeracy hours, SATs, league tables and the like. We know that dramatic improvements can and must be made in standards. There is everything to do. But the heady energy of central initiatives, however purposeful, well planned and well intentioned, can have an enervating effect on the periphery – especially when it feels seriously detached from the decision- and policy-making process. Purpose seen from a victim's perspective can seem like obstinacy, poor communication and insensitivity.

Paradoxically, then, this urgency is always in danger of promoting a counter: a paralysis of ideas, of creative alternatives, of entries into places unknown where we're certainly going to have to go if only to keep up with the marketplace of ideas, which will constantly come up with new and improving notions of how to do things better. For centralist policy making tends to avoid the issue of the ever-growing importance of the *diversity* of the marketplace. And in another market, the employment market in education, as in health, there are many professionals voting with their feet, leading to a looming recruitment problem. (The treatment of doctors and social workers over the last decade has been every bit as cavalier as the treatment of teachers.) It might be argued that we are encouraging low-initiative, low-risk and narrowing institutional thinking at precisely the moment that the business world is moving in a new direction. The cutting edge of management thinking is focusing on the development of creativity, initiative – and above all, *trust* – in its workforce. The 'glass ceiling' principle is precisely the model being put aside. Even the last Conservative Government had its doubts and set up an unannounced investigative group run by business, with a seconded headteacher from Sheffield to explore alternative models of school inspection and self-evaluation.

In a world in which contemporary business management increasingly devolves, encourages trust, inspires teamwork, responds fast to initiatives, the centralist approach to down-the-line policy-making and policing looks increasingly vulnerable and out of date. It inhibits the development of new models of inspection, advice and institutional consultancy. It undermines the best aspects of market forces, which is the rigour of economic scrutiny and the exploration of better, cheaper and possibly more effective models. With so much to play for, Ofsted's Grand Plan starts to look maladaptive to the rapidly developmental forces that a high-quality contemporary business approach requires in a changing world, which is perhaps why most other countries in the Western world and the Far East alike are pursuing evaluative and quality control models that look radically different from ours.

THE MEANING OF OFSTED

There is a strong political case to be made in defence of Ofsted. Ofsted will be seen by its apologists as an important reflection of centralist political momentum, a function of the Labour Government's legitimate passion to improve standards. Moreover, it is symptomatic of a fashionable shift to performance measurement of all manner of professional activities. There has been a movement in some influential academic quarters to argue that teaching is in most important respects a science – successful teaching can be described, replicated and measured. It has definitive rules and method-ologies, and it is pure romance to support otherwise. Ofsted enters this debate, proposing its own definition of quality based on a set of well-defined criteria. The outcome is a mass of new – some would say refresh-ingly new – information about the link between good teaching and measured outcomes. The Ofsted database is (theoretically) able to map out the performance of the country's schools and to pinpoint areas of strength and weakness. One outcome of this process is to identify the schools that are models for the rest eg Beacon Schools – and to make use of their skills in bringing successful practice to everyone's attention. Defenders of Ofsted will argue that the inspection process has the integrity of a piece of quality social research – depersonalized, indifferent to opinion, quality controlled, analysed and delivered by trained researchers (the inspectors). Indifference to outcome, and lack of commitment to the schools inspected becomes a virtue. Judgements are not linked to future business commitments or to any future involvement with the people surveyed.

The final report thus provides a detached, clear, snapshot of the state of the schools. Moreover, anyone who disputes the importance of such 'snapshots' underestimates the current public interest in performance indicators: parents have every right to as much knowledge as possible about the schools which their children do or might attend – including academic performance. It is the nature of a developing democracy that the clients (or customers) should have as many choices as possible in matters which affect them most – the most convincing of the theoretical argu-ments underlying the Conservative's position in relation to consumer knowledge and consumer rights. Schools are important places, and a mature society should provide as much information as possible to assist proper choice.

A further argument is that there is a huge range of quality not only between schools, but between teachers. It is demeaning to the best teachers and unfair on the pupils of the worst to allow such a wide range of inequity of provision.

There has been as a consequence an exponential growth of inspection and scrutiny in every corner of educational (and indeed public) life. To this we can add the razor of competition – the cult of the best – with football league table types of analysis applied to every manner of social and cultural life from pop records (the best 100) to politicians (league tables of the 'cleverest' ministers were recently published). No one is immune from such categorization, so why not schools, teachers or even pupils themselves? An ever-growing exam culture generates excitement in the press and opportunity to publish information about the best of this and the worst of that.

The much criticized tendency for the HMCI and Ofsted to command the headlines could be seen as sensible opportunism, educating the public by attracting media attention – if you don't then someone else will. Ofsted might well argue that its judgements carry more substance, given its enormous range of data compared with most tinpot small-scale research projects. If John Marks and the like can declare as they do from time to time that 'Standards are getting worse', then is it not better to hear a prestigious and informed – moreover independent – voice of the state? Chris Woodhead has argued that he speaks from firmly established data, and his message (like the messages of many who speak to the press) is often misheard, oversimplified and misunderstood and his view of events, though far from complacent, is more complex than people realize. The problem, if there is a problem, is the media not the message.

The argument that the professionals are not happy with what is happening is, maybe, no argument at all. Professionals everywhere do not like to be overly scrutinized and overly criticized, but then maybe we've been allowed to get away with too much in the past. Those paid out of the public purse, whose jobs are invariably more secure than those in the private sector, have to put up with a level of accountability which is rigorous (a buzzword of the 1980s) and above board. Furthermore, such scrutiny at least shows that the activity matters – and matters greatly.

Through the 1970s and early 1980s the primary education sector was low on the DES's agenda. Throughout the 1970s more than 80 per cent of HMIs were secondary inspectors, despite 60 per cent of the child population being in primary schools. There is no evidence that primary education was much scrutinized, and maybe not much cared about, accounting for the one-third less per capita allowance that primary schools receive. Increase scrutiny reflects increased interest. It could be that the barrage of concern about literacy and numeracy standards in schools has helped to underpin David Blunkett's important initiative in developing a preschool multi-disciplinary agenda supported by £450 million ('Surestart') – development that might have been unlikely without the Blitzkrieg approach on standards which the Government has been taking. The downside of much increased scrutiny and public knowledge may be linked to the upside of a far more intelligent and sustained concern for educational sectors that in some ways has been hiding neglected under stones.

And so, the argument goes, maybe the critics of Ofsted are making too much of a fuss, failing to see the wood for the trees, and harping after an old lost (and not so wonderful) world that is past and gone. There are, however, legitimate doubts. The question of the scientific validity of the Ofsted data must be raised. A close analysis of the inspection process reveals unpredictability and insecurity in its assessment process: it falls uneasily between a quasi-scientific process of measurement and a critical interpretative process in which the style and attitude of the team (and especially the registered inspector) are of great importance. Moreover, there appears to be at best only a loose connection between the internal Ofsted analysis and SAT results, ie standards as academically conceived.

Ofsted outcomes, like SAT results, are demonstrably linked to social class. The study commissioned by the Channel 4 *Dispatches* programme on Ofsted found that 59 of 83 failing secondary schools had to cope with poverty levels which were twice the national average: only one of the failing secondary schools was in an area that could be described as prosperous. At the other end of the spectrum the vast majority of schools with outstanding reports – many subsequently featured as Beacon Schools – are from relatively well-off socio-economic areas.

The depersonalization of the inspection process has arguably damaged school and teacher morale. We are short of teachers and getting seriously worried about recruitment and yet the Ofsted process appears to be a key factor in depressing the morale of the profession. On the evidence of our questionnaire to 200 recently inspected schools, the Ofsted experience has an undeniably negative effect. At a recent seminar at Cambridge University a group of highly rated heads and teachers confirmed universally that Ofsted has had a damaging effect on teacher recruitment and morale among the best professionals by generating the mythology that teachers are by and large second-rate and if they were told what to do and worked to a much tighter structure of competencies they would perform better – the notion that morale, personal commitment, independence and intelligence are side issues.

Ofsted discourages both imagination and risk. The inspection process encourages conservatism and as such is hardly likely to make much difference to pupil standards or to energize school quality. The vast number of observation grades are in the middle rank. This is, of course, exactly what statistically we should expect, but there is something in Tony Wenham's point (in a letter to the *Times Educational Supplement*, 10 April 1998) '… inspections encourage lots of safe teaching … had the inspector not been there teachers would have approached lessons in a much more interesting and stimulating way'. The inspection process eliminates the opportunity for dialectic and exploration: a highly controlling, and bureaucratic approach presumes that all is known about successful teaching and learning at a time when, as we approach the millennium, there is a pressing need to explore new approaches, new ideas.

There is little evidence that Ofsted had made any genuine difference to standards, except in the obvious case of a minority of poor schools closed or revamped following a critical inspection. The argument is that for the vast majority of schools and teachers, where they are not actively depressed or even damaged by the inspectorial experience, they are confirmed into making only the most marginal changes to their *modus operandi*: there is little motivation or reason for the kind of regenerating reform which some of our most creative thinkers – including some Government agitators – think may be needed.

Ofsted may be a way of avoiding issues, of smokescreening the situation, of (eg) tackling the problems of the inner city school by mere exhortation, of avoiding considering funding, social and socio-economic issues. The evidence is that the independent school sector outperforms the State sector on every criterion, without either Ofsted or the National Curriculum, but with double the per capita finance. There is the further issue that the same patterns of results between schools emerge in the very many Western world nations that do not have the traumas of Ofsted (or even in some cases a national curriculum) and yet whose results seem to outperform England. There is little to show that rigorous inspection has made even the most marginal difference to the great national cause of improving standards, which raises the question of value for money and what might have been otherwise done with the £1 billion plus cost of this particular department – some £60,000 per annum for every secondary school in the land – over 10 years £600,000 per school. To this we might add the issue of lack of accountability, a failure to institute an independent financial and performance audit.

It could then, by the harshest of critics, be argued that Ofsted is the poor man's substitute for action, based on dodgy evidence, helping deny the need for massive political action requiring resourcing – or at least radical rethinking of the educative process. It has damaged the personal will of precisely the most creative and committed teachers; it has created an excuse for inaction by exhorting action. Its focus on negativity has had the fallout via the media that teaching is seen by most of our best educated youngsters as a no-no. Unreliable, overweening and damaging to schools: poor value for money. A political device to avoid a more disturbing and radical analysis of social and educational problems. Libby Purves (1998) put it ferociously ...

'It was abruptly decided that education was a vote-winner; a succession of careerist education ministers brought in compulsory change at bewildering speed, declining to target real failure but instead throwing hundreds of perfectly good schools into anxious uproar with their scattergun directives ... The habit of insulting teachers, once confined mainly to disaffected intelligentsia and *The Beano*, was made mainstream by Government.

She only misses one point – that it was Ofsted that led the way in its public statements, and produced the evidence to justify its own invective.

The key issues are presented here starkly: they represent dilemmas which at the very least call for close examination. There is no disputing that the education service needs to be made accountable, though inspection has historically never been seen as anything other than a conservative phenomenon, an insurance policy, a public protector on the margins of the activity it inspects, a public security against abuse and incompetence. The whole business of inspection, in fact, has been seriously under-researched. Apart from my own book on local authority advisers and management (Winkley, 1986), there has been little systematic investigation in recent years. By far the most comprehensive general survey of the inspection process was by Rhodes (1981), and its strong conclusion was that inspection in virtually all areas of public and industrial life is by and large an inefficient and ineffective way to quality control. It can also be argued, however, that there is no way that poor schools – however tiny they are as a proportion – can be allowed to proceed unmolested, and Ofsted has in some cases offered parents and children a better deal by picking up and dealing with some of the worst schools (and subsequently LEAs).

The problems seem to be of balance and perspective – and of cost. How can we put together an adequate inspection service that is up to the complexity of the interpretative process, that is value for money and acts not as a distraction or a demoralization, but as a spur to further action and improvement? How can we link the need to make the best of our professional expertise? At a deeper level how can we move away from the encamped centralist position that assumes that top-down management exhortation based upon a fancifully quasi-scientific and largely negative process is moderated by drawing upon the positive support of those who actually work in the most beleaguered of our institutions? How can we create a cost-effective system that is more useful than one that indulges in examination of everything that moves once every few years in a programme of analysis that has dubious intellectual standing either with the teachers or from a rational examination of the evidence? There has developed an undeniable rift between those who face children every day of the week and those who plan in offices well away from the field with (as teachers perceive) considerably higher pay. There is an interesting managerial rule at play – that management perceptions of situations unless countered by complicating and refining evidence or real sustained experience, tend by a law of attrition, to theorise, reduce and simplify: which explains in part the tensions that currently exist between management and professionals in almost every area of public life.

This tension is recognized at the heart of Antony Giddens's (1998) recent examination of 'the Third Way': do we register a centrally driven moral authoritarianism in the public sphere, or (as Giddens' argument from the sketch of his programme seems to imply) do we genuinely practise inclusion, seeking to incorporate local and professional participation in revitalized conceptions of democracy? The definition, role, implementation and control of accountability systems mirror the to and from of this tension in the analysis of current social democratic politics, and become key indicators of which way the political wind is blowing.

There are certainly many alternative accountability models to draw from – industry, other professions and walks of life. Numerous ideas were thrown up by head-teachers in our questionnaires, as part of an overwhelming feeling that change is needed. There were many who wish to return to the old LEA adviser-inspector arrangements. Many thought that Ofsted is an enormous hammer to crack a small nut, and needs substantially thinning down and streamlining. Some thought a new model altogether is called for, which is more participative and breaks down existing defences. Many noted that the current arrangements are barrier creators. The teachers try to put on their best costumes while the inspectors set out to strip them naked. However people try to be pleasant to each other, conflict and subversion, performance and pretence are built into the agenda.

If we want to look in new directions altogether there is an interesting working model worth looking at in the way doctors who teach other doctors are assessed. Thirteen thousand doctors have so far been assessed by expert assessors, based on clear ethical principles: 'education is a morally charged activity. Ethically, therefore, it is crucial that the location of the power should be constantly under question, that the learners should be empowered to take responsibility for their own learning ... the moral imperative is to help and not to harm' (Playdon and Goodsman, 1997).

It distinguishes between 'training' as a learning process which deals with known outcomes with the central concern that the same product should be produced identically each time, and 'education' which is a learning process which deals with unknown outcomes. The Ofsted model to date has increasingly edged to a view of school teaching as 'training': it would benefit from looking at the model described by Playdon and Goodsman, of Kings College, University of London, as appropriate for doctors that education refers its questions and actions to principles and values rather than merely standards and criteria. In a clinical setting, therefore, 'a major means of communicating these (principles and values) is the activity which we identify as the professional conversation, the ongoing interchanges about patients, principles and procedures through which doctors learn and update their clinical practice' (Playdon and Goodsman, 1997).

Here, then, are two key notions on how to improve professional practice: high-quality dialectic – the searching forward for improvement – which is located in a strong sense of self-worth, in a belief that 'I can achieve the goals I set myself'. These notions are not only not in evidence in the Ofsted process, the process of inspection it advocates seems to undermine them by design. It is for teachers to offer their own analysis of how to move forward in the spirit of constructive criticism. We might argue that there is clearly an urgent case for the introduction of a quick surveying process or 'light touch inspection', with intervention in indirect proportion to school success.

We need to estimate the kind of support a school needs to move itself forward. The teachers themselves need to be drawn into this exercise. The accountability process should be far less bureaucratic. It should ensure good ongoing quality control. It should link to a medium- and long-term development programme. It should be far more cost effective. A subsidiary aspect of this should be to greatly improve the business of school/institutional consultancy. The use of highly adaptive and trained external analysis in the business of improvement has been long established in industry. We need to press for a national programme to set parameters for institutional consultants to work with head-teachers and schools on school improvement. The Ofsted Polaroid photograph is not enough; institutional consultancy is not the same as inspection.

Schools with serious weaknesses come into a different category. Here something like the current inspection process can justifiably be taken, though there are aspects of the measuring, number-crunching, and impersonal bureaucratic nature of the process that need addressing. Some of the criticisms outlined above need in all circumstances to be taken seriously: some aspects of the current programme are unreasonable, and have been damaging by an obsessive, unbalanced emphasis on negative features. Teachers need to be drawn into the school accountability and improvement business in more direct and general ways by developing symposia and forums that assess and feedback on Ofsted. It is unconstructive to create a management-professional divide of the kind we have at the moment.

Teachers need to be drawn from the periphery more to the centre of things and feel that they can genuinely influence events and be listened to as part of the policy-making process. The Beacon School idea is potentially a step forward here: we must move to pressing our brightest teachers to engage in dialectic in ways in which they feel they can be listened to. We think the NPC has a role here, along with other evolving professional organizations, including hopefully, the putative General Council of Teachers (GCT). There is a real concern by this Government that quality teachers and head-teachers should be identified and drawn into the dissemination and development process, celebrating and building on the work of successful schools.

It would be a mistake to suppose that some of these messages have not reached the current Government. The whole notion of accountability if open to reappraisal in a new generation of thinking. The next tranche of inspection – though it will continue through Ofsted for the foreseeable future – is likely to look different. The quality and transparency of the inspection process ought to improve, and (hopefully) the debate about 'quality practice' deepen and refine. More decisive action will be taken by Ofsted in the case of justifiable complaints. The emphasis will need to be increasingly on support and the relationship between the future Ofsted and other developments – particularly the Qualifications and Curriculum Authority (QCA) and the Standards and Effectiveness Unit – will need closer attention. It is likely that the new brief for the HMCI will give greater emphasis to the need to improve teacher morale, which may – ought – to lead to a sea change in attitude in the public arena. Particular sensitivity will be needed in handling the problems of inner city schools, if we want to retrain staff. Good reasons have to be given for teachers to work in schools in difficult circumstances, and the current perception – rightly or wrongly – of abuse, underestimation and victimization must be dramatically reappraised.

The complex nature of the relationships between poverty, SAT results and high-quality school cultures needs close reappraisal; the resurrection of a great debate begun in the 1960s here lies waiting in the wings. Quality education is not simply about SAT results, and in many cases long-term improvements will need huge sustained multi-disciplinary efforts from preschool onwards. The debate about teaching as training or education, teaching as art or science, also needs revising in much greater depth.

And yet many hardworking teachers (and nurses and doctors) are going to ask: does any of this seriously address the immediate crisis in schools – and hospitals – in recruitment and professional confidence? Are we doing too little too late? How long is it going to take to reverse the distracting and demotivating bureaucratic mountain that surrounds the life of the working professional? How do we regenerate trust? How do we recon-struct the fierce and powerful vision of teaching described by John Steinbeck, and quoted approvingly by Muriel Spark, that most acerbically unromantic of writers ...? 'I have come to believe that a great teacher is a great artist ... Teaching might even be greater than the arts since the medium is the human mind and spirit'.[1]

Does the problem lie deeper: signalled in the glass ceiling of perceptions and understanding between those who practise a profession and those who manage it? I leave the last word to that most famous of inspectors, Matthew Arnold, commenting on the uneasy balance lying at the core of the inspection business, between feeling superior to those you inspect and yet being humbled by their commitment.

> I met daily in the schools men and women discharging duties akin to mine, duties as irksome as mine, duties less well paid than mine: I saw them making the best of it; I saw the cheerfulness and efficiency with which they did their

work and I asked myself again, How do they do it? Gradually it grew into a habit with me to put myself into their places to try to enter into their feelings, to represent to myself their life and ... I got many lessons from them.[2]

NOTES

1. Quoted by Muriel Spark (1992) in 'Curriculum Vitae', Penguin Books.
2. From Matthew Arnold's retirement speech at Westminster School.

REFERENCES

Giddens, A (1998) *The Third Way: The Renewal of Social Democracy*, Polity Press, Cambridge

Playdon, JZ and Goodsman, D (1997) *British Medical Journal*, March

Purves, L (1998) in *The Independent*, 1 October

Rhodes, G (1981) *Inspectorates in British Government*, Allen and Unwin, London

Szreter, S, 'Staff and resources in the State Education System', Primary Practice, **13**, January 1998

Spark, M (1992) Curriculum Vitae, Penguin Books, London

Winkley, DR (1986) *Diplomats and Detectives: A Study of Local Authority Management and Advisory Services*, Cassell, London

Effects of Ofsted inspections on school performance

Cedric Cullingford and Sandra Daniels

At the heart of the policy of successive governments lies the firm belief that the raising of educational standards is largely a matter of will. The often repeated mantra of 'Targets, targets, targets' encapsulates this belief. All the policies since the introduction of the National Curriculum have been examples of this. Whether expressed in the relatively neutral term 'accountability' or through 'naming and shaming', the policies have been dependent on the accumulation of evidence; the gathering of all kinds of data for the purposes of comparison.

Beyond the publication of raw statistics that make up the league tables, the most significant demonstration of the belief in measures of external control is the power invested in Ofsted. While there are all kinds of doubts expressed about the side-effects like stress on teachers and pupils and disruption to the normal routines of school, inspection remains at the heart of Government policy. If weaknesses are to be put right, and if all pupils are to receive their entitlement, then, so runs the argument, a vigorous succession of inspections need to take place on a regular basis in all schools. The official policy documents and statements all make this clear. 'The purpose of inspection is to identify strengths and weaknesses so that schools may improve the quality of education they provide and raise the educational standards achieved by their pupils' (Ofsted, 1998).

The more tightly controlled and the more consistent the formula of inspection the more useful is supposed to be the result. This suggests that any suspicion of the regime of inspections is deemed to be short-sighted. Temporary difficulties, like individual pain, are as nothing compared to the overall raising of standards. If the policy is right then standards will inexorably rise as a result of Ofsted inspections.

Many of the doubts about the system are to do with all kinds of possible side-effects. They do not really question the overall results. The questions that arise are to do with the narrowness of the focus and the mechanistic nature of the exercise (Gray, 1997). They question the criteria that are used and whether enough allowance is made for socio-economic differences. They worry about the side-effects on the school, on staff morale, which is well documented, and on the pupils (Jeffrey and Woods, 1997). Parents also are concerned about the impact of inspection on their children (Cullingford, 1996).

The central argument about Ofsted inspections is the intention between the essential purpose and the side-effects. Even in research commissioned by Ofsted itself, parents and the community generally demonstrate no particular interest or involvement (Tabberer, 1995).

Schools are left isolated and unsupported. Parents detect this and express their subsequent doubts about the whole process (Ouston and Klenowski, 1995). But these matters are deemed to be peripheral. The abiding concern with attainment targets remains. If inspections work then the outcomes will be clear: standards will rise, inexorably, over the years.

Putting aside all the philosophical and cultural arguments about inspections and their aftermath leaves us with the simple and fundamental question: does such a system work in its own terms? The research reported here asks a simple and objective question. What is the correlation between Ofsted inspections and exam results? The information is openly available, both in terms of dates and outcomes. The objective and disinterested hypothesis is the extent to which the Government's claims about the efficacy of such a programme are justified.

THE REPRESENTATIVE SAMPLE

Sample description

Examination results were obtained from a representative sample of pupils throughout the country. Firstly, all the Local Education Authorities (LEAs) (except the London boroughs) were stratified by type (metropolitan, non-metropolitan) in order that the sample would reflect the respective proportions in the country (approximately 35:40). Given their very diverse nature and the requirement to make the sample representative of the country as a whole, one LEA was selected at random to represent the London boroughs (Kensington).

The metropolitan and non-metropolitan LEAs were then stratified, where possible, by region (North, the Midlands and South). One LEA was then selected at random to represent each region. Given the absence of metropolitan boroughs in the South, the London borough provided a balance. Having selected the LEAs the whole cluster of schools (and hence pupils) within its area were included in the sample. Information was collected for all children in these schools during the period September 1993 until February 1998. This sampling procedure was intended to allow a representative sample of pupils from the country in terms of social background, gender and other background features.

As from September 1995, one of the selected LEAs, Avon, was subdivided into four smaller unity authorities. The Avon schools were crossreferenced and their results were combined to give a comparative data set for the rest of the study (see Table 3.1).

Each year the Secondary School Performance Tables and School and College (16–18) Performance Tables are freely available on the World Wide Web (page http://www.open.gov.uk/dfee/perform.htm) subject to copyright. Similarly, the Ofsted Report dates for all secondary schools in all LEAs are available on the Web (page http://www.ofsted.gov.uk/htm/seclea.htm). These two data sources were used to produce a combined data file for the analyses in this chapter.

Methodology

Logistic regression is useful for situations in which you want to be able to predict the presence or absence of a characteristic or outcome (proportion of pupils achieving five or more grade A$\star$ to C GCSEs) based on values of a set of predictor variables (year, inspection period). It is similar to a linear regression model but is suited to models where the dependent variable is

Table 3.1 *Composition of sample schools*

Type of LEA	Region	Selected LEAs	Schools (per year)	Pupils (average/year)
Metropolitan	North	Kirklees	126	4,285
	Midlands	Birmingham	158	11,459
Non-metropolitan	North	North Yorkshire	72	7,714
	Midlands	Nottinghamshire	86	11,574
	South	Avon$\star$	119	11,837
London boroughs	South	Kensington	23	976
Total		6$\star$	426	47,846

Note:
$\star$ Unitary authorities were: West Somerset, City of Bristol, Bath and north-east Somerset, South Gloucestershire.

dichotomous. Logistic regression coefficients can be used to estimate odds ratios for each of the independent variables in the model. An illustrated example, related to the types of variables being considered here, is given in the Technical Appendix.

Results

Figure 3.1 shows the distribution of all the school examination results according to their period of inspection. This code took the value 0 if the school was not inspected and 1 (inspected during September/October 1993), 2 (inspected during November/December 1993) etc up to 27 (inspected during January/February 1998) for schools that were inspected. It can be seen that, generally, the proportion of pupils attaining five or more A* to C grades at GCSE was higher for the non-inspected schools than for those receiving an inspection during the period 1994–98. This may have been due to some selection criteria of Ofsted but there is no record of that being the case.

The boxplots in Figure 3.2 shows the range in the proportion of pupils obtaining five or more grade A* to C at GCSE in schools in June 1996. The results were subdivided between schools that were inspected during that year and those that were not inspected.

It can be seen that generally the schools inspected during 1996 had lower proportions of pupils obtaining five or more A* to C GCSEs than did the schools that were not inspected. Similarly, Table 3.2 below shows

Table 3.2   *Average percentage of pupils obtaining five or more A* to C grades at GCSE in inspected schools compared to schools not inspected and overall percentages*

	1993–94	1994–95	1995–96	1996–97
Overall pass rate (national)*	43	44	45	45
Overall pass rate (sample)	42	43	44	45
Not inspected	49	53	56	51
Sept/Oct inspection	39	57	51	47
Nov/Dec inspection	34	39	39	40
Jan/Feb inspection	44	36	40	49
Mar/April inspection	42	44	35	32
May/June inspection	29	33	25	10**

Notes:

*   England.

** Based on information available at the time for a small number of inspections during this period.

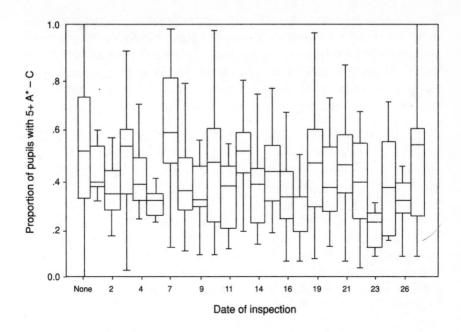

Figure 3.1 *Distribution of examination results by period of inspection*

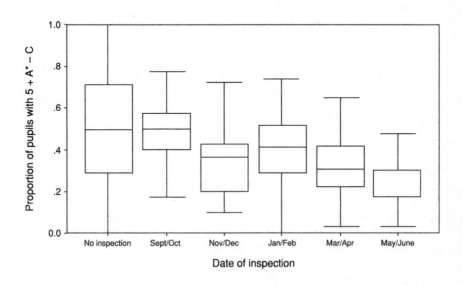

Figure 3.2 *The proportion of pupils obtaining five or more A* to C grades in schools in June 1996*

that a similar pattern emerges for the other school years covered by the study. Firstly, the national percentage of pupils obtaining five or more grade A* to C GCSEs during the four school years September 1993 to June 1997 are shown. Secondly, the overall percentages for the sample are given for comparison with the national statistics. Lastly, the percentages for schools inspected (or not) during each of the inspection periods are provided.

It can be seen that the estimates of the overall pass rate in the sample were very close to the national pass rates as provided by official Government statistics. This should provide some measure of confidence that the sample was representative of the national population.

In each of the school years the percentage of pupils obtaining five or more grade A* to C GCSEs was least for schools that were inspected during the period immediately prior to the June examinations. However, care must be taken when interpreting these findings so as not to imply causality. The outcomes could be attributed to several influences. Firstly, Ofsted may have a policy of inspecting the worst schools during the May/June period. Secondly, they may have a policy of inspecting only poor performing schools and hence the lower performance of the inspected schools could be anticipated. Lastly, it could be that the inspections placed an extra burden on teachers at a time when they were needed most prior to examinations. Nevertheless, given that the sample was representative of the national statistics and the pattern is generally replicated over each of the four school years it should provide some cause for concern over the timing of inspections.

The results of the logistic regression model are given in full in Appendix A but a summary is shown below.

$$\log_e (p/(1-p)) = 0.515 + 0.02 \text{ (years)} - 0.16 \text{ (Sept/Nov)} - 0.56 \text{ (Nov/Dec)} - 0.39 \text{ (Jan/Feb)} - 0.57 \text{ (Mar/Apr)} - 1.02 \text{ (May/June)}$$

A summary of the variables is shown in Table 3.3.

Table 3.3   *Summary of regression model variables*

Variable	Description	Code
Years	Year of examination results	1994 = 0, 1995 = 1 etc
Sept/Oct	School was inspected during Sept/Oct	yes = 1, no = 0
Nov/Dec	School was inspected during Nov/Dec	yes = 1, no = 0
Jan/Feb	School was inspected during Jan/Feb	yes = 1, no = 0
Mar/Apr	School was inspected during Mar/Apr	yes = 1, no = 0
May/June	School was inspected during May/June	yes = 1, no = 0

Using this model, each additional year produced a 0.02 increase in the log odds of having five or more grade A★ to C GCSEs, when the inspection period was kept constant. Using the regression equation, May/June has a log odds value of −1.02 and a corresponding odds value 0.36. Consequently, for an inspected school in May/June, the odds in favour of getting five or more grade A★ to C GCSEs are approximately 0.36 of that of a non-inspected school (years kept constant).

It can be seen that all the inspection periods produced a significant reduction in the log odds of a pupil obtaining the higher grades. All the regression coefficients were significant ($p < 0.01$) and negative except for the year that had a positive effect on the outcomes. That is to say, each year the overall picture was of a rising proportion of pupils obtaining higher grades but the actual proportions were restricted by the inspections.

The average difference in the percentage of pupils obtaining five or more grade A★ to C GCSEs between 1994 and 1997 varied between schools having inspections at different periods of the year. Appendix B shows that there was some evidence of an interaction between the years and period of inspection. However, this interaction was found only for the September/October and the March/April inspection periods. For convenience, using the regression model as described in Appendix B, the odds have been calculated and used to produce the predicted average percentages for school in each inspection period. These are shown in Table 3.4.

The September/October inspection appeared, over time, to be having a decreasingly negative effect. This could imply teachers were adjusting to these early inspections or that these inspections have, apparently, been having an increasingly more positive effect over time. However, the opposite case appeared for the March/April period. The apparent interaction effect was negative and implied an increasingly negative effect over time for inspections during this period. This is not to imply a cause and effect

Table 3.4 *Predicted percentages of pupils obtaining five or more grade A★ to C at GCSE in schools inspected during different inspection periods*

Inspection	Sept 1993– June 1994 %	Sept 1994– June 1995 %	Sept 1995– June 1996 %	Sept 1996– June 1997 %
None	51	52	52	53
Sept/Oct	46	46	47	48
Nov/Dec	37	37	37	38
Jan/Feb	41	41	42	42
Mar/Apr	39	38	37	36
May/June	28	28	29	29

relationship between the time of inspection and a school's educational outcomes. For example, changing the period of inspection would not imply that a school would necessarily improve its performance. The model reflects the relationship between the inspection period and outcomes as it appeared from the sample data set over time.

Conclusions and Recommendations

The research reported here was to measure the success, or otherwise, of Ofsted in its own terms. It did not explore all the issues of whether the kinds of things being measured are worth measuring. It simply took a neutral look at the effect of inspections on the 'raising of educational standards'.

Generally, there appeared to be a modest increase in the proportion of pupils obtaining five or more grades A★ to C year on year however, associated with Ofsted inspections a slower rate of increase as observed, ie schools falling behind other schools. All the inspection periods appeared to have had a significant negative effect on grades achieved. There was some evidence that this observed negative effect was not constant over time for all the inspection periods. It would appear that while September/October inspections were apparently having an increasingly less negative effect over time the March/April inspections were increasingly becoming more disruptive in terms of examination results.

There are two clear results that emerge from the statistics. The first is that the time of inspections is significant. This might not seem surprising to those who have witnessed or reported on the disruptions caused by inspections. The nearer to the exam period that inspections take place the worse the results.

The more significant finding is the fact that whatever the inspection period Ofsted has a negative effect on the percentage of pupils' successful in gaining higher grades. Putting it more bluntly, Ofsted inspections have the opposite effect to that intended. Year on year they lower standards.

Such clear findings, meticulously carried out, should not be discussed in the same way that Ofsted tends to treat other empirical evidence.

APPENDIX A

Table A.3.1 shows the output from the logistic regression model.

Dependent variable: the log odds of the proportion obtaining five or more A★ to C GCSE grades.

Table A.3.1   *Logistic regression model*

Variable	Regression coefficient	Standard error	Exp (coeff)
Jan/Feb	− 0.3918	0.0141★★★	0.6758
Mar/Apr	− 0.5723	0.0143★★★	0.5642
May/June	− 1.0165	0.0235★★★	0.3619
Nov/Dec	− 0.5893	0.0151★★★	0.5547
Sep/Oct	− 0.1639	0.0144★★★	0.8488
Years	0.0189	0.0043★★★	1.0191
Constant	0.0515	0.0115	

Model statistics

−2 Log likelihood	257312.153
Goodness of fit	190652.824
Chi-square	3703.111★★★ (6df p < 0.001)

Note:
★★★ Statistically significant (p < 0.001).

APPENDIX B

Table A.3.2 shows the output from the logistic regression model including interactions.

Dependent variable: the log odds of the proportion obtaining five or more A★ to C GCSE grades.

TECHNICAL APPENDIX

Logistic regression can be illustrated with a simple example as shown in Table A.3.3. This example shows a relationship between the number of pupils obtaining five or more grade A★ to C GCSEs (*higher grades*) or not achieving those grades (*lower grades*) and whether their school had been inspected during that year or not.

Is school inspection an influential factor on educational outcomes? Given a sample of pupils measured by their educational achievement (obtaining five or more grade A★ to C GCSE), a model can be built using the inspection period variable to predict the presence or absence of achievement in a sample of pupils. The model can then be used to derive estimates of the odds ratios for each factor to tell, eg, how much more likely pupils in a school that had been inspected were to achieve five or

Table A.3.2   *Model statistics*

Variable	Regression coefficient	Standard error	Exp (coeff)
Jan/Feb	− 0.4269	0.0241★★★	0.6525
Mar/Apr	− 0.5036	0.0244★★★	0.6044
May/June	− 1.0066	0.0390★★★	0.3655
Nov/Dec	− 0.5998	0.0259★★★	0.5489
Sep/Oct	− 0.2116	0.0253★★★	0.8093
Years	0.0169	0.0078★	1.0171
Jan/Feb by years	0.0238	0.0127	1.0241
Mar/Apr by years	− 0.0479	0.0130★★★	0.9532
May/June by years	− 0.0074	0.0215	0.9927
Nov/Dec by years	0.0068	0.0136	1.0069
Sep/Oct by years	0.0308	0.0131★	1.0313
Constant	0.0548	0.0159★★★	

Model statistics

− 2 Log likelihood	257276
Goodness of fit	190650
Chi-square	3739★★★ (11 df, $p < 0.001$)

Notes:
★ Statistically significant (p < 0.05).
★★★ Statistically significant (p < 0.001).

more grade A★ to C GCSEs than were pupils in schools that had not been inspected.

In Table A.3.3, the *odds* of a pupil obtaining the five or more grade A★ to C GCSEs (*higher grades*) coming from a school that had been inspected were 55/145 = 0.38. The corresponding odds for pupils obtaining five or more grade A★ to C GCSEs (*higher grades*) from schools that were not inspected were 51/49 = 1.04. The *relative odds* of a pupil obtaining five or more grade A★ to C GCSEs (higher grades) from a non-inspected school compared with a pupil from an inspected school are 1.04/0.38 or 2.7 to 1. In other words a non-inspected school was almost three times as likely to produce pupils with five or more grade A★ to C GCSEs than an inspected school. Equally, pupils with five or more grade A★ to C GCSEs were three times more likely to have been in a school that had not been inspected than one that had.

Since the data set here consists of the proportions of pupils achieving five or more grade A★ to C GCSEs, the outcomes are considered to be binary (ie the pupil did/did not achieve higher grades). Consequently, a simple regression equation is not an appropriate model in this situation. It

Table A.3.3 *GCSE outcomes by inspection levels: number of pupils*

Grades	Not inspected (0)	Inspected (1)	Total
Lower	49	145	194
Higher	51	55	106
	100	200	300

is widely acknowledged that proportions have a binomial distribution with a mean of **p** (proportion of pupils obtaining higher grades) and variance p (1 − p) / n (**n** is the number of pupils in each school). A logistics regression equation can then be used to model the logarithm of the odds. Using the example in Table A.3.3 and some statistical software the logistic regression model was found to be:

$$\log_e[p/(1 - p)] = 0.05 - 1.02\ (\textbf{\textit{inspection}})$$

where **p** is the probabilities of pupils obtaining five or more grade A★ to C GCSEs (higher grades) and **inspection** takes the value 0 for no inspection and 1 for an inspected school.

So, the log odds of a non-inspected school (inspection = 0) having pupils with five or more grade A★ to C GCSEs (*higher grades*) was 0.05, which in turn means that the odds of a pupil having five or more grade A★ to C GCSEs (*higher grades*) was exponential (0.05) = 1.04. This corresponds to the odds as calculated previously in the example. Similarly, the log odds of a pupil having five or more grade A★ to C GCSEs (*higher grades*) from an inspected school (inspection = 1) are 0.97 lower (0.05 − 1.02) which means the odds of a non-inspected school producing a pupil with five or more grade A★ to C GCSEs (*higher grades*) is exponential (−0.97) or 0.38, as before. Alternatively, we can say the odds for an inspected school are exponential (1.01) or 2.7 times lower than they were for a non-inspected school. In other words the relative odds are 2.7.

REFERENCES

Cullingford, C (1996) *Parents, Education and the State*, Ashgate, Aldershot.

Gray, J (1997) A bit of a curate's egg? Three decades of official thinking about the quality of schools, *British Journal of Educational Studies*, **45**, pp 4–21

Jeffrey, B and Woods, P (1997) Feeling Deprofessionalised: The Social Construction of emotions during an Ofsted inspection, *Cambridge Journal of Education*, **26**, pp 325–43

Ofsted (1998) *Guidance on the Inspection of Secondary Schools*, Ofsted, London

Ousten, J and Klenowski, V (1995) *The Ofsted Experience Parents' Eye View*, Research and Information on State Education Trust, London

Tabberer, R (1995) *Parents Perceptions of Ofsted's Work*, NFER, Slough

*Chapter Four*_____

Improvement or control? A US view of English inspection

W Norton Grubb

In the United States, the classroom is normally a secret place. Even though it is full of people, what goes on is rarely reported, and even less often used to discuss what teaching is and might be. As generations of reformers have lamented, anything can happen when the teacher closes the door, and so the most carefully constructed reforms are undone when teachers revert to old and familiar practices. And the price of privacy falls on teachers, too, as their life-work is so rarely discussed and their own perspectives ignored in public debate. The nature of teaching is, sometimes and fitfully, the subject of reform efforts punctuating business as usual, but it is not the stuff of daily conversation in most schools.

This explains in part why Americans have been fascinated by Great Britain's traditions of inspection (Stearns, 1995, Chapter 1; Wilson, 1996). Inspection – or, more broadly, school assessments in which classroom observations play a central role – promise to open up classrooms, to convert teaching from a hidden activity to one about which more public discussions take place, and where different approaches and improvements become more routine conversations. They can serve as vehicles for a broad and continuous discussions about teaching, providing ideas for teachers and fostering expertise about instruction located in teachers, in administrators who participate in the inspection process, and in inspectors themselves. These processes have the potential to generate much richer and more appropriate information about how schools are performing than do the simple assessments that now take place – like standardized tests. This is teacher improvement writ much larger than the episodic staff development days and summer workshops that take place in the United States.

However, like any assessment procedure, inspection can be used for regulation and control as well as discussion and improvement. As it has been implemented in English elementary and secondary schools since 1993, inspection has become stressful and punitive. Its benefits, only grudgingly admitted by teachers and administrators, are hardly worth the costs, and the conversation about teaching it has engendered is limited and awkward, constrained rather than facilitated by the specific form it has taken. An important story of English inspection is how a system, fondly remembered from bygone days before 1993, has been so quickly transformed into a widely detested mechanism that teachers view as an agent of Conservative control over education.

And that's part of my point: inspection isn't a single system, but a multitude of approaches to classroom observation. Even in Great Britain, it can therefore be modified to fit different perceptions of what schools and colleges need; the practices that create so much controversy and resistance in elementary secondary schools can be changed. In this chapter I examine four approaches to inspection[1]: inspection in the pre-1993 days (Section 1), only briefly described; the current inspection system in elementary secondary education (Section 2); inspections initiated by schools themselves (Section 3); and inspections in further education (FE) colleges, similar to community colleges in the United States (Section 4). I concentrate mostly on current inspection in elementary-secondary education, because this has been the most controversial and best researched, and because it clarifies a broad range of issues better than any other. Mine is definitely an outsider's view of inspection, based on observations in two schools undergoing inspection, in one of which I was the guest of the inspection team; interviews in two schools that had recently undergone inspection; and interviews with other heads, former Her Majesty's Inspectors (HMIs), researchers and the Office for Standards in Education (Ofsted) personnel.[2]

1   INSPECTION BEFORE 1993: THE MODEL OF CONNOISSEURSHIP

The long history of inspection, beginning in 1839, helps explain the widespread acceptance in Great Britain of classroom observations. Virtually all British educators accept the idea that educational effectiveness requires external assessment, in contrast to the United States where the sanctity of the classroom is often a sacred creed. In addition, the dual and possible conflicting roles of inspection – as a mechanism of accountability, and a process of school improvement – were part of inspection from the beginning, since the periodic observations were intended to determine both whether public money was well spent, and whether the central office of education could help schools improve.

As the practice developed, a cadre of HMIs carried out periodic inspections. Unless a school was failing these were rare, occurring perhaps every 10 years or so, and unsystematic. Among individuals who went through an HMI inspection, HMIs themselves are almost universally remembered as wise and helpful individuals; they were men (almost always) of great experience in the classroom, of quiet and thoughtful temperament, who could come into a classroom and understand quickly what was going on. Their expertise was that of practitioners, not of researchers or evaluators, and they are remembered as both understanding teaching and able to help teachers in ways that others cannot. A common comment was that 'they saw everything', or 'you couldn't fool an HMI'. An HMI inspection was 'tough', one teacher mentioned, but the compensation was that they provided advice about how to improve teaching. HMIs often created continuing relationships with schools and would visit periodically, provide information about specific problems, and be available for consultation. The Inspectorate also published 'red books' for specific areas of the curriculum, entitled *Curriculum Matters*, detailing good practice in specific subjects so that their accumulated expertise was compiled and made available to others.

Prior to 1993; there were no published principles or guidelines for schools to follow, though HMI had an inspection manual that was not public. Because the basis for inspections was uncodified and based on the experience and wisdom of HMIs, it is widely described as a model of 'connoisseurship' – of individuals with a certain sense of what teaching should be. The process of selecting HMIs and the training process, including a two-year apprenticeship with a senior HMI, may have contributed to a certain uniformity in their tastes; however, when inspections were published beginning in 1983 there were many complaints about inconsistencies in judgement (Gray and Hannon, 1996). Even though inspection prior to 1993 is widely viewed as improving education, it didn't have a consistent influence. It was, as one administrator mentioned, 'a great vision but with no management', too infrequent and unsystematic to affect all schools.

In addition to HMI inspections, local education authorities (LEAs) also carried out inspections of schools within their purview (Hargreaves, 1990). This process had the advantage that the institution carrying out inspections would also have the responsibility for 'picking up the pieces' and improving the schools found wanting. These inspections varied enormously, and some paid less attention to classroom observation than to other ways of gathering information and providing staff development; as one ex-inspector mentioned, 'We were making it up as we went along' (Wilcox, Gray and Tranmer, 1993). But, together with HMI efforts, LEA inspections contributed to a system were classroom observations where routine and accepted parts of school improvement.

2 ELEMENTARY-SECONDARY INSPECTION: THE REIGN OF OFSTED

The changes in elementary secondary inspection in the Education (Schools) Act of 1992 are well known to Britons, and I need not review them here. From my perspective, a critical change was that the balance of improvement and accountability shifted markedly, as inspection was reconstituted principally to enforce the National Curriculum with a regular schedule where each school would be inspected every five years (now modified to every six years, though more frequently for weaker schools). Rather than expand the number of HMIs, Ofsted was created; it carries out its work by contracting inspections to teams that bid to perform clusters of inspections in areas of their expertise. Teams are selected based on quality and cost, at least in theory. In practice Ofsted evaluates whether team members have sufficient experience, and as long as the quality of a team appears adequate Ofsted appears to choose on the basis of cost, since it has neither the information nor the resources to make more detailed judgements about quality. (At least this is the prevailing opinion, among team members themselves as well as teachers and administrators.) This contracting process and the squeeze on costs proves to be one of many factors influencing the information available from inspections, as we shall see; as one school head noted, 'it's necessarily a cut-rate production' compared to prior HMI inspections.

Because inspection now had a specific purpose – the enforcement of the National Curriculum – the old 'connoisseurship' model was inappropriate. Ofsted therefore codified the criteria for evaluating schools in guidelines for the inspection process, – eg *Guidance on the Inspection of Secondary Schools* (Ofsted, 1995) – though it apparently relied heavily on the pre-1993 inspection manual. Most teachers and administrators report these *Guidelines* helpful, particularly compared to the absence of guidelines in the pre-1993 era. They may be a little bland, some have commented – they certainly do not illustrate what inspired teaching might look like, and they forego endorsing any particular approach to teaching. But as statements of unexceptionable elements of good teaching, they strike most teachers and administrators (and me, too, for what that's worth) as solid, judicious and helpful. These *Guidelines* have been widely used in schools conducting their own inspections (see Section 3), even those that see Ofsted inspections as destructive. Thus the very process of establishing a framework for inspections has its own educational value, in the effort – necessarily incomplete – to distill what good teaching should be.

The guidelines developed by Ofsted also include prescriptions for school inspections themselves. The majority of time is spent observing classrooms not, as is typical in accreditation visits in the United States, in interviewing administrators or counting resources; by Ofsted regulation, 60 per cent of inspectors' time should be spent observing classrooms, sampling students' work and talking with students. In addition, the inspection process gathers a great deal of other information: schools complete forms providing information about enrolments, student backgrounds, classes offered and the like (the Pre-inspection School Context and Indicator report, or PICSI); the results of national exams are available; inspectors interview groups of parents, students and governors (ie, school board members). Parents are notified about the inspection and invited to submit comments or to speak with inspectors.

Furthermore, elaborate procedures record this information. Every class observed is rated on a sheet that requires a score of 1 (excellent) to 7 (very poor) on teaching, student response, attainment and progress, with a paragraph of support required for each score; other forms are completed for interviews with administrators, parents and governors; and still other forms are completed for observations of non-class activities like assemblies, playgrounds, cafeterias, conduct while passing among classes, physical facilities and the like. Indeed, the process of conducting an inspection is partly a paperwork blizzard, with forms accumulating as the week progresses; offhand comments about observations are likely to be met with the response that 'we need a sheet for that, for Ofsted'. During the inspection week, around Thursday afternoon, the inspection team summarizes its results in 'star charts', with numbers (the ever-present 7-point Likert scale) for each department on a number of dimensions; the 'star chart' is then summarized to the school administrators verbally and translated into writing for a public report. (The numbers on the 'star chart' are never given directly to the school, though they are fed into the Ofsted maw as part of its large database.) So there is a concerted effort to record the information from inspections though, as I argue below, the procedure is still one in which a great deal of information is lost.

Once the inspection is over, the results are written up and presented to the school. Administrators can challenge reports on factual grounds, though this appears to be difficult because the underlying 'facts' have been generated by the inspection team itself.[3] Then a final report is published, for all to see – parents, prospective parents, governors and taxpayers. These reports don't make exciting reading to outsiders because they are written in a peculiar language – 'Ofsted-speak', described below – and because they have boiled down a vast amount of observation into brief sentences. For example, one school's report included the criticisms that 'ineffective use is made of teachers' training and experience', and 'the quality of teaching is poorly targeted in years 7 to 9'; while such comments are based on more specific observations, it's hard to know how schools can respond to such generalizations. Schools prepare a response to criticisms, though the implementation of such plans is left to schools themselves (and their governors). In failing schools, however, Ofsted may conduct periodic reinspections, and schools that fail to progress may be taken over by the Secretary of State.

The procedures devised by Ofsted are, in may ways, substantial improvements over the casual pre-1993 procedures. All schools are inspected on a regular basis; the basis for inspection is clarified in the various *Guidelines*; the conduct of the inspection is standardized, so that differences from team to team are reduced; the information from the inspection is carefully collected; and there are mechanisms for using this information to improve the quality of schools, completing the circle. From a US perspective, the crucial dimension is that classroom observations form the heart of the inspection process. And so teaching is made visible, the subject of discussion and then (potentially) improvement.

But, as in so many areas of education, God is in the details. What happens in practice is powerfully influenced by the specifics of an inspection, the context surrounding the inspection, the way information is conveyed. These details, so different in the inspections schools have created for themselves and in FE colleges, shape the value of inspections for good and evil.

2.1   The conduct of an inspection

The dominant characteristic of an inspection is that is it enormously stressful for all involved. Schools may know a year in advance that they will be inspected, and they typically begin an extensive process of preparing for the inspection not, as one might imagine, by scripting lessons for the inspection week but by completing the enormous amount of paperwork required by the National Curriculum, particularly schemes of work for each lesson, since inspectors may ask for these plans during their visit. Teachers are divided about the value of this preparation: some commented that 'it keeps you sharp', or 'it makes you do what you should have done', but a majority bitterly resent it because the paperwork is carried out for Ofsted, not for the benefit of students. In addition, schools sometimes bring in outsiders to provide specific help, or conduct mock inspections during the months preceding the inspection itself. This period is unanimously described as one of enormous time pressure, with teachers working nights and weekends for many months. This starts to build stress; as one teacher mentioned, 'I don't like the way it's done; I had eight months of hell'. Apparently some people crack: the head-teacher of one school I visited resigned during this period, and there are many stories of teachers taking health-related leaves or falling sick just prior to inspection week. How many of these stories are true is impossible to determine, but the lore and legend of inspection conveys the stress that surrounds the process.

Then comes the inspection week itself. The inspectors enter classes at will, preventing teachers from scripting particular lessons. Often teachers prepare little slips of paper or pages describing the intent of the class, to provide the inspector with some context – since an inspector typically visits a class for 20 minutes or so before moving on, perhaps coming back to a particular teacher for one or two other segments (especially for teachers who appear weak). Teachers are under pressure the entire week, therefore, and there's the sense of constantly looking over one's shoulder to see whether an inspector is entering the classroom – the 'Ofsted twitch', as one teacher described the vigilance for a turning doorknob. Inspectors also observe playgrounds, assemblies, lunchrooms, hallways and every other space, always with clipboards, always filling out Ofsted sheets with 7-point Likert scales. A cartoon in *Private Eye*, with inspectors filling out charts at the Ofsteddy bears' picnic, accurately conveys the sense of inspectors snooping everywhere.

When inspectors visit a class, they typically sit in a corner filling out the required forms; they may also chat with students quietly, though most students seem indifferent to them (as to all visitors) and don't appear to be overly prepped. There's substantial variation in what inspectors say to teachers, however: many, under the pressure of time, simply leave for the next class without a word, while others will take some time – 5–10 minutes at most – to comment on what they saw, what improvements are possible, what practice looks like in other schools. Inspection teams vary in their philosophies about providing advice; some (registered inspectors (RIs), the team leaders) encourage this feedback, other discourage it. Teachers overwhelmingly value this kind of information and the opportunity for discussion with inspectors; it reminds them of the pre-1993 process, where advice was the central purpose. But Ofsted itself has discouraged this advice, portraying the inspection process as a form of monitoring rather than advisement; and the pressure of time makes such discussion fleeting at best.

Despite the attention to classroom observation in the inspection process, the observation turns out to be artificial in several ways. The 20-minute segments are too short; teachers complain that these 'snapshots' don't allow inspectors to see a full lesson, never mind development over a year. Teachers and administrators complain that inspectors behave according to the motto 'If we didn't see it, it didn't happen'; it's therefore difficult to convey to inspectors where a particular class stands in a semester's teaching.[4] Because inspectors will be there for such short periods of time, teachers often feel that they must teach to the plan, not 'on the hoof'; 'teachable moments' and other spontaneous possibilities have to be ignored in favour of presenting a 'typical' lesson. A representative comment is 'Your focus is Ofsted, not the students'; another noted: 'It's strange – you have to pack a whole year into a week'.

In addition, many teachers resent being observed *without* the opportunity to talk with inspectors because it means they are unable to put the lesson in context, to explain how it fits into the year's progress, to interpret the difficulties of particular students. As one noted, 'When someone has been in your lesson, you want to know what went right or wrong. You want to know, because I know if it's Jimmy [who responded inadequately], I understand that; if I've yelled at a student in a particular way [there may be a reason]'. Implicitly, teachers are asking for a discussion around teaching, but the inspection process in elementary secondary education is not a discussion. As one head noted, it's an asymmetric process in which Ofsted and its inspectors have all the power, in which suggestions to teachers are not formally allowed and praise is hard to give, in which teacher corrections of inspectors' perceptions are almost impossible to make.

Finally, teachers widely perceive inspection as a process where Ofsted and its minions are looking for bad teaching, in order to root out the incompetents rather than a process of trying to improve the quality of teaching overall. From my perspective the director of Ofsted, Chris Woodhead, has single-handedly done considerable damage to the process: his public presentations have been consistently demeaning to teachers and other educators and have stressed the large numbers of incompetent teachers. When Ofsted devised a process for identifying failing teachers – those with overall scores of 6 or 7 – it harnessed the inspection process to rooting out incompetent teachers. In return, teachers see Woodhead as one-sided in his appraisal of teachers. As one mentioned, 'He's doing the Government's dirty work', and stories abound (again impossible to verify) of his doctoring reports to make schools and teachers look bad. In this testy atmosphere, teachers play a defensive game: thinking that inspectors are looking for bad teaching, they try to teach by the book so as to avoid the dreaded 6s and 7s. All this is well known to inspectors, of course; one RI complained that 'teachers misunderstand the brief of Ofsted' as teacher-bashing and school-bashing, and this 'misunderstanding' distorts their teaching and limits the value of the process in improving schools.

The end result is that most teachers experience inspection as enormously stressful. Of course, teachers vary in their response to inspection, and a substantial number consider inspection helpful in 'sharpening up' their teaching; these individuals typically look forward to feedback. But many more are crushed by the experience, particularly new teachers, conscientious teachers, those who are insecure in their teaching and dread being found out and those who are timid or introverted. These individuals routinely describe inspection as 'the most stressful process

I've ever been though'; 'it's not as bad as bereavement or divorce, but it's third', commented another.[5] It is so stressful that many teachers are reluctant to acknowledge that it can have any value and they may see the process as so illegitimate that they are unwilling to respond to the recommendations that come from it. Teachers and administrators alike describe a let-down after inspection week, a six-month period in which it's impossible to get teachers to do much of anything. And so some question whether it *can* have any value, since it represents such an intrusion in the normal operation of a school. With a long period of preparation and a long period of recuperation, it may take a year and a half in the life of a school.

So, from the perspective of most (but not all) teachers, inspection is not a particularly supportive process. But the details that make it so stressful can be readily changed, as subsequent sections on self-initiated inspections and FE inspections illustrate. The problem is less with the idea of classroom observations as the basis of school improvement than with the specific way Ofsted and Chris Woodhead have implemented this process.

2.2   The truncation of information and expertise

A remarkable feature of inspection is the amount of information and expertise about teaching that it generates. The inspectors themselves are typically highly experienced: many are former HMIs or LEA advisers who used to provide advice in specific curricular areas to local schools.[6] The process of inspecting schools increases their expertise, as they are able to observe practices in a great many schools. Indeed, two RIs on two different teams described inspection in much the same terms: 'the inspection process is a gift', one said, while another called it 'a privilege and a joy' because of the opportunity to observe many schools. (Teachers might be incredulous to hear inspection described in these terms; particularly in the first school, where there were many distraught and weeping teachers; it's hard to imagine that they considered inspection a gift to anyone.) While, unavoidably, a few inspectors are incompetent (and generate a large number of negative stories), the majority I observed are experienced, dedicated to education, highly informed and therefore – when they have the time and inclination – quite effective in suggesting alternatives for teachers to consider. Their advice is based on practices they have observed rather than their personal views of teaching; they are able to provide recommendations about specific teaching problems since they can comment on the details of a particular lesson rather than providing only general advice abstracted from the specifics of a particular school, class and subject. The real promise of inspection, then, is that it can move between the specific and the general settings of education: inspectors observe specific classes and can provide advice tailored to those situations, while their wide familiarity with other schools enables them to understand how any one class fits into a much broader range of practices.

Unfortunately, an enormous amount of information collected in the inspection process is simply thrown away, and the tremendous expertise on an inspection team is rendered largely irrelevant. The truncation of information starts with each classroom observation: while some inspectors provide feedback on the spot, this is limited by time schedules, by the overwhelming burden of paperwork, by the philosophies of certain teams, and by Ofsted policy which discourages such feedback. Then, when the results of each classroom observation are recorded, four aspects of the class (teaching, response, attainment and progress) are reduced to numbers (1–7 again[7]) with a supporting paragraph of perhaps 100–200 words, but the paragraphs are typically general, rather than referring to specific details. The immediacy of the classroom experience is lost forever.

Then, results are summarized for specific departments on the 'star sheets' during a pressured Thursday afternoon meeting, causing further loss of information across all teachers in a department. The process of generating numbers for each department requires inspectors to provide some justification for their ratings, which they generally base on evidence from particular classrooms. In the rating session I observed, there was a tendency to start with a 4 (the mid-point of the Likert scale) and then demand evidence of any departure from 4, with 3s and 5s requiring some evidence – 'well, it might be 3-ish, but I'm not sure' – but 1s and 2s and 6s and 7s require a great deal more concrete evidence. Reportedly, many inspectors are reluctant to give 6s and 7s, because of the enormous effects this can have on a teacher and school. (Indeed, some RIs have resigned rather than participate in the search for failing teaching and failing schools.) This procedure presses the final scores towards the middle and eliminates high and especially low scores, but it also throws away the rich information about what happened in specific classrooms.

The results of the star sheets are not given to the schools[8]; instead the results are summarized in a few written paragraphs. Any writing which goes to school personnel, as well as the draft reports and the published final reports, translates the numbers from the star sheets into bureaucratic language ('below average for this department', 'well above average for schools of this type'), without any detail about the teaching practices observed or specific strengths and weaknesses. Many teachers and administrators refer to this as 'Ofsted-speak' since it is so standardized and conveys so little information. Thus, rich and generally informed classroom observations by experienced inspectors are converted into numbers with supporting paragraphs, summarized across teachers into yet other numbers, and reported back to the school in impersonal language. Along the way, the information that would be most useful to teachers is lost unless an inspector has managed to have a quick conversation on the run.

In the process, the expertise of the inspectors themselves is wasted. Their increasing experience may enable them to carry out inspections more smoothly, to come more quickly to a summary judgement about a class or department, or to write a supporting paragraph more precisely; as one inspector responded, when I asked what difference her background made to observations, 'it helps me write the paragraph'. However, the form in which information is reported from inspections limits what they can say. If they see systemic problems in a region, or in a particular curriculum area – eg a lack of imaginative practice in technology that one inspector reported to me, or a general inability to educate handicapped students appropriately – there is no forum for their observations. If there are trends in the regions where they practise, for good or ill, they have no official way to record this information. The inspection process may be a 'gift' to inspectors but – unlike the continuing exchanges in gift-giving societies (Hyde, 1983) – the gift falls into a black hole, with no way it can continue to enrich the community.

2.3   The effects of inspection: regulation versus school improvement

The most important question is whether inspection can improve the quality of education. This is, of course, a complex issue because it is entangled with perception of the inspection process itself, and some participants are reluctant to acknowledge that it could help; one teacher complained that 'you've pulled it out of me' when I finally got her to acknowledge some benefit. But there are few clear benefits, and – more to the point – some negative consequences where changes in inspection could make it much more effective.

One consequence, often forgotten in the turmoil over the process itself, is that inspection has served to reinforce the National Curriculum. Because the precepts of the National Curriculum are the basis for observations, a school that departs from this standardized curriculum will fare badly in its inspections, and will, therefore, be subjected to various corrective pressures. At least, this is generally true; in practice inspectors have their own conceptions of what good teaching is and look for practices – eg student initiation, genuine discussions, particular approaches to problem-solving whether in theatre or math classes – that are nowhere mentioned in the *Guidelines*. Inspectors often look for elements that they have taken from their experience and from observations in many other schools, in addition to the National Curriculum itself. But despite these departures from orthodoxy, in the main inspectors are required to judge teaching against the standards of the National Curriculum. Indeed, the four criteria by which each class is judged are not equally weighted: one inspector reported that attainment of national standards is the most important criteria, followed by progress; the response of students – a category reflecting motivation, engagement and interactions within the classroom – comes third, and teaching is last among equals. To the extent this is true,[9] the requirements of the National Curriculum are even more powerful.

Unfortunately, following the National Curriculum constrains the inspection process in obvious ways. For example, I observed a math class for 16-year-olds, solving a perimeter problem ('if a field contains 10,000 square feet and is square, how many feet of fencing are required …'). By US standards this is a 7th or 8th grade activity; the teaching was extremely mediocre, with formulaic inquiry, response, evaluation (IRE) questions and desultory responses. But the students did understand the lesson and made progress. The inspector admitted that in the pre-1993 inspection system he could have critiqued the low content level, the pedestrian teaching and the reluctant student participation, but he couldn't find much fault according to the National Curriculum guidelines. It's difficult, then, for a highly constrained inspection process to be any better than the guidelines it follows.

Beyond its enforcement of the National Curriculum, the effects of inspection are widely debated. Even those teachers most resentful of inspection admitted that it had forced them to think more about their teaching and to complete the lesson plans they should have developed anyway; many received some constructive feedback, and a few teachers received a great deal and found the entire process worth while. But the difficult question, almost always posed by teachers themselves in economic terms, is whether these benefits are worth the costs of the process itself. Most teachers and administrators do admit, albeit grudgingly, that inspection has some benefits, but that they are not worth the costs. In this calculation, my own view is that the alternative inspection procedures that schools have created on their own, and the process in FE colleges, are modifications that generate greater improvements with much smaller costs overall – as I argue in Sections 3 and 4. However, one problem with this economic formulation is that costs take different forms: the real costs of elementary-secondary inspection come in the forms of stress, unpaid work by teachers, and the lack of progress after inspection, none of which are monetized; the more careful and lengthy procedures developed for FE colleges undoubtedly cost more in monetary terms but are much lower in intangible costs. For those concerned only with public budgets, therefore, the FE inspections may not look like they are worth the higher costs, but they certainly are from the perspective of instructors.

From the vantage of administrators and schools, a different calculus about the effects of inspections is typical. Often, of course, inspection finds problems in schools that administrators and head of departments have known about; some observers feel that LEAs, not wanting confrontation, wait for Ofsted's reports to close or reconstitute failing schools. In such cases, inspection reinforces the efforts of administrators to reform schools. But when administrators disagree with the results of inspections, or when inspectors raise points about the quality of management itself, then a different problem arises. Several managers reported that if the results are seen to be illegitimate, then schools are much more likely to resist changes – not surprisingly. There are many different grounds for finding an inspection flawed: sometimes the reggie is rigid and unfriendly, sometimes individual inspectors (particularly the lay inspector) are unobservant or ignorant about practice, sometimes inspection teams see what teachers consider atypical days.

The process by which a school comes to view an inspection as legitimate does not work the same in all schools. Those schools which are basically working well are likely to draw praise as well as criticism; but mediocre schools, or schools with high proportions of low-achieving students, are likely to find themselves with dismal ratings that teachers and administrators then reject. In contrast to the old inspection system, where HMIs were viewed almost with awe and widely thought to be concerned only with the well-being of students, there are many more ways to reject any negative results of inspection: educators can fault the qualifications of the inspection team, or the thoroughness of the inspection process, or the political motives underlying inspection and can, therefore, reject the conclusions of an inspection. As a result there is a general consensus that inspection works better as a mechanism of school improvement with good schools than with mediocre and failing schools (Hargreaves, 1990).

Certainly, if the purpose of inspection is to improve the quality of education by closing failing schools, the process has itself been a failure. Between 1993 and 1996, perhaps 20 or 30 schools have been closed, a tiny fraction of the nation's 25,000 schools – hardly enough to improve the quality of education in Britain. It's still hard to close poor schools, even when external observers and LEA administrators agree.

In my reading, therefore, inspections in elementary secondary education haven't been particularly effective as a mechanism of school improvement. They may 'sharpen up' some teaching, and provide some feedback to teachers who are particularly receptive, but that advice costs a great deal in terms of anxiety, perhaps pointless paperwork, and the inevitable post-inspection let-down. The results may help some schools improve, particularly when inspectors ratify what administrators already know, but they are less effective with precisely those schools that need the most help.

To be sure, official policy is that inspection is a mechanism of regulation, not advice and improvement. But calling inspection a mechanism of regulation rather than school improvement gives away the real potential of an observation-based system. Indeed, the most distressing aspect of the 1993 changes under Ofsted and Chris Woodhead is that a widely respected (though unstandardized) system of inspection, providing highly regarded advice, was converted into a much-dreaded process with such checkered results. As I argue in subsequent sections, other systems of inspection have been much more successful.

2.4 The focus of inspection: the teacher, the school and the system

One of the most promising aspects of inspection, at least from a US perspective, is that it collects information both about individual practice – the activities of teachers in classrooms – and about a school's policies, through interviews with administrators.[10] In theory, this allows the inspection team to link the two – to understand the ways in which individual teaching results from school policies, rather than viewing teaching as individual and idiosyncratic (as is common in the United States).

Many inspection teams appear to stress the institutional origins of good and bad teaching. In one team I observed, there was general consensus that eliminating bad teachers is the responsibility of the school head and other administrators – that they should have a system in place to monitor the quality of teaching, to provide help to weak teachers, but then to begin the process of dismissing teachers ('It's difficult, but it can be done') if efforts at improvement fail. In the eyes of this team, an Ofsted inspection should not be the mechanism for dismissing incompetent teachers; indeed, this would be a sign of a system failing badly. Similarly, this particular school suffered from an awkward physical plant, which might be seen as beyond the control of school administrators; however, the inspection team faulted the head for not going to his board of governors for improvement and for failing to make better use of space, including changes that they had seen work successfully in other schools with poor facilities. In the same school there was general concern that career guidance was not being carefully coordinated – 'things are hit and miss, and students miss out if their tutors are not interested' – rather than having systemic practices providing all students with consistent guidance. While the inspection process focussed on individual classrooms and teachers, the central concerns of the team were institutional and administrative.[11]

However, Ofsted has not been clear about this kind of institutional responsibility, and many of its activities have reinforced a view of teaching as individual and idiosyncratic. Woodhead's constant harping on incompetent teachers and his campaign to rid the schools of failing teachers reinforces the tendency to see poor teaching as an individual characteristic rather than the fault of a system with relatively low pay, poor conditions in many urban schools, and professional strains caused by Woodhead and his fellow officials. Ofsted's requirement of certificates for outstanding teachers (with 1s and 2s) and failing teachers (with 6s and 7s) returns the focus to individuals, and requires inspection teams to focus more carefully on individual ratings than on institutional strengths and weaknesses.

Of course, a reconciliation is possible: surely we should admit that the improvement of teaching has certain institutional dimensions, but that these sometimes fail and that individual teachers should be dismissed. The strength of the inspection mechanism is that it can provide information necessary for both of these. It can identify where schools are failing to provide necessary support for teaching, and can document these patterns by systematic evidence from classrooms. It can also identify 'outliers' where, for example, a department (or school) has strong teachers but with one or two exceptions who have failed to respond to attempts at improvement; in these cases the external authority of inspectors can add to the evidence internal to the school. But – as in the value of inspection as a mechanism of school improvement – the balance between the two matters a great deal to the success of either: if inspection is viewed principally as a form of teacher-bashing, then it may lose its legitimacy as a mechanism for either institutional improvement or individual dismissal.

In one other dimension, the inspection process in England has failed to take advantage of its potential. Inspection is only one mechanism of improving teaching, after all: teacher training, in-service education, administrator preparation, the National Curriculum itself, the structure of salaries and patterns of shortages (or unqualified teachers), the schedules and demands placed on teachers, and the overall morale of the teaching force are other factors influencing the quality of instruction. But the inspection mechanism doesn't provide any evidence about the effects of these alternative influences, partly because it doesn't interview teachers and partly because it emphasizes the National Curriculum. If, for example, there are systemic problems in teaching that should be addressed in pre-service education, or a preponderance of 'failing' teachers in urban schools because shortages of trained teachers are covered by substitutes, or problems in salary scales or teaching conditions that cause the best teachers to leave, there is no way for the inspection process to cumulate this information across schools. The process of contracting out inspections to different teams means that – even though individual inspectors may develop tremendous experience – results are institutionally fragmented in a series of reports on individual schools.

In contrast, inspection was initially created in order to make recommendations to the Crown about schools, and in the days before 1993 its expertise and authority made it a respected voice in policy deliberations. But this aspect of the Inspectorate has changed, because of the inspection process itself as well as the Conservative distrust of educators and the destruction of expertise among HMIs. The irony is that a mechanism created to improve the quality of British education can no longer address the most pressing issues of the system.

2.5 The inspection team and 'role strain'

Finally, what of the inspectors themselves? In England, there seems to be little concern with inspectors. Teachers and administrators usually view them as agents of Ofsted, with a mixture of dread and hostility; there are many stories about their incompetence that circulate among teachers, without any countervailing positive stories. Ofsted seems to view inspectors merely as vendors carrying out contracts, no more special than fishmongers or parts suppliers, even though Ofsted often points to inspectors as responsible for outcomes. A great deal of national discussion seems to view inspectors merely as money-grubbers, getting rich from inspection contracts. The contrast with HMIs of bygone days, revered and respected, is stark.

Inspectors deserve much more sympathy than they have received, in my view. They are usually, in my contact with them, experienced individuals, deeply committed to improving schools, who have been forced out of earlier positions (as HMIs, LEA staff and department heads) by the relentless pressures of Conservative policy. They often participate in inspection as a way of staying in education and continuing to contribute to the good of schools. While they have not sunk into poverty, the competitive pressures in contracting make it implausible that anyone could get rich through inspection; indeed, teams with retired individuals are said to have a competitive advantage because they can charge less than teams whose members still have children to support and mortgages to pay. Inspectors now may not be as wise as the former HMIs, and there are some among them who can inflict damage, but as a body of individuals they encompass an expertise about teaching unmatched by anything else in England, or certainly in the United States.

But they have an impossible task, and I detect signs of 'role strain' that has not been widely recognized in England.[12] On the one hand, many inspectors are committed to education; on the other, they work for an agency – Ofsted – which spends a great of energy in school-and-teacher-bashing. They accumulate a great deal of information about teaching practices, but they are constrained to report it in Likert scales and paperwork that strip the life out of what they've seen. They want to improve teaching, but despite their experience they are unable to provide much direct feedback; for the short period they inhabit a school, they spend their time as snoops and snitches, recording everything they see on their omnipresent clipboards and scaring all the teachers they come across. As a former LEA inspector noted about current inspectors, 'There are lots of conflicted people around'.

The strain of these incompatible roles emerges in many small ways. In the work sessions I observed, there was a great deal of gallows humour, including many comments about the 'bureaucracy' (Ofsted) and its requirements. In referring to computer-based paperwork, one inspector noted that 'if you cut off the Ofsted logo, the computer likes it much better'. 'Don't we all?', another replied. There were many complaints about the pace of work and fatigue at the end of a stressful week, and grumbling about a procedure that requires the enormously complex task of teaching to be summarized in a single number. The team was trying its best to act responsibly – to provide some accurate assessment of the school's strengths and weaknesses that might help it to improve, while still following the guidelines required by Ofsted – but these were difficult to carry out simultaneously.

On another team, the RI – the individual who considered inspection a 'gift' of insight to her and her team – forthrightly acknowledged that the inspection process, her current life work, has been a failure. The purpose, in her view, was to give schools themselves insight into their strengths and weakness, to operate – like the improvement of teaching itself – by building on the strengths of individuals rather than disparaging their weaknesses. But despite the enormous promise of inspection, she admitted (to a complete stranger) that it had failed because the time demands were so severe and because teachers misunderstood the purpose as teacher-bashing rather than instructional improvement. Others admitted that the process worked under some conditions, particularly in schools that were already quite competent, but not in the schools most needing advice. These kinds of admissions must be quite rare, since it's hard for people to admit that their work is ineffective, and it's almost unbearable to hear well-intentioned educators confess their complicity in an ineffective and often destructive system. But the process has put them in an impossible position.

And what of the remaining HMIs, now employed by Ofsted? For the most part, they administer contracts – though a few of them carry out confirmatory inspections or reinspections of failing schools, or schools with low attendance or high rates of excluding students – and, therefore, still serve in the old roles. But the old Inspectorate has scattered to the winds, no longer the repository of experience it once was. Some HMIs retired; some of them still carry out inspections but in new and constrained forms; and some turned into bureaucrats.

And so the saddest story of the current inspection system in elementary-secondary education is that it converted a process that provided substantial help to teachers, albeit in an unsystematic way, into one that thwarts such help, constrains the development of expertise, and imposes enormous costs in the process. Fortunately, there are many other ways to carry out inspections.

3   SELF-INITIATED INSPECTIONS

One consequence of Ofsted inspections is that many schools have created their own inspection systems, to prepare their teachers for the official inspection.[13] Often, administrators visit classrooms, using the Ofsted procedures and requiring their teachers to complete the paperwork required by Ofsted. Sometimes they hire outsiders – particularly individuals who work for inspection teams, or members of LEA staff – to provide an outside view and some 'inside' advice about how an inspection will take place. As a result, there is considerably more routine observation of classes, for the purposes of improving teaching, than takes place in US schools. Such efforts are generally focused on preparing for the inspection itself and, therefore, end when the inspection is over.

However, in a few cases, schools (and some FE colleges) have set up their own permanent inspection systems.[14] One such school began its effort after an Ofsted inspection: they first created an inspection system in which their own teachers and administrators, joined by members of the board of governors, carried out classroom observations with Ofsted's procedures. However, the school found that it was unable to judge standards with only internal observers. The next year, therefore, it added an 'outsider' – a member of the LEA staff who participated in inspections – to the inspection team long with the 'insiders'. Subsequently, they added an 'outsider' for each curriculum area.

While this inspection process follows Ofsted's guidelines, the atmosphere surrounding it is completely different. This system was not imposed on teachers, since the administration consulted with teachers on its design; 'it will be positive and developmental', intended to provide support and encouragement, declared the administrator in charge of it. No individual scores were reported, eliminating the sense of trying to root out incompetent teachers; instead, the faculty as a whole examined scores for various groups of teachers (grade levels and curriculum areas) and proposed collectively how to improve them. Finally, while the Ofsted process is a snapshot taking place in a single week, the internal inspection process for a department took place over several weeks, allowing observers to see teaching over a longer span of time. A serious flaw of Ofsted inspectors – the maxim that 'if we didn't see it, it didn't happen' – was obviated by the longer period of time. Teacher interviews were part of the process and, therefore, teachers had the opportunity to explain to observers the special characteristics of their approach and their students; the resentment at being observed without being able to interpret their teaching to outsiders was thereby avoided.

Unless I was systematically fooled, the teachers in this school generally supported the internal inspection process. Certainly there's some apprehension about being observed; but the process provides them with helpful comments on their teaching, both from their peers and from curriculum experts outside the school, and it enables them to see the range of teaching within the school. There's more discussion about teaching as a result, because there's more shared information. The head declared that teachers change when they participate *as inspectors* in such a system: because the Ofsted forms require justification for any particular rating, teachers begin looking more closely at the details of classroom interactions rather than simple reacting on their feelings about the *Gestalt* of a class, and thereby become more sensitive to the interactions in their own classrooms. Finally, the internal inspection process incorporates the school's governors, making them aware of educational issues in a way that had not been possible before.

In this self-initiated inspection, one school has modified the Ofsted process in relatively small ways, but the results are quite different. The issues – the atmosphere and purposes that surround the inspection process, the balance of insiders and outsiders, the period of time over which observations take place – all prove to be crucial to FE inspections as well.

4   INSPECTIONS IN FE COLLEGES

Inspections in FE colleges are also descended from the old HMI system, though they have developed in very different directions.[15] As Ofsted did, the Further Education Funding Council (FEFC) created a schedule for inspections and a manual to guide them (FEFC, 1993), in place of irregular inspections based on unknown guidelines of the 'connoisseurship' approach.[16] Inspection also had a regulatory purpose; in 1992 FE colleges were required to incorporate as autonomous institutions free of LEA control, allowing them local control of their finances and programmes. Inspection was then instituted as a form of external regulation, to prevent autonomous institutions from watering down the content of their programmes.[17]

However, from the outset the FE inspection process was structured in subtly different ways. Self-assessment has played a more important role: each college must complete a self-assessment report prior to the formal inspection, in which they clarify their own views of the strengths and weaknesses, and formulate a process of improvement. FE colleges often undertake their own inspections to prepare for the official inspection. (In one case, heads of colleges switched places, with each inspecting the other's college.) Since 1997 FEFC has placed even more emphasis on self-assessment; while there are still external visitors, their role is much more to validate a college's self-assessment than to create an assessment from scratch.

In addition, the inspection team is differently constituted. A full-time inspector from the FEFC Office of the Inspectorate puts together the team in consultation with the college head; team members come from a pool of about 60 full-time inspectors and 600 part-time inspectors, who are usually instructors in FE colleges or employers in specific areas. The lead inspector therefore provides continuity among inspections because he or she is in charge of all inspections within a region, in contrast to the Ofsted process where each inspection is a separate event and contract.[18] The team then includes subject area specialists from other colleges and a 'nominee' – an individual from the college being inspected. While there is only one such nominee on a team of perhaps 15, he or she plays a critical role: the nominee can interpret the school to the inspection team, and in turn conveys the conclusions of the team back to the college. Information from the inspection comes not only in the form of impersonal reports, but also in direct discussion with the nominee, the lead inspector and subject specialists.

The inspection process takes place in a more extended fashion. The inspectors responsible for a particular curriculum area are likely to return to the college two or three times, observing classes at different points during a semester – avoiding the 'snapshot' problem of Ofsted inspections.[19] After all the curriculum areas have been inspected, the 'cross-college' inspection takes place, examining college-wide functions (career education, registration, extra-curricular activities and the like) as well as administrative procedures intended to improve teaching; thus the cross-college inspection has all the information from the curriculum inspections available to it. Because subsequent visits can be scheduled after some information about teaching conditions has been developed, the inspection team can concentrate on areas of weakness, or areas that the college would like to improve; the necessity for observing every teacher that makes Ofsted inspections so pressed is thereby avoided. Of course, inspection teams may still miss some weak areas, as one nominee complained; in this particular case the administration was hoping that the inspection would reinforce its own initiatives in a particular department. But there are more opportunities to observe over longer periods of time, and consultation with administrators and the nominee can help prevent errors of omission. And there is much less chance of committing the other kind of error – declaring a competent teacher to be deficient, based on a misinterpretation of a class or a too short period of observation – because there are many more opportunities to discuss observations and interpretations.

Much more clearly than Ofsted, FEFC has articulated a 'corporate' view of inspections – that improving the quality of teaching is an institutional responsibility, not an individual issue.[20] Particularly through the cross-college examination, inspectors evaluate institutional practices related to teaching much more consistently, and the recommendations of inspections are directed at college administrators rather than individual teachers. It helps that FEFC has avoided the strident teacher-bashing of Chris Woodhead and the constant references to incompetent and failing teachers; while FE inspections can certainly identify individuals in need of improvement or dismissal, the aura surrounding FE inspections is much less charged. Most FE personnel view the FEFC inspectorate as supportive of colleges,[21] in contrast to the situation in elementary-secondary education where the Government is widely viewed as being hostile to the education establishment.

In addition, FE inspection is much more thorough in providing information to instructors and colleges. The role of the nominee is crucial to this process; in addition, the chief inspector discusses findings with the college head throughout the process. After an inspection is complete, the college prepares a plan of improvement, and the chief inspector continues to work with the administration as it carries out this plan, providing more continuity in advice and consultation than the Ofsted process allows. The expertise developed among inspectors is used in more consistent ways: subject areas specialists are available for consultation to other colleges, and the inspectorate has published a series of booklets (Further Education Funding Council, 1996a; 1996b) describing overall findings in particular curriculum areas and providing recommendations for good practice. The annual report of the chief inspector, *Quality and Standards in Further Education in England,* is also an informative document, judicious and balanced in its identification of strengths and weaknesses. The FEFC seems to have learnt from experience: one senior inspector noted that early reports were 'terrible' – poorly justified and badly written – and the process changed in response.

Finally, the inspection process forces administrators to think about issues of teaching and learning. By contrast, many (though not all) community colleges in the United States are led by administrators who spend almost no time in the classroom, who are poorly informed about what instructors face and seem to be unsympathetic to the difficult teaching issues in community colleges; faculty refer to them as 'bean counters', and the level of hostility toward them is dreadful to see (Grubb and Associates, 1999, Chapter 8). But administrators in England at least know more about what happens in classrooms. They may choose to be 'bean counters', and the competition engendered by Conservative Governments has definitely pushed them in this direction; but the inspection system at least provides them with the information necessary to improve the quality of instruction.

Of course, no one thinks that FE inspections are fun. There remain complaints about the vagueness of requirements, about the amount of documentation necessary, and about the tight timetable. However, on all of these dimensions FE inspections are vast improvements over elementary secondary inspections. Furthermore, FE administrators and instructors generally accept the need for improving the quality of teaching, and largely approve of the FE process. When inspection is carried out in ways that maintain the dignity of instructors, then it need not generate the controversy and resistance typical in elementary secondary education.

5   TRANSLATING INSPECTION TO OTHER COUNTRIES

There's considerable interest in inspection in other countries. In the United States, Thomas Wilson, who has examined British inspection carefully (Wilson, 1996), has been working to incorporate classroom observations, or 'school visits', into the procedures used by the New England Association of Schools and Colleges, Rhode Island, Illinois and Chicago, and has developed a handbook to help schools structure such observations (Wilson, 1999); based on his work, Rhode Island has developed School Accountability for Learning and Teaching (SALT) as a statewide procedure including a four-day school visit (Olson, 1999). David Green, a former HMI, has worked with schools in Chicago on the School Change and Inquiry Program and in New York State on the School Quality Review Initiative.[22] In California, the former governor of California, Pete Wilson, consulted with Ofsted before proposing a state inspectorate that failed to pass (thankfully, given Wilson's mean-spirited views); Governor Gray Davis's proposal of peer review for California schools has started a debate over the propriety and efficacy of observations in that state (Archer, 1999). A very few community colleges have their own programmes of observation, and many more instructors would welcome observations in order to more towards the ideal of 'teaching colleges' (Grubb and Associates, 1999, Chapter 8). British Columbia has an inspection process with both an internal and an external assessment that is said to be more supportive than the English model. New South Wales (Australia) also has a multi-method approach to school quality that includes classroom observations (Cuttance, 1995), and the Netherlands is currently implementing an inspection process.

The English experience provides several warnings about how best to institute inspection, in other countries and various types of institutions. Most obviously, the details of the inspection process matter a great deal: the specific composition of the inspection team, the balance of insiders and outsiders, the period of time over which an inspection takes place, the relative roles of self-assessments and external assessment, and the ways information is reported back to instructors and administrators are procedural issues that can be endlessly varied, and that affect the quality and the legitimacy of information gathered through classroom observations. And some way must be found to capitalize on the expertise developed by inspectors themselves, to make this available to teachers and administrators, eg through individual consultation during inspections, or through workshops and publications. Under the best conditions, inspection procedures generate a source of expertise around teaching, grounded in practice and experience, that can continue to improve schools and colleges.

Second, the culture of inspection is important. The relative emphasis on advice and improvement versus regulation and control is established both by the responsibilities of the inspectors and by the less tangible aspects of the atmosphere surrounding inspection – poisonous in the cases of Chris Woodhead and (potentially) Pete Wilson, more supportive in the case of FEFC and school-initiated inspections. The goal of school improvement requires a climate of trust, a sense that teachers, administrators, and policy-makers are joined in a common enterprise to improve schools. Where this trust does not exist – eg where policy-makers are trying to impose an unwelcome agenda, as in English elementary-secondary education, or where teacher unions and administrators are antagonistic, or where personal relations within schools are antagonistic, as in many urban schools in the United States (Payne, 1997) – then the inspection process itself may be undermined as teachers engage in defensive teaching, and any recommendations are likely to be undermined as teachers and administrators see them as illegitimate.

Third, inspection requires some generally accepted standard of what teaching should be. The model of 'connoisseurship', although it may work well with certain individuals, is likely to be too unsystematic for widespread use, and the lack of any guidelines makes it difficult for teachers to know how they should improve their teaching. Observation-based procedures may be best viewed as *complementary* to other reforms taking place, and might be most effective in conjunction with other reforms that have clarified what practice should look like. And groups of schools engaged in the same kind of reform – as in the loose networks of schools taking the same general approach to reform in the United States – might also see themselves as part of a community of practice and, therefore, be open to inspection teams from other similar schools.

Of course, it's difficult to borrow practices from other countries. The longevity of inspection in Great Britain has made the idea of external observers widely acceptable there, just as the US history has led to the privacy of the classroom. But the secrecy of the classroom doesn't serve anyone well – certainly not students, nor advocates for reform, nor administrators who have little idea what is happening in their classrooms, nor teachers who often find themselves isolated and unsupported. If teaching and learning are to be central to our educational institutions, then inspection provides a way of learning what happens in the classroom and generating the expertise necessary for improvement.

ACKNOWLEDGEMENTS

I visited schools, conducted interviews and collected materials for this article while on sabbatical at Cambridge University during autumn 1996. I particularly wish to thank Paul Ryan, King's College, and the Faculties of Economics and Education at Cambridge University for their hospitality, and the many teachers, administrators and researchers I interviewed for their candor. Neal Finkelstein, John Gray, Harriet Harper, Paul Ryan and Thomas Wilson made helpful comments on an earlier draft, as did several participants at an AERA presentation.

NOTES

1. There are surely more than four, even within Great Britain. A complete review would also examine the Scottish and North Irish systems, which are quite different from the English system, as well as the small modifications in Wales. See also the concluding section in which I mention practices in several other countries.
2. The schools I visited and the individuals I interviewed were all secondary schools; may conclusions may, therefore, be less pertinent to elementary, nursery and special schools. They were also located only in England. I have also relied on Gray and Wilcox (1996); the special issue of the *Cambridge Journal of Education* (1995); the articles in the *British Journal of Educational Studies* (1997) **45**; and *The Times Educational Supplement*, a wonderful source of information about the fray over inspection.
3. Recently Ofsted has announced that it will create a process by which schools can submit their claims of unfair inspections to an independent arbitrator; see Gardiner (1998). But since Ofsted itself has adjudicated complaints up until now, there is a general feeling that schools have been reluctant to complain because 'they realize nothing will happen if they do make a complaint', according to an official with the National Association of Head Teachers (NAHT).
4. The practice of reporting only what inspectors observe leads to another kind of story about inspectors. One such tale involved a school with a ceremony culminating several weeks of work, but it took place on the Friday before inspection started and the RI wouldn't attend because it didn't fall within the specified inspection week.
5. For much more details about the extent and nature of teachers' distress, see many of the articles in the *Cambridge Journal of Education* cited in Note 2.
6. The Conservative Government has required LEAs to subcontract their staff development, breaking up LEA staff and providing a pool of individuals available for inspection teams. The subcontracting requirements have had devastating effects on the coherence and continuity of staff development; see Finkelstein and Grubb (1998).
7. To an outsider, it sometimes seems as if the British have Likert scales embedded in their souls. I was amused to find Sainsbury's providing 5-point rankings for the sharpness of Cheddar cheese, the strength of differing coffees and the dryness of wines. The infamous league tables take this proclivity for ranking on undimensional scales to absurd lengths.
8. The results of the 'star sheets' are accumulated in a vast database, the Education Information System, that Ofsted proudly considers rich resource for research purposes. It would, of course, be wonderful to have such a database describing many different dimensions of teaching based on observations; but Ofsted data doesn't

include any information about how individuals are teaching, and the numbers them-selves almost surely suffer from restricted variation as inspectors tend to avoid very high and low ratings, and biased because inspectors often try to avoid 6s and 7s. In my view it would be foolish to use these data for research, except possibly to describe what Ofsted itself has done.

9. I've been unable to verify this statement, and it isn't clear precisely how such a weighting would be reflected. At the end of the day, however, the stress on perfor-mance levels throughout the British system is so powerful that a school with low performance levels – because of immigration, language backgrounds, student mobility and other aspects of family backgrounds all too familiar from the US experience – is likely to get a low rating regardless of how inspired the teaching is.

10. However, there are no interviews with teachers except the head-teacher of each department. Consequently, the management's activities are viewed through the eyes of administrators, but not the eyes of teachers; it's possible, therefore, that the concep-tion of what administrators in a school are doing is biased.

11. This perspective almost surely varies among teams. Teams are thought to have distinc-tive personalities, often shaped by the RI, and an institutional versus individual perspective may be among them. Other teams are described as going 'by the book' rather than being less formal, or interested in giving advice rather than unapproach-able. However, while teachers and administrators clearly prefer teams that provide more guidance, it's unclear how these 'personalities' affect the reports written.

12. The problem of role strain arises particularly with social welfare workers, who often go into the profession because they want to help the poor and then find they are agents of a repressive and uncaring State.

13. It's impossible to know how common this practice is, though members of LEA staff report that informal pre-inspection observations are quite common, for which they are often brought in.

14. Again, the magnitude of this practice is unknown. The school I visited with its own inspection mechanism knew of one other school in its shire (county) which had done the same; this practice, therefore, appears to be quite rare. This school's head was particularly insistent on improving teaching: he had started classroom observations before Ofsted began its process, and the school employed an adminis-trator in charge of quality assurance whose job was to examine specific teaching issues (eg pupil tracking, different teaching styles, the quality of staff development) and improve each one.

15. One negative consequence of splitting elementary secondary inspections from FE inspections is that there are no longer any individuals observing both secondary and post-secondary institutions and, therefore, able to judge the transition between them in the way that pre-1993 HMIs could. There have been some efforts for Ofsted's and FEFC's Inspectorates to work with one another, particularly on issues of consistency where they may both have jurisdiction over a school. One senior inspector noted to me that Ofsted was difficult to work with because of its rigid approach to inspections. He considered FEFC to be more open, more flexible, providing more feedback to instructors and allowing colleges to participate more actively in designing the inspection.

16. There's much less research about FE inspections than there is about elementary secondary inspections, though Melia (1995), the chief inspector for FEFC, has written an informative article and Spours and Lucas (1996) include some observations. The *Times Educational Supplement* has a special section, 'FE Focus', that is also valuable in following current developments. This section is based on visits to several colleges, interviews with FEFC personnel, FEFC reports and discussions with several individ-uals who provide technical assistance to FE colleges. There's a great deal of uncer-

tainty about what happens in FE colleges since – as is true for community colleges in the United States – good mechanisms do not exist to gather information.

17. The other regulatory mechanisms include the various qualifications that students are trying to pass, including GCSE exams for 16-year-olds, A-level exams to enter university, NVQs and GNVQs for those entering employment. These are in effect the FE college equivalents of the National Curriculum.

18. FEFC has developed a matrix structure for its inspections: each of its senior inspectors is responsible both for a region and for a curriculum area. In the former capacity they have an overview of colleges in their region, and in the latter capacity they collect information from all the subject specialists and summarize the findings in booklets, eg *Engineering* (Further Education Funding Council, 1996a).

19. During autumn 1996 FEFC was discussing whether to replace this kind of 'rolling' inspection (called the 'drip-feed' method) with two-week 'snapshot', mimicking Ofsted's approach.

20. A 'corporate' view would be especially helpful in the United States where most community colleges do not use the institutional mechanisms that could improve the quality of teaching, despite their claims to being 'teaching colleges'. See Grubb and Associates (1999), especially Chapter 8.

21. It's important to distinguish feelings toward the FEFC inspectorate from feelings toward FEFC itself. FEFC has been responsible for establishing competition in post-secondary education, equalizing funding among FE colleges and establishing national policies for what had previously been local institutions. All these responsibilities have caused friction between FEFC and local colleges. Indeed, some observers have suggested that the lack of controversy around inspection has been due to the fact that there are so many other issues in conflict.

22. See Institute for Education and Social Policy (1994); State Education Department and Olson (1994) for a description of the New York efforts. Wilson (1995) mentions some other activities in the United States.

REFERENCES

Archer, W (1999) California bill rekindles debates over teacher peer review, *Education Week*, **18**, pp 1, 31

British Journal of Educational Studies (1997) Various articles, **45**

Cambridge Journal of Education (1995) Inspection at the crossroads: time for review, special issue, **25**

Cuttance, P (1995) An evaluation of quality management and quality assurance systems for schools, *Cambridge Journal of Education*, **25**, 97–108

Finkelstein, N and Grubb, WN (1998) Making sense of educational markets: lessons from England, paper presented at the American Educational Research Association, School of Education, University of California, Berkeley

Further Education Funding Council (1993) *Assessing Achievement*, Circular 93/28. FEFC, Coventry

Further Education Funding Council (1996a) *Engineering*, FEFC, Coventry

Further Education Funding Council (1996b) *Humanities*, FEFC, Coventry

Gardiner, J (1998) Schools to get inspection referee, *Times Educational Supplement*, p 1

Gray, J and Hannon, V (1996) HMI's interpretations of school's examination results, *Journal of Educational Policy*, **1**, 23–33

Gray, J and Wilcox, B (1996) *Inspecting Schools: Holding Schools to Account and Helping Schools to Improve*, Open University Press, Buckingham and Philadelphia

Grubb, WN and Associates (1999) *Honored Even in the Breach: Teaching in Community Colleges*, Routledge, New York and London

Hargreaves, D (1990) Accountability and school improvement in the work of LEA inspectors: the rhetoric and beyond, *Journal of Education Policy*, **5**, 230–39

Hyde, L (1983) *The Gift: Imagination and the Erotic Life of Property*, Vintage Books, New York

Institute for Education and Social Policy (1994) *School change and Inquiry Program*, ILSP, New York University

Melia, T (1995) Quality and its assurance in further education, *Cambridge Journal of Education*, **25**, 35–44

Office for Standards in Education (Ofsted) (1995) *Guidance on the Inspection of Secondary Schools*, HMSO, London

Olson, I (1994) Critical friends, *Education Week*, **13**, 20–7

Olson, L (1999) Moving beyond test scores, *Education Week: Quality Counts '99*, **18**, 67–73

Payne, C (1997) 'I don't want your nasty pot of gold': urban school climate and public policy, working paper QP-97-8, Northwestern University, Evanson IL: Institute for Policy Research

Spours, K and Lucas, N (1996) The formulation of a national sector of incorporated colleges: beyond the FEFC model, working paper no 19, University of London, London: Post-16 Education Centre

State Education Department (1994) *Developing the School Quality Peer Review*, State Education Department, New York

Stearns, K (1995) *School Reform: Lessons from England*, Carnegie Foundation for the Advancement of Teaching, Princeton

Wilcox, B, Gray, J and Tranmer, M (1993) LEA frameworks for the assessment of schools: an interrupted picture, *Educational Research*, **35**, 211–21

Wilson, T (1995) Notes on the American fascination with the English tradition of school inspection, *Cambridge Journal of Education*, **25**, 89–97

Wilson, T (1996) *Reaching for a Better Standard: English School Inspection and the Dilemma of Accountability for American Schools*, Teachers College Press, New York

Wilson, T (1999) *Foundations of the Catalpa School Visit*, 3rd edn, Catalpa, Providence, RI

Is Ofsted helpful?

An Evaluation Using
Social Science Criteria

Carol T Fitz-Gibbon and Nicola J Stephenson-Forster

INTRODUCTION

Her Majesty's Inspectors (HMI), created in 1839, consisted of putatively independent inspectors who visited schools occasionally. HMI included among their numbers the poet Matthew Arnold and although they were widely hated in the early parts of the century (Hogg, 1990), they later came to be seen as generally benign, supportive and highly skilled in their subject specialism. This change in attitude might have been related to their adoption of the stance that their responsibility was primarily to report to the Secretary of State for Education on the state of the nation's schools. They were not to supervise individual schools. Each HMI served a year's apprenticeship before becoming a fully fledged inspector.

A new policy was introduced by the 1992 Education (Schools) Act with the creation of the Office for Standards in Education (Ofsted). HMI were severely reduced in numbers and are now largely working for Ofsted. Ofsted contracts inspections out to teams of inspectors on the basis of competitive tendering. Training for work on such a team, as this new kind of Ofsted inspector, was accomplished in one week for the first year or two although recently distance learning materials have extended the study period.

It has been estimated that about 70 per cent of an inspector's time is spent on classroom observation so it is particularly important to look at the value of this aspect of inspection. The classroom visits are also a source of stress for teachers, providing another reason to consider their value carefully. Furthermore, as researchers into school effectiveness we must be particularly interested to see if inspectors' judgements concur with other methods of evaluating schools.

Conclusions are only as sound as the methods on which they are based and it was clear from the initiation of Ofsted that the normal canons of research were being ignored. Indeed reservations were expressed to the chief inspector before a single inspection had occurred. The letter suggested a way of checking one kind of validity: schools should keep their careful measures of student progress (Value-Added indicators) away from inspectors until after the latter had made their judgements about the quality of teaching and learning in the various school departments. This would provide a chance for cross-validating inspectors' *judgements* about appropriate progress against a *measure* of appropriate progress. Such a check would clearly be worthless if the inspectors saw the data before making their judgements.

This perfectly proper, methodologically sound, proposal was, amazingly, met with a letter drawing attention to the threat of a 'level 2' fine against any school which failed to provide inspectors with data. This threat, which is written into the legislation by which Ofsted was created, naturally aroused suspicions that all was not well.

Although inspection has an important role to play, since nothing can substitute for the direct observation of the way that a school is functioning, the strengths and weaknesses of inspection as currently introduced in England must be frankly confronted. (Scottish and Welsh systems operate rather differently, as does the inspectorate in England for non-compulsory education, run by the Further Education Funding Council.) The current proposals to have inspectors rate teachers on a 7 point scale also make a consideration of the validity of inspection exceedingly urgent: the confidence of the public and the careers of teachers are at stake.

THE SURVEY

Most systems, such as inspection, need systematic and independent monitoring and feedback. The survey reported here represents a move towards creating such monitoring. The survey is indicative rather than conclusive and serves mainly to illustrate one of the ways in which the inspection process should be monitored.

Questionnaires were sent to 322 head-teachers whose schools were chosen on seven criteria described shortly. The opinions of head-teachers were important as an indication of the effect inspection was having on key persons, but it must be noted that we do not suggest that the opinions of the Ofsted process can be validated or challenged on the basis of other opinions. As researchers, there are *methods* which have been developed to ensure basic standards of evidence and to increase the likelihood of observation and judgement yielding valid findings. It is of interest to ask if these proper methods are being used, ie to conduct an evaluation of the Ofsted design, a 'blueprint' evaluation. It would, however, be quite possible for heads and others to believe every finding that emerged from an inspection, and for researchers still to need to criticize the methods.

The sample for the survey

The intention was to compare and contrast results from some deliberate sampling along with results from two random samples.

One random sample was of one in four schools randomly selected from those participating in an unofficial self-monitoring system in collaboration with the university: the Year 11 Information System (YELLIS, this is briefly described in Note 9.) A second random sample was drawn from a list of all schools. Together these two sources accounted for 68 per cent of the mailing. It is not possible to say exactly how many of the obtained responses were from each source since anonymous responses were permitted.

In addition to these random samples, 17 schools had at the time of the study been deemed to be 'failing' secondary schools and these were each sent a questionnaire but only five schools responded. We were well aware that failing schools were coming under intense media scrutiny and have in general tried to cut down on their exposure and simply concentrate on coping with the demands consequent upon a rating of 'failing'. We wished to compare the failing schools with similar schools in the same area and to that end phoned to ask for the names of schools to which they considered that they were similar and this formed a matched sample for the failing schools.

Although we did not have the resources to obtain all inspection reports in order to match the inspectors' judgements of each department against data which we have already provided to schools through the YELLIS project we rank ordered YELLIS schools on the basis of percentage of pupils with positive value-added measures and selected the top 20 schools and the bottom 20 schools out of over 300 schools. Thus, we had schools who were, in 1994, generally seeing their pupils make better than usual or worse than usual progress. (However, based on the experience of monitoring value-added in schools since 1983, we would never recommend identifying a school by a single number from one year's results. Schools are highly complex and contain considerable variation within the school, from department to department. Single numbers cannot represent this variation and any such numbers are likely to vary across the years.)

By random sampling combined with deliberate sampling we had six categories in the sample. A seventh was created from the 8 per cent of schools that chose to remain anonymous.

One hundred and fifty-nine head-teachers responded[1] of whom 88 reported being inspected by Ofsted. All but 10 of these reported the 'rating' of the school arrived at by Ofsted. The rating is a widely reported datum which can strongly affect the image of the school. The ratings reported were 'fail': 5 per cent, 'cause for concern: 6 per cent, 'satisfactory', 65 per cent, 'good': 10 per cent and 'outstanding': 13 per cent.

INSPECTION OF THE INSPECTORS

There is nothing inherently unscientific in using human judgements as measurements. In fact, such procedures may often be essential. However, there are certain fundamental standards to be observed in the collection and analysis of such judgements before there can be confidence in the evidence presented.

Minimally, there should be information on:

- *sampling* a justification of the representativeness and size of the samples used as a basis for judgement;
- *reliability* measures of inter-rater reliability showing that this is sufficiently high to be adequate for the fine judgements made;
- *validity* extensive studies of the validity of the judgements made – are they correct?

These issues are considered below from first principles (the 'blueprint' evaluation) and as illustrated by the survey.

Sampling

The two major methodological issues relating to the sample used in a school inspection are its representativeness and size.

Representatives of the sample

Does what the inspectors see constitute a representative sample of the lessons, pupils and parents? It seems unlikely that the announced visits of Ofsted inspectors provides them with a view of the school as it is normally functioning. Indeed none of the questionnaire respondents agreed strongly with the statement 'An Ofsted inspector sees a school as it is normally'. Only 7 per cent agreed and 81 per cent of respondents disagreed. The week of the Ofsted visit is a highly unusual week and the presence of inspectors in classrooms will have a major impact on the lessons presented. It may be thought that these lessons will be excellent, better than usual and, therefore, misleadingly good. However, such a hypothesis needs testing. If it were true then there would be reason for making inspections unannounced. There are numerous accounts of subterfuges to impress inspectors (Hogg, 1990; Fitz-Gibbon, 1995). There is also a contrary widespread view that the lessons taught in front of inspectors should be very safe. In sum, the representativeness of the lessons observed is in question and no studies have been provided to show that this is not a matter for serious concern. Researchers in classrooms go to considerable lengths to be present so often that they eventually exert little influence on events and can ideally be 'a fly on the wall'. Observations should ideally be random and unannounced so that they are more likely to represent reality.

The size of the sample

Even if the lessons observed were representative, we would still need to ask whether the number of lessons constituted a sufficiently large sample on which to base important judgements. There have long been methods available for estimating how many lessons need to be observed by how many persons in order to obtain measures with acceptable levels of reliability (Medley and Mitzle, 1963; Fitz-Gibbon and Clark, 1982; Winer 1971). Ofsted has presented no justification for the number of lessons observed, no studies as to whether different subjects require different lengths of observation and no studies of the proportion of a lesson that needs to be observed for the kinds of judgements that are being made. Nor have they shown any cognizance of the methodological fact that to judge individuals rather than, say, departments or schools, will require unprecedently high levels of reliability, probably requiring long periods observation. Nor have any justifications been presented for the numbers of pupils interviewed in the course of an inspection.

The entire design seems to be based on received wisdom rather than checked by proper methods. The problem here is that the received 'wisdom' may not be adequate. HMI were highly respected but they were not experts in checking the adequacy of their methods, methods which had developed before there were good foundations for the statistical procedures needed for careful analyses of judgements. Using methods of the last century, uniformed by this century's advances, might well be considered as indefensible in social science as it would be in medicine.

Reliability

Even if we overlook the inadequacies of the sampling methods, we still have to deal with issues of reliability and validity. To establish that Ofsted judgements are 'reliable' requires that Ofsted demonstrate that it does not matter which inspection team inspects a school or when they visit. Equally, does it matter which inspector is observing a classroom? Would all observers agree to a sufficient extent, ie are the judgements of the classroom reliable?

There does not seem to have been a single study of 'inter-rater reliability' from Ofsted, yet the issue as to agreement among inspectors is critical. If there is variation in the judgements two inspectors would make of the same lesson, department or school, which inspector is to be believed? The whole system is called into question if reliability is not demonstrated.

How did head-teachers view this issue? Two questions related to reliability:

1. *Question 13* Two Ofsted teams working without contact would come to the same conclusions about a school and;
2. *Question 17* I believe the Ofsted teams have no difficulty in reconciling the judgements of each team member to provide a corporate view.

Neither proposition attracted majority support. 'Disagree' or 'strongly disagree' was chosen by 48 per cent for question 13 and 61 per cent for question 17.[2]

Further evidence that inspectors actually disagree a good deal comes from reports of those who have trained to be inspectors, particularly from an exercise in which they all watch a video of a lesson and generally fail to agree on a rating for the lesson. Furthermore, in print, it was stated that 'the majority of Rgls[3] were able to make appropriate decisions about conflicting evidence' (Coopers and Lybrand, 1994: 10), a statement which clearly implies that the majority of registered inspectors were presented with conflicting evidence, as did a subsequent statement on the same page: 'a few hasty compromises or unresolved conflicts were evident', but we were assured that inspectors could '... move towards a corporate view on the range of issues prescribed by the Framework ... Four fifths of such meetings were successful in involving all or almost all inspectors, and sometimes the discussion was outstanding in producing corporate judgement'.

In summary, there does not seem to be any evidence to assure us that Ofsted inspectors' judgements are reliable, and head-teachers predominantly do not believe them to be reliable.

Validity

If the sample observed is inadequate and judgements do not agree, there's an end to the issue: inspections are not secure judgements. Validity cannot be obtained without an adequate sample and reasonable consistency in the measurements. However, there can be arguments about how 'adequate' and what is 'reasonable' consistency, so, in the absence of data on reliability, we will leave the issue as unresolved and move to the question of validity: the question as to whether Ofsted's judgements are correct.

Has the public been provided with evidence that the judgements inspectors make are correct? Can governors trust these judgements? Can parents rely on them? Ofsted's approach to validity has been to have a second team, fully aware of the report of the first team, re-examine the school. This is poor methodology since the second team is not a fresh, independent inspection. It is already biased by knowledge of the first report. Even agreement only establishes consistency, which could be a consistency of bias. Agreement does not constitute validity.

The issue of validity is one to which there is rarely a single or simple answer. To establish validity generally requires the accumulation of a variety of kinds of evidence, a collection which adds up to what Cronbach and Meehl (1995) called the 'nomological net'. Various kinds of validity are described in any basic test on measurement: construct, concurrent, predictive, face and discriminant validity. These are discussed below.

Face validity

Does the demand seem reasonable? Do the various judgements rendered appear reasonably feasible ones to make? Face validity is very much a matter of opinion. The notion that one can judge a school in a matter of hours is fairly widely accepted and hence inspection tends to have face validity. This does not mean it is correct. Face validity – an agreement that the procedure seems reasonable – may simply represent the shared misconceptions of persons who have never had the sobering experience of subjecting their judgements to the test of proper validity studies. The history of science is the history of replacing guesses and 'the obvious' with careful measures which sometimes disconfirm what we thought we knew. The careful checks are represented by the other kinds of validity.

Construct validity

Is the very construct of a single rating for a complex school reasonable? Is a 'failing school', for example, adequately defined? Is it methodologically valid to apply a single label to a whole school given that there is almost certainly considerable variation within every school? Has Ofsted published any consideration of the validity of the constructs given to it by the legislation, or must it simply accept these? (Who wrote the legislation and from what empirical base? Is it too much to ask that legislation be informed by knowledge as we approach the 21st century?)

Concurrent and predictive validity

Are there some concurrent measures which would show differences in line with inspectors' judgements, and thus tend to confirm those judgements? Do the judgements predict detectable differences in the future performance of schools? Since Ofsted has defined effective schools as ones in which pupils make average or better progress, value-added measures are clearly the ideal concurrent measure which should agree with inspectors' judgements. Discrepancies between value-added measures and the Ofsted rating might certainly occur for good reasons, but the ratings should show considerable match with value-added measures.

The response of Ofsted's first chief to suggestions to check this relationship was mentioned earlier. Despite the widespread availability of value-added measures Ofsted has failed to publish any studies of this fundamentally important question relating to the validity of their judgements.

View of heads regarding the validity of the Ofsted process

It could well be that head-teachers believe that visiting a school for a week provides an adequate basis for precise ratings. This would not prove that the view was correct. However, if heads did not have confidence in the validity of the judgements this would have serious implications for the capacity of the system to have any positive effects on schools.

Nine questions in the form of statements to which respondents answered on a Likert scale[4] were used to assess validity as perceived by head-teachers. Statements which checked on validity were those in items 3, 4, 5, 6, 9, 10, 11, 12 and 16, namely:

3. *An Ofsted inspector can judge the achievement of a school against national expectations.*
4. *An Ofsted inspector can judge the achievement of a school taking into account pupils' capabilities.*
5. *The distinctions between moral and spiritual, cultural and social are clear.*
6. *An Ofsted inspector can assess moral and spiritual, cultural and social aspects of the school.*
9. *Ofsted inspectors rely on what they see, not on what they are told.*
10. *An Ofsted inspector knows what constitutes 'good practice'.*
11. *Ofsted teams have ways of assessing pupils' capabilities which provide better judgements than those made by staff in the school.*
12. *Ofsted can accurately, reliably recognize 'failing schools'.*

16. If the judgement of the Ofsted team differed from data available to me on value-added I would tend to believe the Ofsted judgement.

Correlations were sufficiently high for the responses to the items to be added and averaged thus producing a scale for the perception of validity by the head-teachers.[5]

On only one of the items assessing validity did more than half the head-teachers register a positive belief in the validity of the Ofsted judgement. This was Question 3: 'An Ofsted inspector can judge the achievement of the school against national expectations', with 51 per cent of head-teachers opting for 'agree' or 'strongly agree'. However, on two other items (9 and 10) the positive responses were as high as 41 per cent and 48 per cent. A study to check empirically the accuracy of perceptions regarding Question 3, for example, would need to test inspectors about their evaluation of the statistical data relating to national 'expectations'. So far as the authors are aware there is no test of statistical reasoning required before inspectors are sent to interpret statistical data.

As for the knowledge of 'good practice', this can be a shared prejudice rather than accurate knowledge. Indeed, teachers are all too aware that views on what constitutes 'good practice' have changed over the years, like a fashion. The evaluation of processes, in an endeavour as complex as teaching, is hazardous since the link between processes and outcomes may be tenuous indeed.

Item 4 was the next most positive response. Even so only about a third of heads agreed that Ofsted inspectors can correctly judge the achievement of a school taking into account pupils' capabilities. In their recently revised procedures Ofsted itself has dropped this claim to an ability to intuit the capabilities of pupils and no longer demands that its inspectors do so. Schools that failed partly on such judgements will not, however, receive apologies.

The next least negative item was Question 12. Fewer than one in three heads (29 per cent) agreed that Ofsted inspectors can 'correctly identify failing schools'. Twelve per cent of head-teachers agreed that inspectors 'can assess pupils' abilities better than can the staff of the school',[6] with 69 per cent disagreeing and 19 per cent taking a neutral position. For questions 5 and 6, the belief in inspectors' capabilities to assess the spiritual, moral, social and cultural aspects of schools, accurately or separately, sank to 7 per cent and 6 per cent agreeing (see example below).

A primary school was declared to be failing in the year that the head-teacher, who had worked there for the last 19 years, was retiring. One of the few negative comments to explain why the school failed was the following: The school promotes satisfactorily the social and moral development of the pupils, but not their spiritual and cultural development. This seems extraordinarily unconvincing. There was no evidence presented to illustrate which observations convinced the inspectors of such finely differentiated effects.

Evidence of discriminant validity

If the claim is that inspection measures the effectiveness of a school, we need to ask if it actually measures this or if it is accidentally confused by other factors. This is the issue of discriminant validity. For example, a decade ago Gray and Hannon (1986) showed that HMI almost never praised schools in inner cities. HMI seemed unable to recognize good teaching in a context which was not predominantly middle class. The problem identified by Gray and Hannon may be still with us. Being a school with a high percentage of free school meals was associated with a significantly higher likelihood of a poor rating. The simple correlation between a rating and free school meals was found to be 0.44 ($p < 0.001$, $N = 75$). Is it possible that the strong relationship between a poor inspection rating and being an inner city school reflects the incapacity of the inspectors to make adjustments for the difficulties of working in these schools and for the handicaps that pupils continue to experience in the urban environment, as suggested years ago by Gray and Hannon? However, the association could be an indication of genuine, remediable problems in some inner city schools in which case there needs to be adequate research into what remediation is effective.

Whatever the reason for a strong association between receiving a poor rating and having a high poverty indicator, we can take the relationship into account statistically, and then ask whether there are yet other factors which relate to the ratings received from inspectors. Amount spent on obtaining pre-inspection help turned out to be such a factor.

Even after taking account of free school meals, there remained a relationship between the amount spent buying in pre-inspection help and the rating received by a school.[7] If inspectors judge what they see and not what they are told and if they are evaluating a school as it actually is, not on the basis of a self-presentation exercise, why should the purchase of pre-inspection help apparently have such a noticeable impact? One interpretation is a frankly quid pro quo arrangement. Indeed, an explicit complaint has been received of Local Education Authority (LEA) inspectors pointing out to schools that they would be undertaking inspection and a pre-inspection visit could be helpful to the school. Do heads feel at all obliged to buy in advance from inspectors? If heads are so confident as not to buy in pre-inspection help they apparently risk a lowered rating. Of course, these findings are just correlations. The actual mechanisms cannot be established from correlations but they do raise hypotheses and this link between money expended and rating received is a situation which needs monitoring and further investigation.

Validity of different kinds of information

Despite the limitations of numerical indicators, they appear to carry more weight than inspectors' judgements in measurable areas. Question 16 invited agreement or disagreement with the following statement, 'If the judgement of the Ofsted team differed from data available to me on value-added I would tend to believe the Ofsted judgement'. Only 8 per cent agreed with this statement (only 1 per cent 'strongly') and 72 per cent rejected the statement. If these heads were representative of heads in general, the inspection system of the future could be vastly reduced in cost, be far more economical and have higher perceived validity if value-added indicators replaced the guesses of inspectors.

Impact

The actual impact of inspections will have to be monitored in a variety of ways but here we consider the perceived impact in terms of the value put on the inspection process by head-teachers. We then look at the difference in perceptions of those who have and have not been inspected, and we then consider the impact on the school of the pending inspection with regard to cost in time, money and staff illness.

Perceived outcomes as reported by head-teachers

For those who had had an inspection, there was the question:

> *Q. & How much information of use to you in improving schooling did you gain from the inspection?*

Since this last question in a sense went to the heart of the slogan for Ofsted 'Improvement through inspection', it is worth looking at the distribution of results on that item alone: Only 4 heads reported having learnt nothing; 14 reported not much; 34 reported 'some' (the middle of the scale) 28 reported 'quite a lot' and 5 reported 'a large amount'. The modal response was thus 40 per cent of the sample in the middle of the scale suggesting that they had learnt something in between 'not much' and 'quite a lot'; a result not overwhelmingly positive nor overwhelmingly negative.

Three items that did not require the experience of inspection were used to create the 'usefulness' scale[8]:

- *(1) an Ofsted inspection provides good value for money;*
- *(15) I believe it is better for my school to receive an Ofsted inspection every four years than to receive the money it costs (eg £20,000);*
- *(18) For my school the net impact of the whole Ofsted process is positive.*

The most positive item on the outcome scale related to the net impact of the 'whole Ofsted process' with 45 per cent agreeing that it had been positive and only 22 per cent disagreeing. This resulted in an average on the 5-point scale of 3.25 just above the mid-point. Since none of the other indicators of inpact was positive this needed some explanation. It could be that the 'whole Ofsted process' was seen to include the very existence of inspections and the use of the popular 'framework' (Ofsted, 1995). Seventy per cent agreed with the statement 'the framework had a useful impact on school management and organization'. In the view of head-teachers the original framework was a welcome document. Whether it in fact constituted 'advice' and put across a philosophy of management that was not necessarily helpful, are questions which may now be academic since the framework has been revised from a £40 tome down to a slim, 26-page glossy (Ofsted, 1995).

Responses to Question 15 which asked if the schools would prefer to have the money that an inspection cost, rather than an inspection, leaned heavily towards the money. Only 16 per cent would prefer the inspection. The question about value for money yielded 13 per cent agreeing that 'Ofsted provides good value for money', but more than twice as many, 54 per cent, disagreed.

Summary of findings regarding reliability, validity and impact (outcomes)

We have now considered the reliability, validity and outcomes as perceived by various groups of head-teachers. We found that, with the exception of one group, all attitudes were below neutral, ie negative (see Figure 5.1). Reliability was seen as a problem. Validity was generally seen as not quite as much of a problem and for one group the outcome scale was above neutral. The unusually positive group consisted of schools nominated by the failing-according-to-Ofsted (FAO) schools as being nearby and very similar. Could it be that one outcome of a nearby school being declared 'failing' was seen by these nearby schools as improving their own position in the market? Mere speculation but interesting.

Among all this evidence of the rather negative view of inspection by head-teachers it must be said that there was some strong support for inspection. This seemed to come particularly from inexperienced and newly appointed heads, a finding report also by Outson, Fidler and Earley

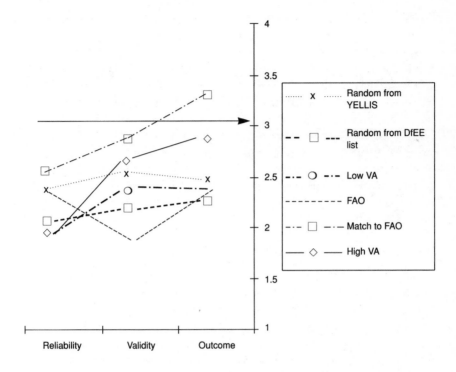

Head-teachers' views of Ofsted inspection on three dimensions (3 is neutral, higher is positive, lower is negative. FAO = Failed according to Ofsted. VA = value-added score)

Notes:
The six target groups consisted of two random samples, one from schools participating in the Year 11 Information System (YELLIS) and one from the DfEE list of schools; schools which, in YELLIS, had low value-added scores ('low VA') or high value-added scores; schools which were 'failing' according to Ofsted (FAO) and schools which were nominated by the FAO schools as being similar and nearby (matched to FAO).

Figure 5.1 *Head-teachers' views of Ofsted inspections*

(1996: pp 117): 'There was a trend for acting Heads to be more positive than permanent Heads'.

COSTS

Value for money (VFM) studies are the heart of management decisions and strategic planning for the nation as a whole. Now that the Ofsted trial has had time to bed down, it is a suitable time for VFM studies to be conducted by the appropriate bodies. Meanwhile, an important feature on the cost side of the balance sheet is not just the £70 to £100 million spent by Ofsted but the consequences of inspection for school budgets, money taken directly from schools' services to children. Several sorts of costs were investigated: costs due to stress-related absence as well as photocopying and other costs of preparation for the pre-announced inspection.

The cost of stress

An inspection is undoubtedly a source of stress for staff. Were the stress minor it might well be dismissed as a necessary evil in protecting the well-being of children. As the stress becomes more serious the necessity for proving that inspection does in fact, look after the well-being of children becomes the more urgent. At the very least, in any value for money study the cost of stress in the profession must be counted in, both in the short- and long-term possible effects on morale and recruitment.

One way to do this, and to put a realistic figure on the impact of the stress, is to look at absences which heads attributed to the inspection process. On the questionnaire heads were asked 'In your view, were there any stress-related absences before, during and after the inspection? This part of the questionnaire was often written over with statements such as 'too many' or 'too difficult to estimate'. There was a wide range of response in terms of staff absence. Absences before inspection were substantial and reported by half the heads. The overall average was 15.1 staff days. Absences during inspection dropped to a level of 2.3 staff days on average, but then shot up again after inspection to 28 staff days on average. For the 50 per cent of heads reporting some absences the average was 45 staff days.

One assumption sometimes implied rather than stated is that the worst teachers feel the most stress and will be encouraged to leave the profession. This is strongly denied by many heads and many teachers who feel that the people most stressed are often the most conscientious and excellent teachers. If staff absence were a sign of nervousness because of incompetence it would be expected that the amount of absence would be related to

	Pre-inspection	During inspection	Post inspection
Number of respondents (out of 61)	40	47	42
All respondents	14.7 staff-days	2.6 staff-days	32 staff-days
% reporting some staff absences	50%	30%	57%
Those reporting some absence	30 staff-days	8.5 staff-days	57 staff-days

Ofsted inspections: Staff absences attributed to stress

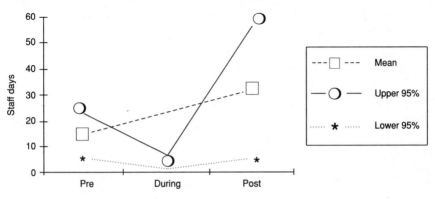

Intercorrelation between staff absences before, during and after an inspection and the rating received

	Pre	During	Post	Rating
Pre	1.00	0.80	0.64	−0.15
During	0.80	1.00	0.67	−0.13
Post	0.64	0.67	1.00	−1.10
Rating	−0.15	−0.13	−0.10	1.00

Note: Absences were more common in some schools than others but the extent of staff absence was unrelated to the rating of the school by Ofsted. The rating was coded with a positive rating as 5. None of the correlations reached the 0.05 level of statistical significance.

Figure 5.2 *Absences pre-, during and post-inspection*

the rating the inspectors attached to the school. No such relationship was found. Despite a considerable search through the variables little could be said about stress other than that it was apparently related to little else, certainly not to the Ofsted rating of the school.

Costs of preparing for inspection

Mention has already been made of the average expenditure of £1192 on pre-inspection advice. The more spent on pre-inspection help the higher the rating subsequently received. Because there are some extremely high values on other costs, the medians are a better representation than the means. Median values were 40 staff days preparing documents, 10 days of the head's time on documents, £250 on reprographics and photocopying, 5 staff days on extra meetings of staff, but zero on extra meetings with parents although some schools reported high values such as 300 staff days. Two staff days were reported as the median for extra meetings with governors and zero with the press, though again some schools reported very large amounts such as 90 staff days.

The costs of (bad?) advice

Ofsted's official position is that inspectors do not give advice. This seems an entirely reasonable position in that if inspectors give help and advice then, when they return, they will be returning to evaluate the effectiveness of their own work. The two functions can, perhaps profitably, be kept entirely separate. However, the rhetoric of keeping inspection and advice separate does not match the practice.

Despite the claimed principle that inspection should be separated from advice there appears to be a sub-text of advice implied by Ofsted's framework. Thus, it pushes schools towards target-setting and detailed planning, both short and long-term, without there being adequate evidence that this 'gradgrind' ethos or five-year plans are effective. There are alternative views as to good management. W Edwards Deming, for example, widely credited with transforming Japanese industry from the shoddy goods of the 1950s to the world-class quality of the 1980s and 1990s, was explicitly opposed to targets, and to appraisal. He advised, rather, the constant collection of hard statistical data, well interpreted, and an ongoing striving for improvement, combined with an insistence on joy in work (Neave, 1992; Hinkley and Seddon, 1996). Furthermore, he urged the search for 'profound knowledge', ie soundly based research results. 'Don't work harder work smarter'. It has been argued elsewhere that Deming's philosophy fits with the conclusions reached by many other eminent scholars such as Popper and Simon (Fitz-Gibbon, 1996). These issues may well be oversimplified and not easily resolved. What is clear is that Ofsted's unthinking adoption of one approach to management and improvement is going beyond its brief and may conceivably be damaging.

The perception that Ofsted advises is clear from parents' comments as reported by Taberer (1995). Quite reasonably they suppose that a plan identifying the 'key issues for action' (Ofsted, 1995: 11) constitutes advice. It directs behaviour and not, necessarily, effectively. For example, the report which failed Breeze Hill Comprehensive School in Oldham complained that the school had done nothing about the underachievement of boys at GCSE. Since this achievement discrepancy is a country-wide phenomenon, mainly in English rather than science or mathematics, it might have been a reasonable management decision that efforts could be better expended in areas more likely to yield results. Is Ofsted usurping school's rights under local management of schools? Who is then subsequently responsible?

The psychodynamics and legal position of inspection

Ofsted has been given unchallengeable power. When Breeze Hill was rerated as 'failing' less than a year after being rated as 'satisfactory' it wished to take Ofsted to court. The LEA was prepared to back this challenge. Unfortunately a QC stated it could not be shown that the judgements were 'perverse' or 'unreasonable' and a case would not be successful. Yet it would seem both perverse and unreasonable that Ofsted should demonstrate clearly in one school the unreliability of its procedures and not be subject to review. Is it not fundamentally perverse and unreasonable that Ofsted is not held accountable for being able to demonstrate its levels of reliability and validity?

Lord Acton warned that power corrupts and absolute power corrupts absolutely. Again this is a very difficult area to deal with, not one in which the authors feel in the least bit competent. There are numerous instances coming to our attention of inspection acting as a poison in the system and concern has been expressed at the appearance of subterfuge among grown-ups being less than educationally sound for children who observe the inspection process and its impact on their teachers. Inspection has certainly created much bad blood between between teachers and their LEA and it has undermined the confidence of parents in their schools, without good evidence. Because there is considerable fear in the system we can only urge that an enquiry is needed in which those with some responsibility for Ofsted can hear statements given in confidence which many inspectors and others feel unable to provide publicly.

DISCUSSION

The aspect of inspection which is the most expensive in inspectors' time, the most costly to schools in staff stress, and the least validated, is the practice of having inspectors sit in classrooms using classroom observation methods which have not been demonstrated to meet any level of quality standards and drawing unchallengeable conclusions which have yet to be subjected to proper scrutiny for their reliability, validity or sufficiency for the purpose of publicly rating an entire school. It is this aspect of inspection which should be immediately suspended pending the application of proper standards.

It is doubtful that business or industry would permit an inspection regime, centrally imposed, that was based on opinion about how the business or industry should be run, not on sound research. This is what is being imposed upon schools in the public sector, despite the intentions of the welcome local management of schools legislation.

Inspection should do what inspection can do best and should not pretend to second-guess what is better measured such as rates of progress or 'value-added'. There should be compliance indicators (Richards, 1988) as, for example, with the delivery of the National Curriculum, maintaining a safe environment, maintaining proper financial records and showing a duty of care to children and staff in the school. Such compliance should be assessed by unannounced visits as is practised in industry. Furthermore, the differing responsibilities of Ofsted inspectors and those of such bodies as the Audit Commission, the Health and Safety Executive and the Teacher Training Agency need to be clarified.

We have received complaints from science teachers' organizations that Ofsted inspectors are not well trained in health and safety and some make poor judgements and recommendations. This raises the entire issue of what competencies inspectors need. If they are interpreting a body of statistical data, then they should be examined in their understanding of such data. If they are interpreting the adequacy of account-keeping then they should be examined in their knowledge of accounts. If the are serving as health and safety officers they should be qualified to the highest standards since nothing is of greater concern to parents than the health and safety of their children. There can be no substitute for inspection, but as it is presently operating it is an embarrassment to anyone who understands social science, its complexities and methods, and it is apparently a source of grave distress to a teaching profession on which we rely for the care of our children and grandchildren.

SUMMARY

A simple blueprint evaluation starting from the proposition that 'Inspections are as good as their methodological foundations' (Gray and Wilcox, 1995: 127) and considering Ofsted's procedures would seem to raise grave concerns since Ofsted's methods have:

- been amateurish and far from 'state of the art' in that they have failed to meet even the most elementary standards with regard to sampling, reliability and validity;
- failed to implement the organization's own principles, such as separating advice from inspection;
- failed to keep abreast of modern approaches to management and to research evidence;
- demanded analysis skills from inspectors without having demonstrated that inspectors have these skills to a degree which gives them authority in the interpretation of complex data and research evidence;
- confused its mission with that of other bodies;
- included methods which have now been quietly repudiated by Ofsted itself, but without apology or compensation made to the schools damaged by those methods now admitted to be indefensible.

The survey of 159 head-teachers reported above indicated that Ofsted has:

- failed to win the confidence of head-teachers;
- caused schools considerable expense which must now figure in value for money studies;
- possibly caused schools to spend money to find out how to improve the rating they will obtain in an inspection;
- delivered ratings of schools which are worse for schools in the most difficult circumstances.

Because of all these failings Ofsted may have substantially damaged the quality of education provided by schools by causing them to spend time, money and energy unproductively. The pretence to unlikely levels of wisdom, so inherent in an inspection system which has avoided any routine and proper checks on the adequacy of its methods, is the greatest enemy of empirical investigation, effective problem-solving and real improvement. There should immediately be an expert panel to consider the role and methodology of the inspection process, with representatives from business, industry, medicine, and statistics as well as education.

NOTES

1. This was a response rate of 51 per cent which is considered high for a response to a one-off survey.
2. These two items were not as mutually consistent as might have been expected. There was only a weak tendency – only $r = 0.41$ – for those heads who believed that independent teams would agree to be also those who agreed that differences within an inspection team would be easily resolved. On further investigation, this low correlation turned out to be partly due to a difference between heads whose schools were rated 'failing' or 'cause for concern' (henceforth referred to together as the so-called problem schools) and other heads. Among the heads of so-called problem schools, the correlation between the two reliability questions was actually negative. (-0.30). These heads tended to have seen the inspection teams as monolithic, easily resolving conflicts, but strongly believed other teams might have arrived at different judgements (see Figure 1). It must be remembered that the school is not allowed to hear the inspection team's deliberations. These are conducted behind closed doors, unlike practice in the Further Education Funding Council (FEFC) where a member of the staff of the college is included in inspectors' meetings. Among the heads whose schools were rated satisfactory or better ($n = 69$) the correlation was 0.5. Perhaps the difference in perceptions represented a difference in the behaviour of the inspection teams or perhaps it was a reaction to the rating.
3. Registered inspectors, ie leaders of Ofsted teams.
4. In a Likert scale a statement is made and the respondent selects responses from 'strongly disagree', 'disagree', 'neutral', 'agree', or 'strongly agree'.
5. Scales are preferable to single items because the true variance becomes a larger proportion of the whole variance as more items are added. An individual items may attract some odd responses due to a particular interpretation but if all items are answered in a particular direction this provides a strong indication of the respondent's view. The extent of agreement among items is called the *internal consistency* and is often measured by Cronbach's alpha (Cronbach, 1951; McKennell, 1970; Fitz-Gibbon and Morris, 1987). For the validity scale in this study Cronbach's alpha was 0.79.
6. This was such an extraordinary view in our opinion that it seemed interesting to ask what characteristics were shared by these heads. They appears to be from every sample source and from schools with a range of free school meals though predominantly low on this indicator of poverty. Of those inspected, the ratings were significantly higher than the whole group's, with none in the 'cause for concern' or 'failing' categories.& check significance
7. The correlation between residuals and the amount spent on pre-inspection help was 0.23 ($p = 0.07$ for the 58 heads who answered the question on expenditures on pre-inspection help. For schools which had spent over £1000 the residuals were positive for 11 schools and negative for 3. The 5 schools which had failed had all spent nothing on pre-inspection advice, usually provided by inspectors.
8. The measure of internal consistency for this scale, Cronbach's alpha, was 0.73.
9. YELLIS, the Year Eleven Information System, collects data from 100 per cent samples of pupils and relates pupils' reports of aspirations, attitudes, and school experiences to a test of developed abilities given in Year 10 and external examination results, in over 50 subjects, from Year 11 (15-year-old pupils). Run by the CEM Centre, University of Durham, YELLIS tracks value-added and many other indicators.

10. Ofstin, the Office for Standards in Inspection, has been formed by concerned educators and welcomes submissions regarding the proper role of inspectors in the 21st century. Please address these to The Ofstin Secretary, 9 Quatre Bras, Hexham, Northumberland, NE46 3EY, tel: 01434 604747.

REFERENCES

Bryan, C (1995) Inspection, in IMAC Research (ed) *Education and Training Statistics,* Statistics Users' Council

Cronbach, LJ and Meehl, PE (1955) Construct validity in psychological tests, *Psychological Bulletin,* **52**, May, pp 281–302

Cronbach, LJ and Meehl, PE (1955) 'Construct validity in psychological tests', *Psychological Bulletin,* **52**, May, pp 281–302

Fitz-Gibbon, CT (1995) Ofsted, schmofsted, in *School Inspection,* ed T Brighouse and T Moon, Pitman Publishing, London

Fitz-Gibbon, CT (1996) *Monitoring Education: Indicators, Quality and Effectiveness,* Cassell, London and New York

Fitz-Gibbon, CT and Clark, KS (1982) Time variables in classroom research: a study of eight urban secondary school mathematics classes, *British Journal of Educational Psychology,* **52**, 301–16

Fitz-Gibbon, CT and Vincent, LS (1994) Candidates' performance in science and mathematics at A-level, School Curriculum and Assessment Authority.

Gray, J and Hannon, V (1986) HMI interpretation of schools' examination results, *Journal of Educational Policy,* **1**, 23–33

Gray, J and Wilcox, B (1995) The methodologies of inspection: issues and dilemmas, in *School Inspection,* eds T Brighouse and B Moon, Pitman Publisher, London

Hinkley, T and Seddon, J (1996) The Deming approach to school improvement, P Earley, B Fidler and J Ouston in *Improvement through Inspection? Complementary approaches to school development,* David Fulton Publishers Ltd, pp 71–93, London

Hogg, GW (1990) Great performance indicators of the past, ed C T Fitz-Gibbon in *Performance Indicators,* Multilingual Matters Ltd, Clevedon, Philadelphia

Kelly, A (1976) A study of the comparability of external examinations in different subjects, *Research in Education,* **16**, 50–63

McKennell, AC (1970) Attitude Scale Construction, in eds O'Muirchearthaigh and Payne, *The Analysis of Survey Data. 1: Exploring data structures,* Wiley, Chichester

Medley, DM and Mitzel, HE (1963) Measuring classroom behavior by systematic observation in *Handbook of Research on Teaching,* ed NL Gabe, Rand McNally, Chicago

Neave, H (1992) *The Deming Dimension,* SPC press, Knoxville, Tennessee

Ofsted (1995) *Framework for the Inspection of Schools,* HMSO, London

Ouston, J, Fidler, B and Earley, P (1996) Secondary schools' responses to Ofsted: improvement through inspection? in *Ofsted Inspections: the Early Experience* eds J Ouston, P Earley and B Fidler, pp 110–25, David Fulton Publishers Ltd, London

Richards, CE (1988) A typology of educational monitoring systems, *Educational Evaluation and Policy Analysis,* **10**, 106–16

Rutter, M, Maughan, B, Mortimer, P and Ousten, J (1979) *Fifteen Thousand Hours: Secondary Schools and their Effects on Children,* Open Books, London

Taberer, R (1995) Parents' perceptions of Ofsted, National Foundation for Educational Research

Winer, BJ, 1971) *Statistical Principles in Experimental Design*, 2nd edn, McGraw-Hill, London and New York

Inspection and education: the indivisibility of standards

Robin Alexander

INTRODUCTION

What follows is a lightly edited version of evidence submitted to the 1998–9 Commons Education Sub-Committee Inquiry into the Work of Ofsted. The editing has removed paragraph numbering, the executive summary and the conclusions, but has incorporated a further brief statement which the author submitted to the Committee in the light of its reported meeting with Her Majesty's Chief Inspector (HMCI) in February 1999. If there is a theme, it is that 'standards' – the obligatory educational watchword of all governments these days – are a moral absolute rather than merely something to be measured on an 8-level scale, and that they must, therefore, be applied with equal rigour to all aspects of the education service: to those who inspect no less than those who are inspected, to those who make policy no less than those who implement it.

THE STATUS OF OFSTED

Ofsted is a non-ministerial government department. The non-ministerial aspect and HMCI's status as Crown office holder are presumed to guarantee the same independence of judgement possessed by Her Majesty's Senior Chief Inspector (HMSCI) under the old HMI system until 1992.[1]

In practice, that independence has not as yet been demonstrated, and certainly not in the way it was asserted – eg over resource levels – by HMCI's predecessors HMSCIs Eric Bolton and Sheila Browne. HMCI statements are invariably premised on unqualified support for the policies of the government of the day. His annual report focuses upon the performance of schools and teachers, but exempts from comment the policy framework within which they work. This implies that policy is sacrosanct, and that it enables but never frustrates, whereas it is very evident from a decade of highly interventive education policy since the 1988 Education Reform Act (ERA) watershed that it can do both.

There are several instances where this lack of objective, independent scrutiny of education policy has been badly needed: eg the previous administration's claim that class sizes have no impact on teaching quality;[2] the failure of successive administrations to address the problems caused by the primary/secondary funding differential;[3] the present administration's National Curriculum for teacher training; its literacy and numeracy strategies, including the literacy hour. In the latter case, Ofsted has been asked to 'monitor the implementation' of the strategies.[4] Since these are essentially experiments, based on a contestable reading of the international evidence on pedagogy and pupil attainment, they should be objectively evaluated rather than merely policed to ensure compliance.

My own 1986–91 research on the condition of primary education in one of Britain's largest cities showed that an approach to school improvement which is based on teacher compliance to standardized models of 'best practice' can prove deeply counterproductive, and indeed damaging in terms of the quality of children's learning. (Alexander, 1991, 1997). Nobody offers other than wholehearted support for goals such as that of raising standards of literacy and numeracy, but a national system of inspection must provide impartial and if necessary critical advice on the means chosen to achieve these goals. The more a government engages with the fine detail of educational practice – as the present administration, through the Department for Education and Employment (DfEE) Standards and Effectiveness Unit, has done to an unprecedented degree – the greater the need, and the risks, in this regard. As the Leeds reform programme graphically demonstrated, 'Good educational practice is achieved dialectically and empirically, not by decree' (Alexander, 1997: 287).

OFSTED'S REMIT

Ofsted has a statutory duty to inspect and report on schools, nursery education, colleges, Local Education Authorities (LEAs) and both initial and in-service teacher training. HMCI may also offer advice and reports on any other matter connected with these as he sees fit.[5] This remit is extremely broad, and sensibly so. However, it carries in consequence two dangers.

The first is that the broad scope of the Ofsted remit may infringe and frustrate the legitimate imperatives of people and institutions which fall outside that remit. The most serious example is the interface between teacher training and the work of the universities, where the bulk of teacher training is concentrated. Ofsted initial and in-service teacher training inspections assess universities' compliance with the standards promulgated by the Teacher Training Agency (TTA):[6] the strong emphasis on compliance in the Ofsted teacher training inspection model[7] might be seen to constitute a direct challenge to academic freedom, especially in higher degree advanced in-service provision where the focus is on educational ideas as much as executive skills. The inquiry will not need reminding of the central importance of academic freedom to both higher education and a healthy democracy.

The second danger arises from the potentially limitless scope of HMCI advice and comment. Once these stray beyond the evidential core of Ofsted's work they may constitute little more than the personal opinion, belief or prejudice of whoever happens to be HMCI. Since one person's opinion is not necessarily more valid or informed than another's, the status of these interventions, once they cease to be sustained by Ofsted evidence and the quality assurance procedures by which such evidence is validated, is by definition questionable. Yet because the interventions are made by HMCI, they are presumed to be evidentially grounded and of unimpeachable authority. I return to this issue later.

THE OFSTED MODEL: ONE AMONG MANY

The sub-committee cannot fail to be aware that the current system of inspection has provoked widespread concern: that, after all, is why this inquiry has been initiated. Leaving aside for the moment the specific reservations, the more fundamental point to be made here is that Ofsted's is just one among many possible inspection models, and though it is one of the most extensive and expensive, this does not necessarily make it the most effective. Having developed a centralized education system later than most other countries, we seem unable or unwilling to learn two simple and obvious lessons from those countries which having had highly centralized systems are now striving for a better balance of national, regional and local control: namely, that there is a point beyond which central control and central policing of the fine detail of teaching and learning become counterproductive; and that a high degree of centralization does not guarantee a high level of performance.[8] The more problematic aspects of the Ofsted model are now summarized.

THE BALANCE OF DISRUPTION AND BENEFIT

No inspection system can have so light a touch that it does not interfere to some extent with the day-to-day work of the institutions inspected. The weight of evidence about Ofsted, however, is that the disruption caused by inspection can be excessive, and may well outweigh any benefits. The teachers' unions have substantial dossiers of complaints on this score, and as an instance of these I have one from a primary school in north Yorkshire which attests to acute disruption lasting from a whole term before the inspection to the best part of a term after it. In this case, it is notable that it is parents and governors, rather than the school's teachers, who have made the strongest complaints. To take another example: the University of Warwick will have experienced, over the four years 1996–97 to 2000–01, some 23 inspections of its teacher training and award-bearing in-service courses, each one entailing between two and four visits by inspection teams, sometimes involving 12 days of visits each, not to mention the time required for preparation and follow-up.[9]

To such a massive investment of time, and the consequent financial cost to each institution – which, incidentally, never features in public statements about the cost of Ofsted[10] – should be added the high stress levels which the process provokes. The latter cannot be quantified, and because it tends to be described in somewhat emotive language – stress *is* an emotional matter after all – it is easy to dismiss it as mere griping by an overcosseted profession. That reaction is inadequate: the case material available, eg from the teacher unions, testifies to levels of personal stress and distress induced by Ofsted which are as incompatible with today's supposedly civilized employment ethos as they are counterproductive to the goal of school improvement.[11]

THE COMPETENCE OF INSPECTORS

Ofsted rightly places considerable emphasis on recruiting inspectors with appropriate experience and on providing them with the necessary training. Despite this, there are too many accounts of inspectors exceeding their brief or demonstrating an inadequate grasp of their field for the Inquiry to be sanguine that 100 per cent competence has been achieved. The problem stems partly from the insistence of those who created the system that amateurs (ie registered, team and additional inspectors) can do the job better than professionals (ie tenured Her Majesty's Inspectors HMIs) and partly from the power that inspectors are given to deliver judgements on complex matters which are absolute and unchallengeable. LEA inspections pose a particular problem in this regard, as noted by Maurice Kogan (1996).

THE INSPECTION CRITERIA

The Ofsted model involves the application of criteria set out in the Ofsted *Handbook* (1995a) and glossed in supplementary publications (Ofsted, 1998a). The criteria are extensive and very detailed, and in the case of school inspections cover educational standards, the quality of teaching, curriculum, school management and relationships with parents. There is an overarching rationale which links school context, pupil outcomes and contributory factors.

The criteria as such are in many respects admirable in that they focus on what most would accept are the critical features of successful teaching, learning and educational management. Some might cavil at assumptions embodied in some of the criteria, but the more fundamental issue is this: in the context of a closed model of inspection such as Ofsted's (ie where the criteria are not open to discussion or negotiation and where neither evidence nor judgements may be questioned), the more detailed the criteria, the greater the requirement for unimpeachable inspection expertise and evidence. What matters, then, is not so much the criteria as how they are used. Contrary to the impression created by Ofsted's adoption of numerical rating procedures, the application of these criteria is not at all an exact science. Most require a qualitative judgement[12] rather than a yes or no answer, or (as in the case of pupil attendance and punctuality) a quantitative calculation; and most are phrased in ways which allow scope for different interpretations.

Whether the training provided by Ofsted is adequate to secure absolute consistency in the interpretation and application of the inspection criteria – for in this model nothing less than absolute consistency can be acceptable – is something the sub-committee will no doubt wish to check against the confident claims in Ofsted's submission[13] on the one hand and the somewhat contrary anecdotal evidence from individual schools, colleges and universities on the other.

THE EVIDENTIAL BASIS OF INSPECTORS' JUDGEMENTS

Ofsted aims to offset the problem of criterial ambiguity referred to above by setting out indicators and itemizing the kinds of evidence which inspectors should seek, and through its training programme. By and large, the *Handbook* prompts are sensible and appropriate, but they are no guarantee that the evidential basis of judgements will be watertight. Indeed, given the format and context of inspections – high stakes, high stress and a relatively brief period of time in which to pack a complex procedure on which an institution's future may depend – it is inevitable that some of the evidence will be inadequate, or skewed by the dynamics of the inspection process, thus compounding the problems of criterial ambiguity and judgemental subjectivity referred to above.

These inbuilt frailties demand, in the interests of both methodological accuracy and social justice, that the evidence for particular inspection judgements be open to inspection. At present it is not.

THE STATUS OF INSPECTORS' JUDGEMENTS

This takes me to the heart of my reservations about the Ofsted model: the status of judgements made by Ofsted inspectors. These judgements are absolute. The Ofsted complaints procedure, such as it is, admits complaints about the conduct of inspections and inspectors, but not about evidence and judgements.

To return to the Warwick example. Warwick's Primary Postgraduate Certificate in Education (PGCE) was inspected in 1996–97. On the basis of a disagreement over the assessment of three students[14] between Ofsted inspectors on the one hand, and university lecturers and teachers in partner schools on the other, Warwick was deemed not to be complying with the criteria on the assessment of teaching. The evidential basis for the inspectors' judgements was by any reasonable standards – let alone those applied in academic research or a court of law – open to question. The judgement, however, was final. In the Ofsted model it is impossible for an inspector to be wrong.

The consequence of this disagreement between two groups of professionals over three students, in the context of the problematic inspection dynamics to which I referred earlier, was that the entire course had to be reinspected. Had there been further problems at the reinspection stage (there were not), TTA could have summarily withdrawn teacher training accreditation from Warwick University and its institute of education would have faced closure: all on the strength, I stress, of a divergence of judgement – subjective judgement, at that – concerning three of the institution's 1,200 students.

This, manifestly, is to invest in Ofsted inspection judgements an authority far beyond what they can legitimately bear. I doubt whether for any other profession outside a totalitarian regime this would be even contemplated, let alone sanctioned, and those outside the education service may find it astonishing that in this country it was indeed both contemplated and implemented. Yet the system has the backing of the Secretary of State and the Prime Minister, and is used by the TTA to accredit courses and institutions and to allocate teacher training numbers. Disturbingly, in his reappointment letter to HMCI, the Secretary of State acknowledges the need for flexibility and a 'light touch' where school inspections are concerned, but treats the inspection of initial training as unproblematic.[15] In my view, it stands in even more urgent need of reform than the school inspection system.

I have used the Warwick example by way of illustration. My concern, however, is a general one. The inherent frailty of the Ofsted system in respect of those of its criteria, evidence and judgements which are firmly in the domain of the qualitative and subjective, whether these apply to schools, LEAs or teacher training, is such that its evidence must be open to scrutiny and its judgements must be open to challenge and independent arbitration. Anything less is an affront to the most basic principles of natural justice.

Ofsted's belated appointment, in July 1998, of an external complaints adjudicator might seem to address these concerns, though it is too early to tell. However, if the adjudicator is employed by Ofsted, his or her independence would appear to be compromised from the outset; and if the scope of complaints continues to be restricted to the conduct of inspectors and inspections rather than the adequacy of evidence and the validity of judgements, then all my reservations remain as stated.

OFSTED AND STANDARDS

As Ofsted's name indicates, it is centrally concerned with standards. That being so, it is proper to ask whether the Ofsted regime to date has had the direct and positive impact on standards which was intended and is frequently claimed. The independent evidence on this matter is by no means clear-cut,[16] and where it actually points to a downturn in standards this must be counted – assuming that such research can stand up to methodological scrutiny – a serious indictment of the current inspection arrangements (Cullingford and Daniels, 1999). Beyond this, there are three basic points to be made.

First, the demonstration of cause and effect in this regard is by no means easy. It is most readily demonstrated at the lowest extremes of school performance. It is almost certainly the case that improvements noted in a number of schools placed on special measures, including some which have attracted considerable press attention, can be attributed to Ofsted's intervention: had there been no adverse inspection report and no special measures, then several of these schools would no doubt have continued to perform badly.

Secondly, rather more difficult to demonstrate is Ofsted's positive impact on standards in the large proportion of schools which are already performing satisfactorily. Individual schools confirm the value of having to prepare for inspection, of constructive comments and advice, and of the way an inspection report can provide a lever for school development (Fidler *et al*, 1998). However, for some schools already performing well it is arguable that the disruption factor referred to above may outweigh the benefit. This is tacitly acknowledged by the Secretary of State in his instruction to HMCI to introduce a 'light touch' model of inspection for good schools.[17] Yet he does not specify where the line should be drawn, and the inquiry could usefully press Ofsted on this matter, and on exactly how it proposes to interpret the Secretary of State's requirements that 'schools which fail to secure the results of which their pupils are capable or to sustain continued improvement will be inspected under the current model'.[18] The inquiry might also ask why the proposals for flexibility and a 'light touch' do not apply to teacher training.

Finally, it is pretty obvious that Ofsted's impact on standards is at best indirect. It is teachers who raise the standards of their pupils' achievement, not inspectors. That being so, Ofsted should ensure more effectively in the future than it has in the past that its contribution to school and teacher improvement is a positive one.

INSPECTION AND RESEARCH

HMCI has made several public attacks on the quality and usefulness of educational research[19] and in 1997 he commissioned a study from James Tooley to back his claims. (Tooley and Darby, 1998). Contrary to normal research contract procedure, this research was not open to competitive tender, so there were understandable grounds for suspicion that the project was given to someone in sympathy with HMCI's prejudices. Though Tooley's study was, in fact, a review of a sample of articles in just four journals, and though its authors offered the required caveat about the danger of generalizing from such a small sample, the Ofsted press release was headed 'Majority of academic educational research is second rate' and quoted HMCI as saying of the report: 'It shows that considerable sums of money are being pumped into research of dubious quality and little value [and] ... that the crucial areas of initial teacher education and in-service training are being ill-served by the research community'.[20]

Clearly, HMCI's gloss, which received considerable press coverage and was apparently accepted by the DfEE,[21] went far beyond what could be sustained by the very limited range of material studied by Tooley and Darby and the less than objective way in which they had studied it. Yet it was part of a pattern, which in the context of this inquiry, deserves both comment and investigation.

It is beyond the Inquiry's remit to test claims about the quality and usefulness of educational research as such. However, it *is* relevant for the inquiry to examine HMCI's assertion that Ofsted inspections have made independent research redundant. In fact, despite the somewhat sensationalist claims in the press release quoted above, and HMCI's frequent public attacks on research and researchers, Ofsted's stance on educational research is decidely ambivalent, if not contradictory.

In the first instance, Ofsted itself commissions both research and research reviews from the same academic community which HMCI so frequently excoriates.[22] Once published, these research reports and reviews are frequently endorsed in Ofsted publications and by HMCI himself.

Secondly, HMCI himself refers to other published research, albeit selectively. For example, in the 1995 publication *Teaching Quality* he referred in some detail – and warmly commended – research studies by Maurice Galton and his colleagues at Leicester, by Stevenson and Stigler in the United States, and by myself.[23]

Thirdly, the Ofsted inspection framework is manifestly informed by a generation of published research. To take one example, the section of the *Handbook* for nursery and primary schools dealing with the quality of teaching is clearly derived from the 1992 Department of Education and Science (DES) primary discussion paper (Alexander *et al*, 1992) (the 'three wise men' enquiry, on which I myself served, alongside HMCI Chris Woodhead and Ofsted Director of Inspections, Jim Rose) both as to its focus and in some cases its wording.[24] That document was a distillation of evidence from (HMI) inspection and from research, mainly the latter: the bibliography contained some 90 references.

Fourthly, if we take the most familiar arena for HMCI complaint, and the one which draws the loudest applause from certain sections of the press – the damaging impact of 'progressive' ideas on teaching quality and educational standards in the primary phase – one basic fact needs to be placed firmly on the record. Far from condoning and encouraging woolly thinking, mindless ideology and educationally unchallenging practices in primary education, it was the academic community whose research first exposed these in the 1960s, and investigated them empirically in the 1970s and 1980s. In doing so, they frequently found themselves working against the grain of received opinion among HMIs, LEA advisers and the teaching profession. But in doing so they pursued truth rather than myth and were, therefore, as interested in the strengths of progressivism as its weaknesses, and in ascertaining rather than exaggerating its extent and impact.[25] This commitment to balance, regrettably, was contrary to news values, as is demonstrated in the published accounts of the aftermath of my 1991 Leeds report. (Alexander 1997; Wallace 1993; Woods and Wenham, 1995).

The unsatisfactory scenario of a mismatch between HMCI word and Ofsted deed raises wider questions about the role of HMCI to which I now turn. It also demolishes some of the wilder claims about the quality of educational research and its supposed lack of relevance to Ofsted and to the work of teachers and schools.

THE OFFICE OF HMCI

The present occupant of the position of HMCI has forged for himself a profile markedly higher than that of any HMCI or HMSCI within living memory, higher indeed than that deservedly enjoyed in the last century by Matthew Arnold, arguably the most distinguished and enlightened HMI in the service's 150-year history. As often as not, Ofsted documents open with HMCI Woodhead's portrait and personal message. He has courted – and been courted by – the media, has appeared on numerous public platforms, and is a regular guest on broadcast news and current affairs programmes. Occasionally, his chosen medium has been more politically partisan than might be deemed appropriate for a supposedly impartial inspectorate.[26] Through this activity HMCI has acquired the mantle of fearless crusader for educational standards against the vested interests and outdated ideology of the 'educational establishment'.[27] In many people's eyes the Chief Inspector *is* Ofsted.

The inevitable result of this exposure is that the man and his style have come in for a great deal of comment. Indeed, midway through its deliberations, in February 1999, the Committee questioned HMCI Woodhead about the style and tone of his public pronouncements. Not surprisingly, he saw nothing to apologize about, and though some may prefer a more diplomatic manner it could be argued in HMCI Woodhead's defence that he has a duty to present the facts about education in England as directly and unequivocally as he can, and that if some people find these facts uncomfortable that is their problem rather than his. As a researcher with an equal obligation to discovering the truth about education I support this view, and I myself know what it is like to be labelled 'anti-teacher' for coming up with research findings which some within the profession find unpalatable.

However, more important than style – about which in any case people will rarely agree – is the *substance* of those HMCI pronouncements which claim to represent the state of education as it is. It is my understanding that at the meeting referred to above the Committee did *not* raise with HMCI the suggestion it had received from a number of quarters that what he had on occasions presented as fact may well have been somewhat at variance with the evidence. The well-publicized objections of former HMI Colin Richards and Birmingham Chief Education Officer Tim Brighouse illustrate the kind of unease which has been expressed, as does the mismatch, to which I referred earlier, between the Tooley report and its Ofsted press release. Let me give two further examples to illustrate why this matter is more important than has so far been acknowledged.

The first is an example of how HMCI's preference for the full frontal assault on individuals rather than proper engagement with their ideas allows the truth to be buried under an avalanche of rhetoric and misrepresentation. In his *Blood on the Tracks* 1998 RSA lecture (Woodhead, 1998a), which as always received massive press coverage,[28] HMCI launched a highly personal attack on three Government education advisers, two of them members of the Qualifications and Curriculum Authority (QCA), the third a member of the Government's Standards Task Force, misrepresenting their published views and charging them with being at the 'heart of darkness' of the 'trivialization of culture and the erosion of belief in the intellect'. Those thus denigrated were not the only people disturbed by these unwarranted accusations: the Secretary of State himself expressed concern.[29] HMCI himself made no effort to correct the sensationalizing treatment of his remarks by the press, even though he privately claimed that it did not 'constitute an accurate representation of [his] views'.[30] The attacks were repeated in the press a year later, in March 1999, though this time they were broadened to include other academics and professionals, including QCA as a whole. Much of the language was that used at and after HMCI's 1998 RSA lecture, though this time the article was by-lined 'By Anonymous, an Education Department Insider'.[31] By that time, therefore, the 'heart of darkness' charge had stuck, regardless of its justice or otherwise.

The second example is less sensational, but in its implications for the quality of English education it is perhaps more serious. During the autumn and winter of 1997/8 there was much discussion about how the school curriculum should be modified to meet the demands of the next century while also enabling teachers to deliver on the Government's pledge to raise standards in literacy and numeracy to specified levels by 2002. HMCI's most public and consistent contribution to this debate was to insist, on several occasions from autumn 1997 onwards, that primary schools would not be able to deliver on these targets unless the non-core elements of the curriculum were drastically slimmed down. His interventions polarized the debate into an apparently stark choice between 'curriculum breadth' and 'standards in the basics' and proved influential both in the press and at the DfEE.[32]

However, in November 1997 – that is to say, at exactly the time when HMCI was beginning to press this argument most strongly – Ofsted published a report on its statistical analysis of the relationship between inspection data and national test results at Key Stage 2 whose conclusions directly contradicted HMCI on this matter. The timing was not coincidental, for the DfEE had commissioned the study specifically:

> to provide information which could be taken into account ... in discussions within the education service about curriculum issues. Essentially the question the analysis aimed to address was: had schools which did well in the tests in 1996 done so at the expense of curriculum breadth and diversity?[33]

The Ofsted report concluded:

> The main finding was that schools which did well in the tests [in English, Mathematics and Science at KS2] also provided a broad and balanced curriculum ... On average, schools awarded a high grade for curriculum balance and breadth score well in the tests and those awarded lower grades score less well. This trend persists across all schools analysed regardless of their context.[34]

The November 1997 evidence was in line with findings from HMI inspections and surveys going back to 1978, when the relationship between standards in the 'basics' and the quality of the wider curriculum was first demonstrated. Moreover, I understand that two forthcoming Ofsted reports – one on the Government's literacy strategy and the other a four-year review of primary school inspections – will consolidate the November 1997 finding.

I trust that I do not need to spell out the policy implications of this. HMCI's polarizing of 'breadth' and 'standards' is not just unhelpful and unnecessary: Ofsted's own evidence suggests that it may even damage the very cause it claims to support – the raising of standards in literacy and numeracy. The national (and international) evidence is absolutely clear on this. Provided that the curriculum as a whole is sensibly planned and managed, no choice is required: the way to raise standards in literacy and numeracy is to raise the standards of *teaching* in literacy and numeracy, while embedding those subjects in a broad curriculum which will provide the necessary context for the application and consolidation of the skills in question.

HMCI stresses the importance of reporting on education as he finds it. This laudable aim is entirely unproblematic when there is no divergence between Ofsted evidence and HMCI belief, and when the act of reporting sticks firmly to the facts. But the climate I have described is not conducive to this and during the last few years truth and myth about English education have become hopelessly and damagingly confused. HMCI must bear his share of responsibility for this.

The task of HMCI – any HMCI – is to assemble and assess, dispassionately and even-handedly, evidence about the state of the nation's schools, its LEAs and its teacher training, and to report on what he finds. HMCI, the private individual has, like all of us, his beliefs, affiliations and prejudices. But if what a chief inspector – any chief inspector – believes overrides what the national evidence reveals; if that evidence is used selectively or tendentiously, or as justification for replacing one questionable orthodoxy by another; if an ostensibly impersonal inspection system is used as a platform for parading prejudices or settling scores; if it degenerates into a personality cult: then warning lights should begin to flash, for from that moment a chief inspector can no more claim to present the education system 'as it is' than can anyone else, and his or her authority and credibility as HMCI are irretrievably damaged. Neither truth nor education deserve to be so wantonly compromised.

It is unfortunate that those commenting on Ofsted find themselves calling into question the activities of the person who happens to be its chief officer. It *should* be possible to deal with these matters impersonally, to separate the organization from its head, and the office of HMCI from the person and manner of its holder. Let us hope that before too long the country will regain an inspection system which deals in issues rather than personalities, and whose procedures and evidence command respect because they are secure against caprice.

NOTES

1. DfEE submission to the Inquiry, 9 October 1998.
2. A claim not subscribed to by the present adminstration.
3. It was left to the Education Committee itself to investigate the primary-secondary funding discrepancy (House of Commons, 1994). The previous administration chose to ignore the policy implications of this report's conclusion that primary schools were seriously disadvantaged by the current funding arrangements and although many LEAs have attempted, within tight budgetary constraints, to achieve adjustments, the problem persists. This is an example of the kind of issue to which Ofsted might have devoted more of its attention.
4. Secretary of State's reappointment letter to HMCI, 19 September 1998.
5. Ofsted submission to this inquiry, 6 October 1998.
6. In accordance with section 5(4) of the Education Act (1994) and DfEE (1998a) Circular 4/98.
7. See Ofsted (1997a).
8. For a detailed tracking of the international shift to greater decentralization in educational decision-making, to which England is an increasingly isolated exception, see OECD (1998).
9. See submission from Professors Campbell and Husbands, para 5.1.

10. I believe that the Inquiry should attempt an assessment of the *financial* burden – not just the temporal one – which the Ofsted process places on the institutions which it inspects.

11. See submission to the Inquiry from Professor Colin Richards.

12. The Sub-Committee may wish to consider how it would apply criteria such as 'Do pupils show respect for other people's feelings, values and beliefs?' or 'Does the curriculum promote pupils' intellectual, physical and personal development and prepare pupils for the next stage of education?'

13. See Ofsted (1998b).

14. Warwick University believes this to be the number of students involved: in line with its policy of not discussing its evidence, Ofsted would not expect to confirm or deny this figure.

15. Letter from Secretary of State to HMCI, 18 September 1998, p 2.

16. See, for example, the studies undertaken by Bell, Hunter, Cullingford, Daniels and Brown, and Fidler, Ouston, Earley, Ferguson and Davies; see also other chapters in this volume.

17. Secretary of State's reappointment letter to HMCI, 18 September 1998.

18. *Ibid*.

19. For example, in his lectures to the Royal Geographical Society in January 1997 and to the RSA in January 1998.

20. See Ofsted (1998c).

21. Letter to the author of this submission, from AR Martin of DfEE on behalf of the Secretary of State, 17 August 1998, and public statements by ministers.

22. Ofsted's (1998b) considerable commitment to research is outlined on pp 33–6 of its submission to this Inquiry.

23. See Ofsted 1995b.

24. Compare, with respect to such matters as 'fitness for purpose' and the use of the organizational strategies of individual, group and whole class teaching; Alexander, Rose and Woodhead, 1992 (sections 4 and 6) and Ofsted 1995a (section 5.1).

25. On this issue the list of references would be too long; they can be provided if required. However, it should be noted that as co-author of the 'three wise men' report HMCI presumably endorsed that document's evidence-based refutation of the frequently heard claim of a progressive takeover of the nation's primary schools (Alexander, Rose and Woodhead (1992) paras 18–22). The claim is still frequently heard, though now it tends to be used as a stick with which to beat teacher training institutions and – confusingly – those same academics who exposed the weaknesses of the system they are accused of perpetuating.

26. For example, the Woodhead (1995) paper for Politeia, *A Question of Standards: finding the balance*.

27. For example, Phillips (1996), *The Times*, 20 January 1997.

28. The headlines are instructive: 'Trio at heart of darkness' ... 'The men failing our children, by schools chief ... 'Woodhead blames the academics' ... 'Three influential academics ... accused by the Government's chief schools' watchdog of undermining the drive to improve standards in the classroom' ... etc.

29. Letter from Secretary of State for Education and Employment to the author, 24 March 1998.

30. Letter from HMCI to the author, 3 March 1998.

31. See Anon (1999).

32. Press coverage of education during this period can be checked to confirm this, as can DfEE and Ofsted press releases. See also letter from HMCI to the Secretary of State dated 5 January 1998. This letter is in the public domain: it was circulated to the heads and chairs of governors of all primary schools the following week.

33. See Ofsted (1997b), para 3.
34. Ibid, paras 2 and 7. Clearly both versions of the Ofsted evidence cannot be right. The November 1997 Ofsted report contradicts HMCI's claim, in his widely disseminated letter to the Secretary of Stare of 5 January 1998 (see note 32) that 'there is evidence from inspection that many schools whose pupils are benefiting from the literary and numeracy hours find difficulty in managing the rest of the primary curriculum'. In January 1998, when HMCI wrote this, neither the literacy hour nor the numeracy hour had been introduced (the literacy hour was introduced in September 1998 and the numeracy hour will not come into force until September 1999, nearly two years after HMCI purported to have evidence about its impact). So HMCI's evidence base for his claim to the Secretary of State could only have been that used in the November 1997 report, which of course said the opposite. Thus, in his published advice to the Secretary of State in January 1998, HMCI both contradicted published Ofsted findings and anticipated the impact of policies which had not yet been implemented and inspections which had not yet been undertaken. Readers might take the view that in this matter HMCI misled the Secretary of State and fuelled a panic which was unwarranted.

REFERENCES

Alexander, RJ (1991) *Primary education in Leeds: twelfth and final report from the Primary Needs Independent Evaluation Project*, University of Leeds.

Alexander, RJ (1997) *Policy and Practice in Primary Education: Local Initiative, National Agenda*, Routledge, London

Alexander, RJ, Rose, AJ and Woodhead C (1992) *Curriculum Organisation and Classroom Practice in Primary Schools*, DES, London

Anon (1999) Luddites at the school gate, *Mail on Sunday*, 14 April

Cullingford, C and Daniels S (1999) *The effects of Ofsted inspections on school performance*, University of Huddersfield

DfEE (1998a) *Teaching: High Quality, High Standards*, Circular 4/98, *HMSO*, London

Fidler, B, Ousten, J, Earley, P, Ferguson, N and Davies, J (1998) *The Work of Ofsted*, University of Reading

House of Commons (1994) *The Disparity in Funding Between Primary and Secondary Schools*, HMSO, London

Kogan, M (1996) Independent reviews of Staffordshire and Kirklees LEAs, *Times Education Supplement*, 15 November

OECD (1998) *Education at a Glance*, OECD, Paris, pp 292–304

Ofsted (1995a) *Guidance on the Inspection of Nursery and Primary Schools*, Ofsted, London

Ofsted (1995b) *Teaching Quality: The Primary Debate*, Ofsted, London

Ofsted (1997a) *Framework for the Assessment of Quality and Standards in Initial Training 1997–98*, Ofsted, London

Ofsted (1997b) *National Curriculum Assessment Results and the Wider Curriculum at Key Stage 2: Some Evidence from the Ofsted Database*, Ofsted and DfEE, London

Ofsted (1998a) *Inspection '98: Supplement to the Inspection Handbooks Containing New Requirements and Guidance*, Ofsted, London

Ofsted (1998b) *Memorandum from Ofsted: Inquiry into the Work of Ofsted*, Ofsted, London

Ofsted (1998c) *News release*, 22 July, Ofsted, London

Phillips, M (1996) *All Must Have Prizes*, Little Brown and Co, London

Tooley, J and Darby, D (1998) *Educational Research: a critique*, Ofsted, London

Woodhead, C (1998) *Blood on the Tracks: Lessons from the History of Education Reform*, Ofsted/RSA, London

Wallace, M (1993) Discourse of derision: the role of the mass media within the educational policy process, *Journal of Educational Policy*, **8** (4)

Woods, P and Wenham, P (1995) Politics and pedagogy: a case study in appropriation, *Journal of Education Policy*, **10** (2)

Chapter Seven

Standards and school inspection: the rhetoric and the reality

Gerran Thomas

INTRODUCTION

In this chapter, I seek to cover two aims: to give a brief account of the creation of the Office for Standards in Education (Ofsted), and to review the research evidence which purports to show a link between inspection and improved standards in schools.

It is interesting to note that in one of the earliest government documents to describe the new inspection arrangements (The Parent's Charter, Department of Education and Science (DES), 1991), there is more emphasis on *accountability* (a buzz-word of the period) than on *standards*. The *Charter* starts with a section entitled: 'The right to know', which refers to the new requirement for schools to produce an annual report for parents on each child. The next section, 'Regular reports from independent inspectors', comments that:

> At present Her Majesty's Inspectors (HMI) ... cannot cover all schools regularly ... Under the Government's proposals, every state school will have to be inspected regularly ... (and) when the inspection is finished: you will be sent a report ... which sets out the school's strengths and weaknesses. You will also be sent the governors' plans to tackle the problem areas (DES, 1991: 4).

The rationale of the document appears to be that in the first instance, parents will be informed of the performance of local schools; that they will choose their child's school on the basis of that information; and that 'your right to choose will encourage schools to aim for the highest possible standards' (DES, 1991: 14). In this scenario, inspection plays a part in *informing* parents, rather than in helping schools to improve post inspection. Whether or not inspection, in and of itself, can lead to improvement will be considered later.

THE CREATION OF OFSTED

It is said that Margaret Thatcher, in her time as Secretary of State for Education (1970–74), considered HMI 'to be over-manned, and ... they should spend much more time inspecting schools and colleges' (Lawton and Gordon, 1987: 141). HMI continued to draw more criticism in the 1980s, especially from the right wing of the Conservative party: Kenneth Baker's (Secretary of State for Education, 1986–89) hostility to HMI was summed up by this comment:

> Of all Whitehall Departments, the DES was among those with the strongest in-house ideology. There was a clear 1960s ethos ... rooted in progressive orthodoxies ... It was devoutly anti-excellence, anti- selection and anti-market ... If civil servants were the guardians of this culture, then Her Majesty's Inspectors of Education were its priesthood. Reports on schools were written with an opaque quality which defied any reader to judge whether the school being inspected was any good or not (Baker, 1993: 168).

The Tory perception at this time was that HMI's reports were implicitly critical of Government policy, which led to increasing tensions. By 1991, according to Professor Eric Bolton (Senior Chief Inspector) (1998: 45) 'Kenneth Clarke (the Secretary of State for Education) made it abundantly clear that he, and the Government, found it hugely irritating to determine policies for education and then "have HMI running around the country critically commenting on them".'

Matters reached such a pitch that in May 1991 several Conservative MPs signed a motion in the House of Commons to abolish HMI (Dunford, 1998: 192). These tensions between HMI and the Secretary of State, and other factors (such as the Government's wish to monitor the recently introduced National Curriculum) were soon to force the issue. When John Major took over from Margaret Thatcher as Prime Minister in 1990, an election was already on the horizon. Major's 'big idea' leading up to that (1992) election was the Citizen's Charter (Cabinet Office, 1991), which was intended to lay down standards in many areas of professional activity.

In parallel with this development, Kenneth Clarke announced to Parliament his decision to review the role of HMI. Taking his lead from a pamphlet published by the right-wing think-tank, the Centre for Policy Studies (Burchill, 1991) Clarke set his civil servants to work on developing a brand new independent, market-orientated system of inspection which was to be independent of HMI (Thomas, 1998). These ideas formed part of the education policy outlined in the *Parent's Charter* (DES, 1991).

The proposals listed in the *Parent's Charter* formed the basis of a Bill presented to Parliament in November 1991. Several of these proposals were highly controversial, not least the idea that school governors should be allowed to choose their own inspection teams. A powerful lobby headed by former senior chief inspector Sheila Browne drew up a briefing paper for peers, in the hope that the House of Lords would amend the Bill. This paper 'argue(d) that the Bill's fundamental weakness is in allowing schools to pick their own inspectors. As their ability to attract parents will depend in part upon the inspection reports, schools will have no incentive to choose teams which they think might be critical'. (Hackett, 1992a: 4).

When the Bill reached the Lords for its Second Reading on 11 February 1992, it was roundly condemned by peers from most points on the political spectrum. Baroness Blackstone, Labour's chief education spokesperson in the Lords, described the Bill as 'ignorant, misguided and doctrinaire ... By allowing schools to choose their own inspectors, it will be easier for poor standards to go unnoticed'. Her attack on the Education (Schools) Bill was supported by Lord Beloff (Conservative), Emeritus Fellow at All Souls College, Oxford, who rejected the idea that the schools inspectorate could be run like a commercial organization. He described the bill as 'the silliest one which any Parliament has had to consider' (Looch, 1992). Lord Skidelsky, a member of the SDP, and professor of international relations at Warwick University, said the principle of allowing schools to choose their own inspectors was indefensible (Hackett, 1992b: 1). Following these criticisms, on 2 March 1992 the Government was defeated on an amendment proposed by Lord Peston. This amendment gave the responsibility for selecting inspection teams to the Chief Inspector for England or for Wales (as appropriate), and removed it from the governors of the school concerned. In order to ensure the passage of the Bill before the 1992 general election, the Government was forced to agree to bring in its own amendment, which had the same effect.

Baroness Blatch (for the Government) told peers: 'We regret the fact that a whole new bureaucracy will need to be established to run a centralised system, but we shall make it work' (Hansard/Lords, 1992: 1229–30). Thus the powers and responsibilities which were to be given to the new inspectorates were greatly increased, and the monolithic body now known as Ofsted was created despite the opposition of the Conservative Government.

IMPROVEMENT THROUGH INSPECTION?

'Improvement through inspection' was Ofsted's battle cry in the years immediately following the 1992 Education (Schools) Act. The phrase may have made its first appearance in the *Corporate Plan 1993–4 to 1995–6* (Ofsted, 1993), and thereafter reappears at regular intervals. In the booklet *A Focus on Quality* (Ofsted/Coopers & Lybrand, 1994), the comment is made that 'the driving force (during Ofsted's first year) has been Ofsted's central purpose: **improvement through inspection**' (Ofsted's emphasis). Even at this early stage, however, voices were raised to suggest that the link between inspection and improvement might not be as self-evident or as inevitable as the proponents of the new system would have us believe. Gray and Wilcox (1994) commented that 'we have not encountered a sustained account of how the inspection process might work to bring about ... improvement. Doubtless part of the reason for this omission is that it is all assumed to be "commonsense"'.

An attempt was made to describe how the process might work in practice in the short booklet *Improving Schools* (Ofsted/OHMCI, 1994), which included a chapter entitled 'Improvement through inspection'. Essentially, the process was viewed as one where the inspection led to the identification of key points for action; the school then drew up an action plan to deal with these key points, and the plan was then implemented. Matthews and Smith (1995), who were both employed by Ofsted at the time, comment that:

> some of those critical of Ofsted's programme come close to asserting that inspection cannot of itself bring about improvement: that quality control is by definition not quality assurance ... Disentangling the impact (of the many recent changes in educational policy) is likely to be the subject for research for many years to come. *Whether Ofsted's programme contributes to school improvement has to be established, rather than simply asserted* (my emphasis).

It is encouraging that these authors, from within Ofsted itself, are aware that research evidence is needed to evaluate the effectiveness of inspection as a tool for improving schools. Unfortunately, they go on to state that 'there is growing evidence that the introduction of the inspection system, together with statutory post-inspection action planning, is making a contribution to school improvement'. This may well be the case, but the only evidence cited in their paper comes in a reference to 'surveys in secondary schools' which are not described further. As Peter Earley (1996) pointed out:

> To date, the research undertaken into the Ofsted inspection process and its contribution to school development has largely been undertaken by Ofsted

itself. With the possible exception of the work of Gray and Wilcox (1995) and Shaw and colleagues (Shaw, Brimblecombe and Ormston, 1995), there has been no independent research commissioned by an outside body to investigate the role of Ofsted inspections in *school improvement.*' (Earley's emphasis).

It must be pointed out again here that there is a difference between school improvement as measured against some clear criterion, and a *perception* that the school has improved in some way. The former type of improvement is difficult to measure or quantify for many school activities – and even if there is improvement, it is difficult to say whether any change resulted from the inspection, as Matthews and Smith (1995) noted. Matthews (1995) further admits that 'one weakness in action planning is the difficulty many schools experience in establishing clear indicators for criteria for success against which their progress may be monitored'; however, he does not go the extra mile and question the validity of the criteria used during inspection itself, or the way in which those are used by the inspectors. The theoretical problems of validity have been discussed at length by Wilcox and Gray (1996), and by Gilroy and Wilcox (1997). Wilcox and Gray state that 'the validity of individual inspections can never be assured – all are prone to one or more validity threats (which) can be minimised although never completely eliminated. Inspection, like other forms of educational evaluation, is never unassailable. In the end, an inspection has persuasive power rather than definitive validity'.

Gilroy and Wilcox (1997) are more critical about the criteria used by Ofsted teams:

> Supposedly objective factual criteria are being used to provide the basis for judgements of the complex social situation of teaching governed as it is by conventional criteria means that the subtleties of inter-personal relationships are being crudely ignored … it is this which has generated so much distrust and dislike of Ofsted, in particular the way in which objective factual criteria are supposedly being used to make judgements about a situation which is at heart governed by covert conventional criteria.

Thus – if we accept these arguments – it is not possible to devise (let alone use) wholly 'objective' criteria to assess school improvement in many important areas. As Wilcox and Gray argue, 'objective truth is a *chimera*'. This does not, of course, mean that the search for meaningful methods of measuring school improvement should be abandoned, but it does mean that the limitations of the measuring tools used should be honestly recognized.

On the other hand, it is relatively easy to ask people's *opinions* as to whether their school has improved; there are a number of studies which have followed this course. Several authors have commented on the fact that preparation for inspection was believed to produce various improvements, including *improved teamwork* (NUT, 1994) and *teamwork, policies and documentation* (Thomas, 1995). Fidler, Earley and Ouston (1995) discovered that a high proportion of respondents to their survey (48 per cent) found the preparation valuable.

Some studies have looked at whether the inspection leads to any changes in teacher performance post-inspection. Shaw, Brimblecome and Ormston (1995) found that a high proportion of teachers intended to change some aspects of their practice (38 per cent overall, with 52.6 per cent of classroom teachers intending to change their teaching style/method). Of course, 'change' does not necessarily lead to *improvement*, even though that was undoubtedly the aim of the teachers. It is also possible that the number who did eventually change their methods was rather lower than these figures imply ('The road to Hell is paved with good intentions'). No indication is given of whether the 'changes' envisaged are of a revolutionary nature, or merely 'fine-tuning'. Nevertheless, this study does indicate that inspection can lead a large number of teachers to reassess their methods. The most recent survey was carried out by the NUT late in 1998. According to this survey:

> Probably the most significant finding arose from the penultimate question in the survey. Overwhelmingly, head and deputy head-teacher members rejected the statement that Ofsted inspections led directly to schools improving. Two-thirds of respondents did not believe that inspections helped school improvement, whereas only 17 per cent agreed with this statement (NUT, 1999).

As might be expected, the NUT survey showed up widespread dissatisfaction with Ofsted. In a classic piece of news management, Ofsted released within 24 hours the results of a survey carried out on its behalf by the pollsters MORI. This survey 'showed that four schools in five were satisfied with the way the inspection was conducted, with more than two in five being very satisfied' (Ofsted, 1999). The press release also contained comments from the HMCI, eg:

> Welcoming this major survey of reactions to inspection by primary schools, Her Majesty's Chief Inspector of Schools Chris Woodhead said today:
>
> 'I am greatly encouraged by what MORI has found. It puts firmly in perspective the negative picture of inspection which is created by the tiny but vocal minority of critics who have access to the columns of the educational press'.

However, even the MORI survey contained some rather negative points, eg:

Opinion was divided over whether the benefits of inspection outweighed the detrimental effects, with 35 per cent of schools thinking they did, 37 per cent reckoning there was a balance between the two and 27 per cent thinking inspection did more harm than good. This latter view was strongest amongst those schools who were unhappy with the inspectors' judgements.

For what I hope will be a more balanced view, I shall now present the results of a survey carried out in Welsh schools in 1997. It is worth pointing out that the relationship which exists in Wales between the teachers and the inspection body (OHMCI – the Office for Her Majesty's Chief Inspector) is much more cordial than that in England.

SURVEY OF INSPECTION IN WELSH SECONDARY SCHOOLS

In the summer term of the 1996–7 session, a questionnaire survey was undertaken of all Welsh secondary schools (except special schools) which had been inspected under the Education (Schools) Act 1992 up to the end of the 1995–6 session. Since other evidence (Wilcox and Gray, 1996, Chapter 7) suggests that it takes some time for schools to implement their action plans, it was felt that a time lapse of around 12 months as a minimum was needed for the schools to be able to comment on the effects of their inspection.

One hundred and twenty-five Welsh secondary schools were inspected in the sessions 1993–4 to 1995–6 inclusive, and all were contacted. Eighty schools returned the questionnaire, giving a response rate of 64 per cent. Of these returns, 67 were filled in by the head-teacher (84 per cent of the returns, representing 54 per cent of the total of schools inspected in the period) and 13 were filled in by other senior staff (16 per cent of the returns). In general, the respondents did not answer each and every question.

The aim of the survey was firstly to compare the perceived influence of a number of factors on 'school improvement', which was defined narrowly as 'an improvement in the percentage of pupils gaining five or more GCSE passes as grades A$\star$ (or A) to C', and secondly to discover which areas in the schools had been most altered by the inspection. This key was used for responses:

1. large contribution to improvement
2. medium contribution to improvement
3. small contribution to improvement
4. no contribution to improvement
5. contribution to deterioration

The results are shown in Tables 7.1–7.3. The rank order of the factors listed has been determined by calculating the average 'score' for each factor. The percentages of respondents replying 1 or 2 (large or medium contribution to improvement) and 1, 2 or 3 (large, medium or small contribution to improvement) are also shown in the tables. The rank orders based on percentages show some minor differences from that based on average scores, as one would expect, though the overall pattern is much the same. It is important to realize that, when the average scores and/or percentages for two or more factors are very close, no great significance should be attributed to the *exact* positions in the rankings; however, when the differences are large, then it is safe to conclude that there is a real difference in the effect on improvement or, at least, that the respondents *believe* that such is the case.

DISCUSSION OF SURVEY RESULTS

In Table 7.1, the respondents commented on their own school and, therefore, base their responses on their own experience of what has actually happened. The most significant factor to emerge, by some distance, was *increased monitoring of teaching standards by the senior management team* – 77 per cent felt that this can lead to a large or medium contribution to improvement. This should be seen against the background of Russell and Metcalfe's comment (1996) that 'the rating (calculated by Ofsted) for the

Table 7.1   *Factors which may affect your school's performance*

Rank	Factors which may affect *your* school's performance	Average score	% of 1 and 2 responses
1	Increased monitoring by SMT	1.99	77
2	Effect of INSET on current staff	2.29	59
3	Commitment of Y11 group	2.51	56
4	Better use of current staff	2.52	48
5	New staff	2.59	52
6	Inspection	2.61	45
7	Reducing class sizes	2.67	48
8	League tables	2.72	41
9	Ability level of Y11 group	2.90	38
10	Social background of pupils	3.11	32
11	Target setting (external agency)	3.37	19

effectiveness of reviewing the school's work is one of the poorest scores nationally (i.e. in England) for all the criteria on which schools are judged'.

This weakness was highlighted by the Chief Inspector's (CI) Annual Reports in 1995 and 1996 (Ofsted, 1995; 1996). It may well be that the Chief Inspector's remarks have ensured that monitoring has appeared as a key point for action in many inspection reports – in Wales as well as in England. The fact that 23 per cent of respondents did not expect monitoring to make a significant contribution provides some support for Russell and Metcalfe's warning (1996) that 'there is a danger that innovations in school monitoring and evaluation brought about as a result of inspection recommendations may become detached from their prime purpose of school improvement'.

The scepticism of the 23 per cent of 'dissenters' – coming, as it does, from senior managers – may reflect a deeper doubt about the usefulness of monitoring as a tool for change. If a school's leadership has no faith in the process, it is unlikely to prove effective in those schools: you can lead a horse to water, but you can't make it drink! Monitoring is more likely to have an impact in schools where the senior managers are convinced of its value.

The positive effect of *in-service training (INSET) on current staff* was also felt to be important, with 59 per cent feeling that this would lead to a large or medium improvement, and almost all respondents (99 per cent) expecting some improvement as a result. *Inspection* was ranked only sixth, with 45 per cent indicating a large or medium contribution to improvement and 80 per cent expecting some improvement. The score for *inspection* is not much lower than those obtained for *better use of current staff* (fourth) or for *new staff* (fifth). Whereas supporters of the current system of inspection can draw some comfort from the fact that 45 per cent of heads and senior managers feel that it can make a real difference, it must be worrying that a majority – 55 per cent – feels that the contribution in their school was either small, non-existent or negative.

In Table 7.2, respondents speculate on those factors which might affect other schools. The effect of a *new head-teacher* was by some distance the most popular choice, with 79 per cent seeing the possibility that this might lead to large or medium gains, and 96 per cent seeing a likelihood for some improvement. This confirms the results of other studies, which have identified good leadership as being a key factor in school improvement. Of course, the respondents here are making an assumption about the quality of the new head-teacher, whereas an effective new head-teacher should certainly be able to improve standards – especially in a struggling school – a poor choice by the governors could lead to no improvement, or a deterioration.

The results gained in other schools were believed to be heavily dependent on the *social background of the pupils*, ranked second. The theoretical

Table 7.2   *Factors which may affect other schools' performance*

Rank	Factors which may affect *other* schools' performance	Average score	% of 1 and 2 responses
1	New head-teacher	1.92	79
2	Social background of pupils	2.07	73
3	Reducing class sizes	2.08	69
4	New staff	2.23	67
5	League tables	2.33	62
6	Inspection	2.36	60
7	Future target setting (external agency)	2.88	33
8	'Grade inflation'	3.21	23

possibility of *reducing class sizes* was ranked at approximately the same level; this contrasts with the lower score given to class sizes in the respondents' own schools, probably because no such reduction has taken place or can be foreseen in reality. Once again, *inspection* was ranked only sixth, though the score was not very different to that for *league tables* (fifth). It is worth noting that respondents believed that external pressure (*league tables* and *inspections*) were more likely to affect other schools than their own: for *inspections*, 60 per cent expected a large or medium improvement in other schools as against 45 per cent for their own, and for *league tables* 62 per cent expected a sensible improvement in other schools, but only 41 per cent in their own. There is a hint here of a double standard, with respondents believing that others are more likely to respond to the 'big stick' approach, or perhaps the discrepancy arises from a degree of complacency about their own schools. Whatever the case, a majority (60 per cent against 40 per cent) feels that inspection will have a large or medium effect on other schools.

Table 7.3 shows, in rank order, the areas in the schools which have most improved *as a result of inspection*. Interestingly – and rather unexpectedly, as far as I was concerned – inspection was seen as having had a greater effect on *standards of teaching* than on any other area, with a majority – 54 per cent – believing that a large or medium improvement had resulted. There is a discrepancy, however, between the improvement in *standards of teaching* and the effect on examination results. For GCSE, KS3 SATs and A-levels, inspection was given credit for large or medium improvements by only 28 per cent, 23 per cent and 17 per cent of respondents, respectively.

Forty-three per cent of respondents observed that the inspection has led to large or medium improvements in *stimulating the management team to address weaknesses more urgently*. Around a third (36 per cent) believed that

Table 7.3 *The contribution of school inspection to school improvement*

Rank	Area improved by inspection	Average score	Large or medium %
1	standards of teaching	2.63	54
2	stimulating SMT to tackle problems	2.73	43
3	management	2.83	36
4	GCSE results	3.09	28
5	KS3 SAT results	3.25	23
6	use of resources	3.28	20
7	attendance	3.34	19
8	efficiency in using school finances	3.40	21
9	A level results	3.42	17
10	accommodation	3.56	13
11	behaviour/discipline	3.59	13
12	resources	3.61	11

management had shown large or medium improvements as a result of the inspection, but less than a third of respondents saw such a level of improvement in any of the other categories, and the average scores for all these other factors lay in between 3 ('small contribution to improvement') and 4 ('no contribution to improvement'). Even for *standards of teaching*, the average score at 2.63 only lay roughly mid-way between a 'small' and a 'medium' contribution.

CONCLUSIONS

The weight of the evidence indicates that inspection does lead to some improvement in schools; it does not, however, show that inspection brings about *large* or even *medium* improvements in many areas. According to the survey results, the appointment of a *new headteacher* would be far more likely to have an effect on 'standards' (examination results) than *inspection*. It may be that the training of potential head-teachers will show significant benefits in the medium term. Consideration should also be given to finding ways to re-train current head-teachers who have weaknesses in specific areas, and to moving those heads who are beyond redemption to less demanding work within the education system. The whole role of the head-teacher in modern schools needs re-examination, as the added responsibilities brought about by recent changes such as local management of schools (LMS) are possibly too great for a single individual. It is not surprising that a high proportion of schools now have 'senior management teams' which carry a share of the administrative and decision-making burdens.

It is likely that the increased *monitoring of teaching standards by the senior management team*, which has been identified as an important factor, has been introduced in many schools as a result of inspection reports and/or the Chief Inspector's Annual Reports (Ofsted, 1995; 1996). In this sense, inspection appears to have had a significant effect, though there are other ways which could be used to introduce and improve this practice, short of subjecting schools to full inspections. It is also important that the focus of such monitoring systems should be fixed very clearly on improving teaching and learning (Russell and Metcalfe, 1996).

It is encouraging that a majority of respondents to the survey believes that inspection has led to a *large* or *medium* improvement in teaching standards. The effect of inspection on test and examination results was believed to be much less. One would expect better teaching to lead – almost inevitably – to better examination performance. Either it is too early in the process for the results of better teaching to show up in this way, or the effect on teaching is being overestimated. Further research needs to be undertaken to investigate this point.

It may well be that increased monitoring of action plans by Ofsted (following OHMCI's model in Wales) would reap benefits. A comparative study of the Welsh and English experience should be carried out on a sample of schools in both countries, in order to discover whether such monitoring can be shown to lead to improvements.

The full inspection of secondary schools is a very expensive process (Thomas, 1996) and, in view of the survey results, there must be some doubt as to whether it is a cost-effective method for raising standards. The move from a four-year cycle to a six-year cycle in England is to be welcomed; some of the resources released (money and manpower) should be used to carry out further research into inspection and other policies aimed at raising standards in our schools.

REFERENCES

Baker, K (1993) *The Turbulent Years*, Faber and Faber, London

Bolton, E (1998) HMI – The Thatcher Years, *Oxford Review of Education*, **24**, 44–55

Burchill, J (1991) *Inspecting Schools: Breaking the Monopoly*, Centre for Policy Studies, London

Cabinet Office (1991) *The Citizen's Charter: Raising the Standard*, HMSO, London

Department of Education and Science (1991) *The Parent's Charter: You and Your Child's Education*, Department of Education and Science, London

Dunford, JE (1998) *Her Majesty's Inspectors of Schools Since 1944: Standard Bearers or Turbulent Priests?* Woburn Press, London

Earley, P (1996) School improvement and Ofsted inspection: the research evidence, in *Improvement Through Inspection?* eds P Earley, B Fidler and J Ouston, David Fulton, pp 11–22, London

Fidler, B, Earley, P and Ouston, J (1995) Ofsted school inspections and their impact on school development, University of Bath, ECER/BERA Conference, September

Gilroy, P and Wilcox, B (1997) Ofsted, criteria and the nature of social understanding: a Wittgensteinian critique of the practice of educational judgement, *British Journal of Educational Studies*, **45**, pp 22–38

Gray, J and Wilcox B (1994) In the aftermath of inspection: the nature and fate of inspection report recommendations, University of Oxford, BERA Conference, September

Gray, J and Wilcox, B (1995) *Good School, Bad School: Evaluating Performance and Encouraging Improvement*, Open University Press, Milton Keynes

Hackett, G (1992a) Private inspectors opposed, *Times Educational Supplement*, 24 January

Hackett, G (1992b) Inspection collusion warning heeded, *Times Educational Supplement*, 14 February

Hansard/Lords (1992) 10 March

Lawton, D and Gordon, P (1987) HMI, Routledge Kegan Paul, London

Looch, A (1992) Tory attacks 'silliest Bill', *Daily Telegraph*, 12 February

Matthew, P (1995) Aspects of inspection, improvement and Ofsted, in *School Inspection*, eds T Brighouse and B Moon, Pitman, pp 66–78, London

Matthews, P and Smith, G (1995) Ofsted: inspecting schools and improvement through inspection, *Cambridge Journal of Education*, **25**, pp 23–34

National Union of Teachers (NUT) (1994) Teachers' and headteachers' views of the new inspection arrangements, NUT, London

National Union of Teachers (NUT) (1999) 'Ofsted': the views of headteacher and deputy headteacher members of the National Union of Teachers November/December 1998, 4 January, NUT, London

Ofsted (1993) *Corporate Plan 1993–4 to 1995–6*, Ofsted, London

Ofsted (1995) *Annual Report of Her Majesty's Chief Inspector of Schools: Part I – Standards and Quality in Education 1993/4*, HMSO, London

Ofsted (1996) *Annual Report of Her Majesty's Chief Inspector of Schools: Standards and Quality in Education 1994/5*, HMSO, London

Ofsted (1999) Press Notice 99–1, 5 January, Ofsted, London

Ofsted/Coopers & Lybrand (1994) *A Focus on Quality*, Ofsted, London

Ofsted/OHMCI (1994) *Improving Schools*, HMSO, London

Russell, S and Metcalfe, C (1996) The effects of Ofsted's judgements on the quality of schools' self-evaluation processes, University of Lancaster, BERA Conference, September

Shaw, M, Brimblecombe, N and Ormston, M (1995) Teachers' perceptions of inspection: the potential for improvement in professional practice, University of Bath, BERA Conference, September

Thomas, G (1995) Preparing for inspection: the process and its effects, *Welsh Journal of Education*, **5**, pp 16–26.

Thomas, G (1996) The new schools' inspection system: some problems and possible solutions, *Educational Management & Administration*, **24**, 355–69

Thomas, G (1998) A brief history of the genesis of the new schools' inspection system, *British Journal of Educational Studies*, **46**, 415–27

Wilcox, B and Gray, J (1996) *Inspecting Schools: Holding Schools to Account and Helping Schools to Improve*, Open University Press, Buckingham

Does Ofsted make a difference? Inspection issues and socially deprived schools

Sue Law and Derek Glover

BACKGROUND

The link between inspection and improvement has, over recent years, become a key focus of educational investigation for many authors (Scheerens, 1992, 1997; Hargreaves, 1995; Wilcox and Gray, 1996; Earley, 1998; Stark, 1998; Stoll and Myers, 1998). Moreover, the kind of 'school improvement' strategies and theories outlined in Barber (1998) and Barber and Dann (1996) underpin many of the approaches now framing Government-driven efforts to drive up educational standards across the United Kingdom. Although the establishment of a new Ofsted inspection system in 1992 implicitly suggested that school improvement was a 'new' concern, the reality was that a thriving 'effective schools movement' (ESM) had been in existence for some years, involving researchers, Local Education Authorities (LEAs) and a variety of individual self-evaluating schools (Reynolds, 1992). Indeed, Rutter *et al's* (1979) *Fifteen Thousand Hours* investigation of secondary schooling had, 20 years ago, shown that 'schools can make a difference', while the decades following have seen a growing identification and evaluation of the key factors supporting pupil achievement in even the most difficult of social contexts.

However, while many practitioners and researchers became increasingly convinced that more overt and specific improvement strategies could indeed 'add value', the commitment to school effectiveness and improvement had undoubtedly sometimes been driven by a series of anxieties and desires to face-down increasingly vocal criticisms from Government and industry over declining standards, the apparent failures of 'progressive' education, the 'producer capture' of education (Baker, 1993) and the uneven implementation of comprehensivization which had 'placed schools in the dock' (Gray and Wilcox, 1995). In this respect, schools facing particular difficulties arising from their socio-economic settings have found themselves at a considerable disadvantage compared with those in more favoured locations. Both researchers and practitioners have argued that the published performance tables and the nature of the Ofsted inspection hurdles have been set too high for schools to be confirmed as anything other than failures (Ball, Bowe and Gerwitz, 1995).

Indeed, the inception of the new Ofsted regime has brought considerable cynicism in some quarters about a system which was seemingly so focused on detecting failure. Day, Hall and Whittaker's (1998: 215) comment reflects a frequently expressed view that 'any system of inspection which seems to attach more importance to failure than to success is unlikely to succeed in improving the quality of learning in schools'. Moreover, the ability to secure 'improvement through inspection' (Ofsted's declared mission and motto) would appear to be limited, at least in part, by the social context within which schools are developing. Indeed, schools serving depressed and often inner city areas urge that there should be a more overt recognition of their positive achievements. They contend that they can, in general terms, be effective *within their own context* even though this may not result in a conformity to national statistical norms and the award of associated plaudits from Ofsted.

Reid, Hopkins and Holly (1987: 22) have argued that although 'all reviews assume that effective schools can be differentiated from ineffective ones, there is no consensus yet on just what constitutes an effective school'. More recently, however, there have been signs of growing consensus regarding more rather than less appropriate methodologies for investigating and assessing school effectiveness (McPherson 1992; Sammons, Hillman and Mortimore, 1995). Despite the tendency to conflate the various terminologies associated with the effective schools movement, Mortimore (1991: 9) suggests that an effective school is 'one in which pupils progress further than might be expected from consideration of its intake', while Sammons, Hillman and Mortimore (1995: 3) suggest it is one which 'adds extra value to its students' outcomes in comparison with other schools serving similar intakes'. By these standards, many schools in less favoured areas can clearly be seen to be achieving some success. However, a review of large samples of Ofsted reports (Levacic and Glover, 1994a; Glover *et al*, 1997) has indicated that schools in comparatively disadvantaged social contexts are more likely to have an adverse report with little attention paid to the institution's contextual problems or to those achievements which are less readily measurable in Ofsted's terms.

INSPECTING OFSTED

We set out to undertake an in-depth investigation of the outcomes of the first two Ofsted inspection rounds (based on a four-year cycle) within one shire county – a rural area which is dominated by a large urban area with areas of considerable deprivation and which incorporates four smaller urban areas currently suffering from unemployment as a result of major structural change in the economy. Beyond these urban areas there are substantial rural communities serving as the home base of socially mobile commuters, and some isolated agricultural rural communities. This complex socio-geographical background has resulted in a mixture of secondary schools, ranging from those which serve favoured rural and semi-urban communities to those which are surrounded by extensive areas of run-down private and public housing with few community facilities. Our investigation was undertaken in two stages. It was aimed initially at providing evidence to substantiate the oft-made claim that schools which serve socially deprived areas were unlikely to be judged successful and were, therefore, placed at a disadvantage as a result of the publication of Ofsted reports. We then looked at the progress made by those 10 schools in the county which have so far been through both first and second rounds of inspection. In short, while the rhetoric that 'schools do make a difference' is increasingly acknowledged, we wanted to ask: 'Does Ofsted make a difference?' Ofsted comments are used in this chapter in anonymized form.

The description of some schools as 'failing' by Ofsted inspectors has led to pressure on the management and teaching staff of the schools concerned and the LEA in which they are located in order to establish a greater school improvement focus, conveying a view that there has been some high level of remediable underperformance. Indeed, when judged by the conventional outcomes of GCSE results at the higher grades A–C, course completion, absentee rates and numbers continuing to further education, it is clear that some schools *do* compare unfavourably with others in the same area of broadly similar context. However, the socio-economic difficulties of the environment may impose such a burden on school staff that objectively measured and significant improvements may be jeopardized. If this is so, such schools could never be deemed successful because they are being judged by a set of criteria which, realistically, remain well beyond their grasp in the short term. Failure could, therefore, be seen to be almost an inbuilt feature of schools in some areas.

IDENTIFYING SOCIAL DEPRIVATION

The nature of localized social deprivation is variously outlined by Ofsted inspectors in their summary of the characteristics of each school. Usually these comments include a resume of the soci-economic context, including the age and state of housing, the extent of home ownership, and the level of unemployment in the area. Some reports also highlight unusually high percentages of single-parent family groups, the numbers using English as a second language, and any particular problems arising from the operation of parental choice within the area. Two examples demonstrate that, within the limits of the Ofsted reporting process, inspection teams often have an awareness of the contextual problems faced by school staff:

> The area surrounding the school has fewer people with higher educational qualifications than nationally and the degree of overcrowding in the local wards is above national levels. In terms of 'High Social Class Households', it has half the figures nationally. Currently unemployment locally is around 30 per cent. Currently only four pupils come from the ethnic minorities and only two pupils come from homes where English is not the first language (Ofsted secondary school report, first inspection round).

> The number of pupils is very small for a comprehensive school. The school is set in over thirty acres of playing fields and meadows adjacent to the river. Almost without exception pupils come from an inner city area of high density housing. In the area from which the pupils come, the number of people with higher educational qualifications is well above the national average. There is a considerable level of deprivation. The number of pupils eligible for free school meals is about three times the national average, and an increasing proportion over the last three years. (Ofsted secondary school report, first inspection round).

While the level of deprivation is thus described for each school, Ofsted inspectors during the first round felt that the level of progress being made by pupils in both schools (even allowing for context) was insufficient for a judgement of teaching and learning, outcomes, behaviour and attendance to be other than that the schools are in need of 'special measures'. The establishment of cause and effect was at the heart of the key issues for action offered in each of these reports and these were addressed in subsequent action planning within the schools.

Reference to the free school meal (FSM) entitlement indicates that the inspection system uses this as a ready measure of deprivation. Although initially this was only felt to be a guide to poverty levels, Levacic and Glover's work (1994b) points to a number of potentially significant correlations. Among these, the strength of the link between the number of pupils entitled to free school meals and the percentage excluded is determined by regression analysis to be as high as 42 per cent – a reflection of the difficulties faced by staff in schools within areas of deprivation. In terms of outcomes, the strongest link is between the percentage taking free school meals and the quality of learning, as opposed to teaching.

It appears that 22 per cent of the variation in the achievement of a favourable judgement of learning quality is attributable to the free meal context. This suggests that problematic parental attitudes and the paucity of resources at home for many pupils is such that the kind of home support being given in more favoured homes is lacking. This prompts questions about the ability of schools to be successful when they are fighting, at best, a lack of interest or support in the home situation. Randall (1996) has shown how negative parental attitudes can strongly inhibit pupils' behaviour improvements and may help to create a negative counter culture – a perspective often borne out in Ofsted inspection reports, as the following comment shows:

> The society outside the school often overspills onto the site. Even with a full-time security officer, on occasions intruders come onto the site, climbing over the high fences. On other occasions difficulties within the school invoke quick response from family members, unaware of the full situation, to come onto premises and further inflame delicate situations. The community must be encouraged to have more confidence in the effective, sensible, and caring manner in which the senior managers of the school deal with difficult situations. In this they have been aided by supportive responses from agencies including the police (Ofsted secondary school report).

Payne, Payne and Hyde (1996) have demonstrated that utilizing a *range* of indicators can be valuable in defining social deprivation. While they consider a variety of socio-economic elements which strongly influence the context within which schools work – such as unemployment rates, overcrowded households, children in unsuitable households and low overall GCSE attainment levels – they do not use FSMs as an indicator in their research. Their conclusions do, nevertheless, demonstrate that a clear link exists between their social deprivation indicators and the entitlement to FSMs: those in one category also frequently fall into the other. However, the Department of Education and Employment (DfEE) continues to use FSMs largely as *the* single driver or indicator, leading to unidimensional comparisons being drawn in relation to very different schools. As Payne, Payne and Hyde (1996: 9) conclude: 'Deprivation has a class-connected but independent existence, because it is a way of life'.

If this is the case, using FSMs as *the* most significant indicator of educational deprivation has major implications for those schools which face particular problems in linking with their local communities. It must also raise substantial doubt about the potential of the current inspection system to be a catalyst for institutional change and to influence with any certainty the capacity of schools to improve. In debating these issues, Mortimore and Whitty (1997) conclude that schools in socially deprived areas are inhibited by a range of strong external influences which are simply not capable of modification by the school alone. Gilroy and Wilcox (1994) highlight further problems, arguing that contextual difficulties are being minimized and judgements are being made which are based only upon an imprecise understanding of the nature of criteria for evaluation.

SOCIAL CONTEXT AND OFSTED JUDGEMENTS

Learning at school takes place within a socio-economic context – even though it is frequently assumed that positive approaches to teaching and learning are capable of overcoming the difficulties which arise both at schools and which derive from the external environment and community 'culture'. However, while terms like 'culture' are often commonly utilized in the literature on education management, there is little agreement about definition (Deal and Kennedy, 1982, 1983). Similarly, although often utilized and emphasized as being of key importance in improving schools, the concept of 'culture' remains only infrequently defined in Ofsted reports (Hargreaves, 1995; Stoll and Fink, 1996).

There are, nevertheless, indications that Ofsted teams tend to identify a particular 'feel' about the given institution being inspected, reflecting inspector perceptions about both context and culture most often in relation to attendance, behaviour and/or community relationships. Where one or all of these elements are of serious concern, (or alternatively are particularly commended) they are generally highlighted in the main findings, stressing the implicit accountability focus and emphasizing the value attached to school-based improvement which appears to be centred upon political aspirations to drive schools towards achieving national league table norms (Ball, 1994; Fidler, 1996; Ofsted, 1998).

Our analysis of a range of inspection team comments from the first round of Ofsted reports suggests that all schools are required to follow a developmental pattern which may not be entirely appropriate (Glover *et al*, 1996). Within our own sample of 31 secondary schools operating within one shire county (incorporating city schools prior to the establishment of a unitary authority), the range of comments illustrates the tension and 'pull' between expectations on the one hand, and the realities of the struggle for achievement in different contexts being undertaken in many schools on the other. Perhaps one school's wish that 'We aim to be the sort of school which people want to get up and come to in the morning' removes any high-flown pretence about mission and reveals awareness of the fundamental need to get community support for both attendance and positive behaviour.

(a) Attendance

As the Ofsted reports we analysed frequently note, poor attendance affects the progress of *all* pupils – largely because those infrequently at school can inhibit the learning process for others – especially when the learning of those in regular attendance becomes disrupted when teaching time has to be given over to the infrequent attenders. The lowest attendance rate in the sample was 72 per cent, with the highest being 96 per cent. This, however, masks the problems involved in motivating older pupils to attend – a problem occurring in just under half of the sample studied.

> Attendance, lateness and truancy are a matter of serious weakness for the proper education of pupils. It further disrupts the learning of the more regular attenders as teachers have to go back and revisit earlier work for those who have rejoined the class and leave other learners awaiting tuition (Ofsted secondary school inspection report).

Against such a background, the identified key issue – that the school above should try to improve levels of attendance – does perhaps state the obvious without offering help to the senior management team who are, in other parts of the report, praised for their efforts to develop a positive and supportive culture for those pupils who do attend.

(b) Behaviour issues

While it is axiomatic that teaching and learning is inhibited by poor behaviour the report above draws attention to the need for policies which are effective, based upon rewards and sanctions, and which are consistent and known to all pupils and staff. This reflects the school improvement literature 'lists for effective change' approach indicated by studies like Rutter *et al*'s (1979); Purkey and Smith's (1983) and Sammons, Hillmand Mortimer's (1995). Inspection comments indicate that heavily punitive systems may actually be counterproductive, particularly where a high proportion of pupils have been subject to repeated fixed term exclusions. Commenting on a school in an adverse social context, one Ofsted report notes that:

> Where the situation is difficult, with staff absence restricting specialist subject teaching, irregular attendance by pupils and disruption by some pupils, teaching of the subject fades away and the control of the class becomes paramount – learning has given over to the control of pupil behaviour. This is most often seen in lessons taught by new staff, who have to make their mark

and earn the respect of pupils, and by non-specialist supply teachers (Ofsted secondary school inspection report).

The contrast is shown in another teaching situation where the comment is made that 'based on mutual respect and high expectations, behaviour and relationships are very good and a purposeful, supportive and focused working atmosphere encourages pupils' confidence and progress'.

The problem remains, however, that the instability of home circumstances, the apparently precocious maturity levels and the 'streetwise' nature of many adolescents linked to a negative estate culture, when combined with the resentment felt by parents and pupils about past educational failures, all demands an outreach approach from deprived schools act as community workers to support in-school learning. This is often neither possible nor sustainable – an issue identified by the United States Government in its survey of low-performing schools (US Government, 1998).

(c) Community

Ofsted reports provide an outline of the socio-economic context in which schools operate and comment in general terms on the strength of parental support for the school. As reports either directly or indirectly make clear, without this parental and community support any attempt to change school culture in fundamental ways becomes difficult to achieve – a view echoed by research (Beare, Caldwell and Milliken, 1989). While ideals may be sought, certain problems often appear intractable and school staff may acknowledge that, in reality, there is little prospect of changing community attitudes over the short term. For one school, this issue was seen as arising from the highly dispersed nature of its 'catchment' area and the consequent lack of critical mass in terms of community spirit, while for another, the apparent 'remoteness' of the governing body was identified as a key reason for the lack of community ties and links.

If we are correct in our assertion that socio-economic context can have a significant impact on the ability of pupils to benefit from the educational opportunities placed before them, then this ought to be discernible in certain respects in the relationship between socio-economic context (as determined by the single indicator – FSM – in Ofsted reports) and educational outcomes. This relationship is set out in Table 8.1 for our original sample of 31 schools. It should be noted, however, that we do not intend our comments thus far to be seen as arguing that some form of 'excusable failure' is valid for those schools where managerial, organizational and resource management problems help to inhibit pupil progress. Neither do we argue that low expectations of the pupils, or inappropriate or poorly devised teaching approaches, or inconsistent policies of diagnostic assessment, should be seen as acceptable and excusable. We do, however,

Table 8.1   *The relationship between the percentage of children entitled to FSMs and teaching and learning outcomes*

% FSM	% A–C grades	% Staying on	% Teaching good	% Learning good
> 15 (13 schools)	48 (range 33–65)	72	36	38
16–30 (8 schools)	32 (range 21–46)	54	41	27
> 31 (10 schools)	16 (range 6–30)	46	25	23

contend that precisely the same success criteria may not be generally or easily applicable across *all* schools. While we would not wish to argue that schools should be judged by entirely different criteria, we do argue that if progress is to be more clearly identified, there is a need for Ofsted to provide more *nuanced* understandings – rather than for somewhat simplistic explanations – of failure or success.

The possible contrasts between schools in terms of teaching and learning are shown in the Ofsted reports we reviewed when comparisons are being made between schools drawn from each of the FSMs groups. In one school with a low number of free school meals, inspectors comment that 'Pupils communicate with confidence and standards of reading, writing and numeracy are satisfactory. The majority of lessons are characterized by good behaviour, sound teaching and high expectations' (Ofsted report).

Within the middle group of schools, there is evidence of concern over the relative complacency of the teaching staff – as inspection comments on one school indicate: 'However, on many occasions, the control teachers exercise over the pace and nature of tasks encourages overindependence on the teacher and contributes to pupils' lack of success against national standards' (Ofsted Report).

Finally, as one of the schools in the group (with the highest proportion of FSM problems) indicates, both the approach taken by teachers and the lack of response by the pupils is highlighted where 'Whole classes require strong and effective teaching in order to enable learning to be fostered. Where there is a good pupil–teacher relationship, and problems from outside the school do not impinge, the standards of behaviour can be effectively managed inside the classroom'.

In summarizing the relationships between *context* and *outcomes* in this way, we remain conscious that in the first round of inspections schools were reminded by Ofsted that it was through developing a 'clearer vision', improving their 'institutional ethos', and developing more 'rational planning and organization' that they could promote greater school improvement. For one of the schools deemed to be in need of 'special measures' these recommendations were very explicit indeed. They included the need to: give attention to the pupil–teacher ratio; make adjustments to contact time; develop a greater atmosphere of trust including the opening of premises at break times; make a reduction of accommodation usage to reflect the drop in numbers; and further develop special needs support so that appropriate targets could be set for all pupils. This approach must, however, be set against the comments that 'Most pupils know right from wrong and know what is expected of them in moral and behavioural terms. In practice many of them are unable to exhibit self-discipline and their actions fall well short of the values and published expectation of the school'.

SOCIAL CONTEXT AND SCHOOL IMPROVEMENT

If Ofsted's mission of 'improvement through inspection' is actually paying off and acting as a catalyst to help schools become more effective and successful, then we might expect to find that any progress being made in improving schools would be evident, at least to some degree, in the *outcomes* and performance results of schools in their second round of inspections. Approximately one-third of our identified sample of schools – ie 10 out of 31 – whose earlier experiences had been tracked have now been reinspected and Ofsted reports published. These offer an opportunity to explore further the indications of progress (or otherwise) made over the past four years.

Whilst the original inspection 'Guidance' (Ofsted, 1993) had been revised partly to reduce some of the earlier inspection 'tightness' experienced in round one, subsequent instructions (Ofsted, 1995) have also emphasized more strongly the need to focus on *continuing* improvement. For example, Ofsted has now placed a greater emphasis on the *evaluation* of school improvement (Ofsted, 1998) which, arguably, might be interpreted as an indicator of the Agency's growing concern to take into account the socio-economic context in which learning and teaching takes place. For example, Ofsted suggests that inspectors now need to adopt what might be seen as a more reflective approach, as the following instructions demonstrate:

Questions which you need to consider are:

● *what change could reasonably be expected?*

- *how much change has there been?*
- *how does the change compare with what might be expected?*
- *how have the changes been brought about?*
- *You must also look to the future and decide:*
- *how well the school is placed to continue to improve or maintain high standards? (Ofsted, 1998, Section 6.1: Evaluating School Improvement)*

We have analysed the extent of measurable improvement to the 10 schools which had experienced two Ofsted inspections. The follow-up reports on these schools indicate that four have made significant progress; one has made progress in some areas, but still needs to undertake more work on previously identified aspects of management; another four have made only limited and partial progress; while the last one has deteriorated in performance overall. Table 8.2 summarizes these findings and is again based upon the number of schools operating in the context of significant deprivation (ie using the FSM indicator).

Table 8.2   *Performance data for schools at the second round of inspection*

School group as denoted by Ofsted comments	% FSM average	% Unauthorized absentee rate	% GCSE 5 A–C grades	% Teaching good	Exclusions as % of roll
Satisfactory progress (5 schools)	10.4 (range 4–24)	0.5 (range 0.2–0.7)	52 (range 21–1)	18.6 (range 10–30)	3.9
Unsatisfactory progress (5 schools)	46.4 (range 31–67)	7.1 (range 6–8.4)	12.4 (range 7–24)	10.1 (range 5–14)	25.6

The changes made to Ofsted's reporting are such that it is now no longer possible to note the figures for quality of *learning* in the same format as in the initial round of inspections. It is now only possible to note the percentage of good *teaching* observed. Reporting also now tends to lay greater emphasis on the quality of 'good' as opposed to 'satisfactory' teaching. The danger is that this creates a skewed picture – not giving sufficient explicit credit to those schools which have improved on the percentage of 'satisfactory' teaching shown in the earlier round. Consequently, the danger is that the focus on the amount of 'good' teaching masks improvements in the level of 'satisfactory' teaching overall. In the group of 10 schools which had been inspected twice, the levels of satisfactory teaching ranges from 77 per cent (found in the school deemed as 'failing') to 96 per cent. If the failing school is excluded from the list the average percentage of satisfactory teaching for what might be called the 'lower achieving' group of schools increases to 88 per cent.

These figures indicate that Ofsted's first set of inspections had found that more than 10 per cent of pupils experience levels of 'unsatisfactory' teaching in some lessons. However, reading between the lines in places, the more recent inspection reports imply, rather than state overtly, that over the four years between inspections, there has been an overall improvement of 5.6 per cent in the quality of teaching across previously poorly performing schools. Sadly, despite evidence in these reports that schools have often made considerable efforts to improve in a difficult socio-economic context, the kinds of 'Ofsted language' used in reports (eg the emphasis on the amount of 'good' rather than 'satisfactory' teaching) often fails to fully credit what are often hard-won achievements.

That said, the social-economic indicator of FSMs still points to a range of continuing problems which often inhibits success for schools. The stark figures for absenteeism – particularly in those schools with a high level of FSM entitlement – appear to remain stubbornly high at over 6 per cent. Comments in the reports show that while the reasons behind such statistics are acknowledged by inspection teams (eg the lack of home support) there is what could be interpreted as a 'political' reluctance to argue that schools have often been relatively powerless to bring large-scale changes in the circumstances, as the following comments indicate:

> Attendance is now lower than at the last inspection. The school has tried a number of methods to improve attendance without real success. Procedures to deal with internal truancy are not consistently applied. There has recently been a slight improvement in year 7 attendance which the school attributes to the 'Success for All' programme. However, the school has not tackled effectively the fundamental problem of interesting and motivating pupils so that they attend school regularly (Ofsted report).

Where schools face difficulties, Ofsted Reports now endeavour to offer positive suggestions for improvement. Suggestions include, for example, the development of more efficient, accurate and comprehensive registration procedures, using attendance and assessment data to set targets for different groups of pupils, particularly by gender, and by year, subject and tutor groups. Inevitably, staff changes and a high level of illness may inhibit progress, especially where pupils are aware of weaknesses in the system and where schools face a tension between the need to get pupils into school and the task of dealing with behavioural problems once they are there. Adverse comments are made about the numbers of pupils excluded in four of the five reports on unsatisfactory schools, and action on one front appears to undermine achievement on another. In one school, which Ofsted considers *is* making progress, the report details a number of strategies which focus on involving parents in the life of their offspring and the school. However, it also goes on to note that 'Despite the good efforts of the school, all parents do not co-operate in the children's learning to ensure regular attendance.' Therein lies the hard core of the problem.

Schools which have considerable difficulty appear to have made greater efforts to ensure consistency in behaviour management, although there are also indications of a loss of morale in an uphill struggle. A running theme in Ofsted reports (Ofsted, 1993) is that enhanced expectations of pupils by staff – in lessons and in the hidden curriculum – can make a difference to the schooling experience, but where this is not supported by parents at large, a number of difficulties arise. This dilemma is demonstrated in the juxtaposition of two comments from the same Ofsted report on one of our sample schools:

> Walking round the school during lessons and lunch breaks, and talking to the pupils shows that they are happy in the school and that relationships, with few exceptions, are secure. There are evident opportunities for personal development but rigorous challenge, particularly for the most able, is only evident in a few subjects. There is not a strong, positive ethos for hard work and high achievement.

> In recent times there has been a significant turn-over of staff, the pupil–teacher ratio is very low, made lower by poor attendance. The average time teachers spend in classes is low, but some teachers are overloaded with responsibilities.

As these comments show, there is a clear tension between the positive *community* relationships being established by many schools and the lack of *parental* support many schools experience. The support of commercial interests for a curriculum enhancement programme which is commended for its diversity is clearly giving more point to some of the work undertaken by the pupils in one school, but the failure of parents to take advantage of these opportunities for their children by ensuring they attend school effectively negates these efforts. Tragically, those most at risk are also those most likely to truant or behave badly in school. Indeed, an Ofsted report on one such school in our sample directly comments on the high numbers of pupils on the special needs programme who fall into this group.

The three schools in our sample which had the highest FSM entitlement also had the highest absenteeism rates. They are all small in size, have the highest proportional levels of pupils with special educational needs and have also taken substantial numbers of pupils excluded from other schools. Consequently (and unsurprisingly), they have a very high proportion of excluded pupils in their own school populations. Evidence suggests that such pupils are almost 'bound to fail' in such a context – or more precisely 'cannot succeed' – because of the sheer force of factors weighing against them.

Once again, however, we need to ask why it is that, in similar socio-economic contexts, some schools are deemed to be 'weak' or are even considered to be 'failing' their pupils while others are identifiably more successful. Indeed, we need to consider how far school context and socio-economic context are interrelated. In the sample school which has slipped further towards failure on its second inspection, a number of weaknesses are indicative of the 'typical' problems faced by such schools. For example:

- there is no defined strategy accepted by all staff as a path towards school improvement;
- resource management problems continue to be an issue largely because of the disproportionately high staffing ratio;
- building maintenance issues remain as an unresolved problem often because of inefficient room and space utilization;
- a lack of consistency remains in the application of policy regarding assessment, recording and reporting;
- there is still no evidence that planned professional development is linked to school development planning.

For the other four schools in our sample which, according to Ofsted, have shown only limited improvement, many of the original key issues for action identified in the first inspection round are raised once again. Comments tend to be concerned with:

- the establishment and implementation of rational planning procedures in three schools;
- the need for enhanced monitoring and the evaluation of pupil progress;
- issues of curriculum implementation and resource use in four schools;
- the need for an improvement in home–school relationships including co-operative moves to secure behaviour management in three schools.

In only one school does Ofsted refer to weaknesses in senior management leadership, while in another it comments on the presence of 'low staff morale' indicating perhaps, once again, that despite the efforts to deliver improvements, contextual factors may be strong inhibitors of change.

This leads us to ask whether the range of 'improvement' positives found in schools by Ofsted inspection teams can too often become negated by the overall negative tenor of Ofsted reports. For the five schools which showed the twin indicators of a high FSM entitlement and high absenteeism rates, a range of positive comments are also offered by inspectors. For example, there are commendatory remarks regarding improvements in the physical environment of three schools; better staff–pupil attitudes in three schools; evidence of considerable improvement in subject teaching in certain areas within four schools; and references in four schools to the positive aspects of pupil development through various strategies such as anti-bullying, rewards systems and increased pupil self-esteem.

However, despite the recognition of improvement found in these reports, it would appear that the use of tightly defined and *nationally* developed Ofsted criteria for what is satisfactory or better still inhibits the potential for praise at a local level, which takes account of particular circumstances – on the basis of value-addedness of the schooling experienced by pupils or improvements against a baseline established at the first inspection.

DOES OFSTED MAKE A DIFFERENCE?

Five out of the ten schools in our sample appear to have found that their first experience of Ofsted inspection offered a series of key findings which they have genuinely been able to use as catalysts for development and action planning. For example, second round reports indicate that, in these schools, there have been improvements in terms of attendance, behaviour management, the quality of teaching and learning and resource management. Despite this, however, the gulf between these apparently 'improving' schools and the other five in our sample remains significant, as the data evidences.

For those schools deemed 'underachieving' in our sample, inspection reports indicate that they have been unable to maintain their organizational viability with any real confidence. For example, school rolls in all five schools have dropped and resources are consequently being managed and planned within a declining budget context. Moreover, descriptions of school intakes appear to suggest that four out of the five schools are now starting from a lower baseline of pupil achievement on entry than they had four years ago.

One strategy adopted by Government (and indeed now operating within one local area which we investigated) is to close and reopen the affected school(s) under a 'fresh start' banner, supported by injections of substantial funding to create an educational action zone (EAZ). Potentially, this enables the institution to, quite literally, invest in a new future and attempt to 'slough off' its old image, creating a new expectations' baseline for institutional and pupil achievement. However, our research shows that, according to their inspection reports, approximately half of our sample schools (serving a total of over 3,000 secondary pupils) could readily fall into this category, casting a very different light on the possibilities of implementing such a national policy. While such a move may well secure a number of changes to school organization and staffing, the *contextual* factors do not simply disappear and, indeed, often remain largely unchanged. While Ofsted inspection may identify and articulate the problems (which, of course, are likely to have been previously identified by school personnel, governors and/or LEAs), it remains a truism that implementing strategies to secure school improvement in difficult socio-economic circumstances remains a very different matter.

Ofsted reports may raise awareness of the issues pertinent for individual schools, but our evidence is that they rarely become *specific catalysts* for development and improvement. As Mortimore and Whitty (1997) argue, schools can be helped to make significant improvement if three elements are present. Noting Maden and Hillman's work (1996) which argued that visionary leadership, team cohesiveness, carefully established targets and enhanced community and parent relationships can promote change, Mortimore and Whitty warn of complex interrelationships. For them, the importance of extra commitment, hard work and the maintenance of efforts to achieve improvements in the total environment of the school cannot be minimized. Perhaps more significant, however, is that all the case studies exemplified in Maden and Hillman's exploration of schools *Succeeding Against the Odds* point to the importance of sustained LEA intervention, which brought the various schools concerned a range of additional human and learning resources, a disproportionate investment of time by local inspectors and advisers and a willingness to help organize staffing changes if these are deemed necessary.

Ofsted inspection reports may well be good indicators of the ways in which schools are moving towards further improvement: eg they can readily provide a confirmatory snapshot for schools which are already tracking their progress. Certainly, the detail of the reports in both inspection rounds in our sample schools focuses on areas of weakness in the first round and offers more detailed attention to possible strategies for further change and development in the second. Insofar as any *national* system of school assessment is able to influence – some would argue drive – change at a *local* and *particular* level, the Ofsted inspection process has undoubtedly done so. Clearly, it has focused the attention of managers, teachers and governors on those issues and problems which can be addressed by and within schools, eg the organization of pupil management, curriculum planning and delivery, and human and resource management.

However, the difficulty is that Ofsted cannot provoke or secure changes to the external environment: Ofsted reports inevitably have little or no influence on the socio-economic context in which schools are situated. For example, our evidence argues that:

● while the problem of absenteeism can be readily identified by Ofsted inspection, the hard core of the problem cannot simply be broken by the school alone;

- while schools may actively encourage much broader community participation, parental involvement is doggedly slow to develop and is very precarious (as attendance at parents' evenings and parent–governor meetings show);
- while school–home contracts can produce a formal framework for partnership, the home culture of many pupils in socio-economically deprived areas is often not conducive to the cultural norms of many schools, eg in relation to homework, respect for property and respect for others.

What appears to be missing in the Ofsted regime is the flexibility to address issues which may be of much greater significance in some schools than in others. Clearly, achieving a balance between subscribing to national standards and acknowledging the individuality of schools is extremely hard to establish. However, without seeking to encourage or excuse the perpetuation of mediocrity in some schools, we do urge the development of an inspection system which:

a. pays greater attention to the particular context of each school as a learning community – using more than FSMs as the (only) key indicator of deprivation;
b. allows greater credit to be given to marginal improvements as 'steps along the way' to enhanced outcomes;
c. allows for more flexibility in reporting so that there is scope for greater celebration of success which can be used as a 'building block' within the local community;
d. assesses the contribution made by the LEA and external agencies in securing changes in parental and community attitudes to school;
e. considers the secondary school as part of the progression from nursery to further education rather than as a self-contained unit in isolation.

So 'Does Ofsted make a difference'? We suspect that while, undoubtedly, 'schools do make a difference' (Rutter *et al*, 1979; Sammons, Hillman and Mortimore, 1995) much 'school improvement' work has to be done beyond and outside the school itself. In this respect, it is hard for Ofsted to make much difference. Indeed, the true 'community' school requires a pragmatism which is currently often constrained by national systems. While Ofsted may make *some* difference in certain areas (eg in terms of awareness raising) and can make a *major* difference in others (eg in terms of organizational viability – where a school is deemed as 'failing'), the agency's capacity to stimulate and influence, let alone change, the improvement agenda of schools varies enormously.

Context is the key element here. If it is to have a genuinely deep-rooted influence on schools for the good, Ofsted's methodology would do well to take greater account of socio-economic context by including more scope to incorporate an agreed set of 'local' contextualizing indicators of success or failure. While crude performance indicators may, for all sorts of reasons, have been deemed *necessary* by policy-makers keen to 'get things going' in schools, they are not *sufficient* for deep-rooted change to be facilitated – particularly if Ofsted remains keen to live up to the rhetoric of its mission – 'improvement through inspection'.

There is a real danger that the existing Ofsted methodology may actually *undermine* rather than *enhance* the prospects for school improvement over time – ironically, in those schools which need to improve the most. Essentially, Ofsted needs to create a more nuanced and contextualized methodology which incorporates a slightly wider range of performance indicators beyond FSMs. In this respect, investigating the nature of community education and assessing schools as part of a multi-agency reality in areas of high social class deprivation – rather than seeing each school in relative isolation from its socio-economic context – would be a good starting place.

REFERENCES

Baker, K (1993) *The Turbulent Years: My Life in Politics*, Faber, London

Ball, SJ (1994) *Education Reform: A Critical and Post-structured Approach*, Open University Press, Buckingham

Ball, SJ, Bowe, R and Gerwitz, S (1995) Circuits of schooling: a sociological exploration of parental choice of school in social class contexts, in *Sociological Review*, **43**, pp 52–78

Barber, M (1998) The dark side of the moon: imagining an end to failure in urban education, in *No Quick Fixes* eds L Stoll and K Myers, Falmer, pp 17–23, London

Barber, M and Dann, R (1996) *Raising Educational Standards in the Inner Cities: Practical Initiatives in Action*, Cassell, London

Beare, H, Caldwell, B and Milliken, R (1989) *Creating an Excellent School*, Routledge, London

Day, C, Hall, C and Whitaker, P (1998) *Developing Leadership in Primary Schools*, Paul Chapman, London

Deal, TE and Kennedy, A (1982) *Corporate Cultures: The Rites and Rituals of Corporate Life*, Addison Wesley, Reading, Mass

Deal, TE and Kennedy A (1983) Culture and school performance, *Educational Leadership*, **40**, pp 140–1

Earley, P (ed) (1998) *School improvement after inspection: School and LEA Responses*, Paul Chapman Press/Sage, London

Fidler, B (1996) School development planning and strategic planning for school improvement' in *Improvement Through Inspection: Complementary Approaches to School Development*, eds P Earley, B Fidler and J Ouston, Chapter 6, David Fulton, London

Gilroy, P and Wilcox, B (1994) Ofsted, criteria and the nature of social understanding: a Wittgensteinian critique of the practice of educational judgement, *British Journal of Educational Studies*, **45**, pp 22–38

Glover, D, Levacic, R, Bennett, N and Earley, P (1996) Leadership, planning and resource management in four very effective schools, *School Leadership and Management*, **17**, pp 357–74

Gray, J and Wilcox, B (1995) *Good School, Bad School: Evaluating Performance and Encouraging Improvement*, Open University Press, Buckingham

Hargreaves, D (1995) School culture, school effectiveness and school improvement, School Effectiveness and School Improvement, 6, 23–46

Levacic, R and Glover, D (1994a) *Ofsted Assessment of Schools' Efficiency: An Analysis of 66 Secondary School Inspection Reports*, Open University, Milton Keynes, Centre for Educational Policy and Management

Levacic, R and Glover, D (1994b) *Ofsted assessment of Schools' Efficiency: An Analysis of 66 Secondary School Inspection Reports: Statistical Analysis*, Open University, Milton Keynes, Centre for Educational Policy and Management

Maden, M and Hillman, J (1996) 'Lessons in success' in *Success Against the Odds* National Commission on Education, Routledge, London

McPherson, A (1992) Measuring added value in schools, *National Commission on Education*, Briefing no 1, NCE, London

Mortimore, P School effectiveness research: which way at the crossroads? *School Effectiveness and School Improvement*, **2**, 213–29

Mortimore, P and Whitty, G (1997) *Can School Improvement Overcome the Effects of Disadvantage?* Institute of Education, London

Office for Standards in Education (1993) *Framework for the Inspection of Schools*, HMSO, London

Office for Standards in Education (1995) *Guidance on the Inspection of Secondary Schools*, HMSO, London

Office for Standards in Education (1998) *Further Guidance to Inspectors*, Ofsted, London

Payne, G, Payne, J and Hyde, M (1996) Refuse of all classes? Social indicators and social deprivation, *Sociological Research On-line*, **1**, 1–19

Purkey, SC and Smith, MS (1983) *School Reform: The Policy Implications of the Effective Schools Literature*, Dingle, Washington, DC

Randall, P (1996) *A Community Approach to Bullying*, Trentham Books, Stoke on Trent

Reynolds, D (1992) School effectiveness and school improvement in the 1990s in *School Effectiveness: Research, Policy and Practice*, eds D Reynolds and P Cuttance, Chapter 10, Cassell, London

Reid, K, Hopkins, D and Holly P (1987) *Towards the Effective School*, Blackwell, Oxford

Rutter, M, Maughan, B, Mortimore, P and Ouston, J (1979) *Fifteen Thousand Hours: Secondary Schools and their Effect on Children*, Open Books, London

Sammons, P, Hillman, J and Mortimore, P (1995) *Key Characteristics of Effective Schools*, Institute of Education for Ofsted, London

Scheerens, J (1992) *Effective Schooling*, Cassell, London

Scheerens, J (1997) Conceptual models and theory embedded principles on effective schooling, *School Effectiveness and School Improvement*, **8**, 269–310

Stark, M (1998) No slow fixes either: how failing schools in England are being restored to health, in *No Quick Fixes*, eds L. Stoll and K. Myers (1998), Falmer, London 34–43

Stoll, L and Fink, D (1996) *Changing our Schools*, Open University Press, Buckingham

Stoll, L and Myers, K (1998) *No Quick Fixes*, Falmer, London

US Government: Department of Education (1998) *Turning around Low-Performing Schools: A Guide for State and Local Leaders*, Department of Education, Washington, DC

Wilcox, B and Gray, J (1996) *Inspecting Schools: Holding Schools to Account and Helping Schools to Improve*, Open University Press, Buckingham

The Ofsted lay inspector: to what purpose?

David Hustler

INTRODUCTION

A team at the Manchester Metropolitan University has been researching the role of the lay inspector (LI), within the Ofsted school inspection process, for the last three and a half years. Aspects of this work have been reported on, focusing on the attributes and early perceptions of lay inspectors (Hustler, Goodwin and Roden, 1995), considering how lay inspectors and others seem to be understanding the notion of 'lay' (Hustler and Stone, 1996), and overviewing the general issues in terms of their implication for the inspection process (Hustler *et al*, 1996). At the Lancaster Ofsted British Educational Research Association (BERA) Symposium, we reported on head-teachers' perceptions and experience of lay inspectors (Stone and Hustler, 1996). During this research we have had useful relations with Ofsted and ALI (Association of Lay Inspectors) and aspects of our work have led to recommendations for changes or minor tinkering with the system as it relates to lay inspectors.

In this chapter we start to review some aspects of previous research as well as draw on some of our most recent interviewing programme with some very experienced registered inspectors (RIs), LIs and contractors. In the context of a new Government taking office, it seems appropriate to begin to generate some broad-ranging review of what might be termed 'the lay inspector project'. How has it worked out? What impact has the involvement of LIs had within the Ofsted inspection process? How might we revisit some of the purposes behind introducing LIs? We would have to say, however, that it is our more recent set of interviews which has led us into this review mode, because the data itself is raising questions about 'the purpose of LIs and their future' and now more seriously perhaps than before questions about the meaning of 'lay'.

Our approach in this chapter is to present a variety of extracts from our past data and the more recent work. Some of this links to impending proposed changes as well. Our general argument is that these extracts slowly begin to add up and pose some pretty serious questions about the whole purpose of the LI project. First, though, we shall briefly rehearse some of the arguments for LI involvement as we have come across them in our research. These have already been reported on in the publications cited earlier.

LIs were originally seen as associated with the *Citizen's Charter*, as a means of community representation and accountability, and as a common-sense voice which might serve to cut through and arm consumers against the more esoteric, secretive and self-protective features of educational professionals.

Our interviews with LIs, RIs, and heads, did generate a considerable amount of comment concerning the LI virtues:

- an untainted voice;
- an independent presence;
- someone who could cut through the jargon;
- people who could speak with and for parents;
- those who are not bringing years of professional baggage with them;
- someone who can ask the unexpected question;
- a check on the rest of the team;
- someone who brought freshness with them;
- someone who brought Joe Public's view with them;
- a roving reporter sort of role;
- someone whose very lack of specialism could allow them to get to the heart of the school;
- part of the strength of the British amateur tradition;
- they provide some grit in the system.

Of course there have been a variety of objections raised to LI involvement and considerable resistance and controversy in the early days. However, the above comments capture the flavour (or rather flavours) of what the LI contribution would be and was being experienced as. Several of these features have emerged in other surveys such as Ofsted's 1995 survey of lay inspectors.

This same 1995 survey also noted the view from one contractor that 'there was already evidence that lay inspectors were taking on many of the characteristics and attitudes of their professional colleagues', a similar point to one made in our 1995 article on 'Early days for lay inspectors': 'There seems to be a feeling that the lay inspector will become socialised into the "system" and may have a limited shelf life as truly lay'.

In our contribution to the book *Ofsted Inspections: The Early Experience* (Ouston *et al*, 1996), we also noted that those LIs who had found regular and frequent work were more likely to bring with them considerable experience of education;

> What appears to be happening then is that increasingly the process through which a school finds a Lay Inspector on its doorstep has, not surprisingly, led to that person, in all probability, having either had considerable experience of education themselves, or considerable experience of operating as a Lay Inspector, or being familiar with educationalists through everyday social interaction and discourse (Hustler and Stone, 1996).

The problem concerning the number of trained LIs who had not found work has largely gone away now following the additional inspector (AI) initiative and the use made of relatively unemployed LIs within that initiative. However, the general question concerning the generic role of and purpose of the LI remains. As we noted in closing the 'Early days' article: 'The government's view has certainly been that the lay inspector will contribute to the improvement of schooling; this is certainly a part of "life on the edge of the known universe" (Barber, 1994) where knowledge remains sparse (Hustler, Goodwin and Roden, 1995)'.

RESEARCH EXTRACTS

(a) Our early work on demographic characteristics of LIs, relating well to Ofsted data, suggested that the typical practising LI was around 51, white, male, self-employed/retired; professional background and well qualified. Approximately 1350 have been trained overall and despite an initiative to bring more women and ethnic minority members into the LI population, our typical set of characteristics still holds good. From the outset the invitation into LI training (its timing, associated personal costs etc) made it virtually impossible for there to be good representation from certain sectors of the community. In addition, there has been no addition to that 1,300 in recent years. We have then we believe an average age which is around 54/55 now, with no additional recruits.

(b) Our interviews with heads, and with RIs and contractors, also relates well to Ofsted data and material from other sources, in suggesting that

LIs are well established within the Ofsted inspection system and much more accepted by professional communities than at first. Interviewees talk of the system having bedded down as regards LIs and members of ALI note that the critical comments in the press and from professionals in particular have largely disappeared ... certainly ALI meetings are no longer characterized by discussion regarding how best to handle such criticism. In short, the existence of LIs within the inspection system is now largely unchallenged. There are, of course, rumblings linked with matters such as LIs becoming RIs (a matter we will return to) and the renewed focus on teacher quality within inspection gradings will probably lead to some debates regarding the LI proportional contribution to judgements in certain cases.

(c) Our data suggests that LIs are sticking to, or being required to stick to, certain inspection areas: 'My impression is that LIs are increasingly tramlined into the areas such as attendance, support and guidance and pupil welfare and partnership' and 'You find some working on management, but not many'. The new framework does not seem to have made much of a difference here, except for a greater LI involvement in reporting to parents issues. From some very experienced lay inspectors we have a related concern that many inspections 'side-line the lay inspector ... often the aspects the LI is looking at are viewed as less important and are dealt with rapidly'. This point seems to hold for many despite the experienced LI's recognition that there is tremendous variability in terms of how different RIs use their lay inspectors. The above connects with a point we made in our 1996 BERA paper, though this was seen to be especially true of secondary inspections: 'A cruder, but linked, interpretation of the above is that the lay inspector within secondary inspections has been rendered "safe", having been marginalized to relatively non-threatening areas, which do not involve fundamental trespass on matters at the heart of teaching and learning'.

(d) Although the 'finding work problem' for those trained as LIs has been largely resolved, we find that quite a few LIs are doing a tremendous number of inspections (60 plus and some have notched up well over 100). Here we enter the territory of the full-time lay inspector and connected issues as well as some debate. Some experienced RIs and contractors feel that the very notion of a full-time LI is contrary to the original intentions of the Act, whereas others feel altogether more sanguine about it. Concerns focus around the idea expressed by some that LIs should carry with them, into their inspections, current experience of other occupational areas or everyday experience ... that this is some sort of resource for having or retaining the capacity to operate in a 'lay' framework: 'Lay inspectors are not really "lay" any more if they are working on inspections day in and day out'.

There is an interesting possibility here that some RIs are finding certain very experienced LIs more of a challenge than they are accustomed to: 'Some LIs are out to make inspection a career and clearly want to make an impact ... some are starting to compare schools, seem to be listening less and writing reports which say what schools should be doing' ... 'Their views are becoming more evident and this can irritate heads'. This critique, termed in ways which are suggestive of activities inappropriate to an inspection, are suggestive of some experienced LIs beginning to flex their muscles (recognizing on occasion that they have more experience of inspections than the RI they are working with).

Other comments from RIs take a somewhat different direction: 'My impression is that experienced LIs are pursuing tighter and more routinized inspection roles ... the feeling being they have done it before like this, it went well, etc ... so this is sometimes a self-imposed routinization from more experienced LIs, though it can also be RIs organizing their LI work in an increasingly conventionalized manner'.

The term 'career' was used in one of the earlier quotes in this section and the notion of the career of the lay inspector as an issue for ALI has received some airing in the press (Times Educational Supplement, 1997). Some of this revolves around the issue of whether or not LIs could or should become RIs. Some of our LI respondents point out that in terms of 'career progression', this is the only way forward. As we have noted, the very notion of a 'career' for LIs is viewed as inappropriate by some RIs. The current ruling seems to be that in becoming a registered inspector, a lay inspector must necessarily lose 'lay' status and would, therefore, not be able to revert to operating in LI mode. This obviously gives experienced LIs a problem should they wish to go down the RI road (and training for this is already underway), since they may find inspection work harder to come by. The grounds for the ruling are unclear, but they may stem from concerns about unions' and heads' reactions to LIs operating as RIs. For the purposes of this chapter there are two issues of interest here. First, the attribution of meaning to the notion of 'lay' associated with that ruling. Second, the growth of interest in the career of the LI is in itself an indicator of professionalization.

(e) As noted earlier, there have been worries about LIs becoming 'tainted' by extensive inspection experience ... in the sense that they begin to lose whatever it was that characterized their 'layness'. Certainly our more recent data reinforces these concerns, with some RIs bemoaning the fact that experienced LIs no longer seem to have the freshness, the useful unexpected angle, that they once had to offer. In addition, some have commented to the effect that LIs have themselves now become embedded in the jargon and no longer provide quite the same functions in terms of clarifying communications and in terms of their relations with parents (though LIs often claim capacities as a line into the parental voice and present themselves as such on occasion to parents ... a variant in terms of 'fronts' being presented from those discussed by Jeffrey and Woods (1995), in their ECER 1995 paper on inspection).

LIs too have debated these issues and take different views on it. Some argue that you have to work hard to retain your objectivity and your detachment from the professional viewpoint. Others argue that there is no real issue here as regards losing 'lay' capacities: 'You are still coming from a different direction, not a teacher ... you are prepared to be more critical and prepared to say "that person is a dud" '. Our data is confused here and our understanding is that the people we are talking to are confused at times and that includes LIs, RIs and contractors. The source of the confusion lies in the continuing lack of agreement as to what being an LI should really mean or can really mean as you become experienced.

(f) LIs, like others, have been subject to the changes in the Ofsted approach and particularly to the changes in contracting procedures. Our understanding is that the bidding cycle for 1998–9 is likely to move to an agreed list of suppliers, based on criteria such as contractor quality assurance (QA) arrangements, capacity, region of operation and cost. One possibility is that Ofsted, for reasons of cost-cutting but also standardization, may increasingly shift to the larger contracting organizations. In so doing, and presuming that contractors will continue the marked trend (well known for secondary, but now also for primary) of bidding down, there are, we would argue, some likely knock-on consequences for LI activity. These could include the strengthening of the safe bet LI argument ... ie such pressures will lead contractors to work with pools of LIs who measure up in terms of reliability, extensive experience etc.

(g) We have had some other interesting comments from experienced RIs and contractors as follows: 'My overall worry is that the use of the LI has not really moved on since the beginning ... especially as regards engaging us in some understanding of the uncertainties and interrelationships between professional and non-professional (or lay) judgements' and 'Their role vis-à-vis the community has not developed as broadly as might have been hoped'. This latter point connects with some comments from LIs themselves regarding their view that there is scope for considerable improvement from some RIs regarding meetings with parents (an additional view is that on some inspections scant attention is paid to parents' views anyway). Other contractor comments include: 'The quality of LIs has not really increased ... many are now much more experienced and doing a middle-of-the-road job but not really building up their skills ... some now less thorough perhaps' and 'no one really talks about how LIs should be used, or talks about what being an LI should mean'.

(h) Finally, our more recent data suggests that there has been little change regarding some matters which irritated several LIs. Many RIs do not provide their LIs with draft copies of the report to comment on; LIs often remain surprised regarding how their writing has been amended or changed, sometimes out of all recognition ... though there is sometimes lack of clarity as to whether this is the RI's work or the work of the reader; LIs still do not normally receive any systematic debriefing or feedback on their work; a feeling from some ALI members that they are surprisingly kept in the dark about developments which they would have expected to have some say in ... this is occasionally put in a way which suggests that LIs are rarely thought of in Ofsted developments, ie it is not the case that they are deliberately kept in the dark, rather that no one thinks about the LI perspective.

DISCUSSION

We intend to start with a possibly provocative version of what these extracts might be seen to add up to:

- LIs are not representative of the community at large, and can make no special claim to be representative of non-educational professionals;
- they have become increasingly professionalized in some respects, while remaining essentially marginal to the process and outcomes of inspections;
- their work is becoming increasingly routinized, regularized and focused in certain areas ... undercutting the aspirations which some people have had regarding their distinctive capacity to provide some grit within the system or to pose the unexpected but useful question;
- many of them, and others, are unclear as to what operating in a lay capacity involves or distinctively contributes once they have acquired considerable experience of inspections and even their roving role has become a sort of routinized roaming;

- possibilities for a free-thinking, independent, voice have been, and are increasingly likely to be, undermined given structural, market and cultural pressures for safe-bet, reliables;
- there is little sign of significant development regarding the LI role *vis-à-vis* parents and the local community.

More generally, the overall understanding of the LI role and of the interrelationships between professional and lay judgements has not advanced. In fact, there has been a developing silence regarding the generic contribution of the LI. ALI has clearly been a useful association for many LIs; it maintains a voice with Ofsted and has helped to make visible some of the problems LIs have faced, in particular the early experience of most being that they could not find work as an LI, as well as organizing training possibilities. However, ALI has not been a vehicle for exploring how LIs should or could challenge what some view as professional mystique and control.

The existence of the LI is now largely accepted, but as many RIs and head-teachers have commented to us, acceptance of the LI does not imply that they see the purpose or the need for such a role as currently enacted. In prospect and in their early experience several RIs and others saw the LI as a necessary source of grit in an increasingly routinized system ... some still see the need for that grit, but the LI practice does not seem to be providing it.

For Government, on occasion, and within particular inspections, the existence of the LI has served local or broader political purposes; it can be convenient to talk of the existence of that independent common-sense voice, of that inspector who has in some sense more in common with the community and parents, of a particular expression of the *Citizens' Charter*. There seems here, however, to be an increasing distance between this position and the actual experience. We could read this position as useful, political rhetoric and not much more.

The above should not be taken to be at all critical of LIs. One speculation is that the existence of trained and paid LIs left to function in a market context, as a massive inspection machinery got off the ground, has bequeathed Ofsted precisely what might have been expected: a minor problem, which you try not to think about too much, because if you do it opens up bigger questions which are difficult to answer about how the experience of the LI project relates to accountability, professionality and the improvement of schooling. The minor problem, it could be argued, is that the very systems set up to involve LIs within the Ofsted inspection process have undermined what some originally took to be the essential contributions of an LI. Emerging studies of a lay role across different inspectorates should be of interest here (Mordaunt, 1996).

A general conclusion of the above is that the LI role as currently enacted and structured for seems to operate to no particular purpose. Clearly the argument here is somewhat exaggerated in a variety of respects; however, it does seem that there is a case for a review of the LI experience within Ofsted. Such a review might lead us back into asking how best parents and a school's local community might play a fuller part in inspection and here we might once again revisit the South Australian 'community member' approach. In so doing we might be led to consider how the notion of an effective 'lay' capacity for judgement and influence may possibly be buttressed by notions of representative, voluntary and unpaid features. Alternatively, a review might enable the Ofsted inspection process to harness more fully the existing LIs in relation to more meaningful and *distinctive* contributions.

REFERENCES

Barber, M (1994) Power and control in education, 1944–2004, *Journal of Educational Studies*, **42**, 348–62

Hustler, D, Goodwin, A and Roden, M (1995) Early days for lay inspectors, *Research in Education*, **54**, pp 1–13

Hustler, D and Stone, V (1996) Lay inspectors: insiders and outsiders, in *Ofsted Inspections – The Early Experience*, eds J Ouston, P Earley, B Fidler and D Fulton, London, 61–72

Hustler, D *et al* (1996) Proceedings from the Researching the Lay Inspector Role Conference, Manchester Metropolitan University, January

Jeffrey, B and Woods, P (1995) Reconstructions of reality: schools under inspection, BERA/ECER Ofsted Symposium, Bath

Mordaunt, E (1996) The brave idea: the work of lay people in government inspectorates, BERA Ofsted Symposium, Lancaster

Stone, G and Hustler, D (1996) Head teachers on lay inspectors, BERA Ofsted Symposium, Lancaster

Times Educational Supplement (1997) Letter, 17 January, p 21

Effects of Ofsted inspection on school development and staff morale

Pat Cuckle and Pat Broadhead

EFFECTS OF OFSTED INSPECTIONS

Ofsted inspections are intended to bring about school improvement. However, there is growing evidence that inspection has both positive and negative effects on school development and staff morale. Such evidence is presented and discussed in this chapter. Ofsted's explicit aims (Ofsted, 1994) are to raise standards, enhance quality, increase efficiency and improve the ethos of the school. The framework for inspection is built around these four themes and key issues (KIs) for action are recommended as a basis for improvement (Bennett, 1994). According to Ofsted, schools could 'exploit inspection thoroughly' to bring about development and improvement (Ofsted, 1994: 44). Evidence that the inspection process has both positive and negative effects is described in studies of primary and secondary schools which have been taking place since the early days of Ofsted inspections in 1993; these studies are outlined briefly before discussing our own study.

There are undoubtedly positive effects on school development from inspection. Sharron (1996) described how the first 'failing' school identified by Ofsted improved dramatically over a period of two years. In primary schools, a year after inspection, 'some progress' had been made in the implementation of Ofsted's recommendations on managerial (as opposed to teaching and learning) issues (Gray and Wilcox, 1995).

Brimblecombe, Shaw and Ormston (1996) found that 38 per cent of teachers intended to change practice after inspection, although they also pointed out that intentions are not the same as actions and that the intended changes would not necessarily bring about improvement. Preparation was seen as important, both for coping with the inspection process and as a means of leading to improvement, despite prior fears and anxieties (Matthews and Smith, 1995; Peatfield, 1995). Preparation, verbal feedback and the written report contributed to school development to some extent (Earley, 1995) although less than 10 per cent of schools in their sample considered that inspection made a major improvement. A sample of secondary schools saw potential for development from inspection by providing an external audit, by accelerating and by providing information for parents and accountability for the expenditure of public money (Matthews and Smith, 1995). Ouston, Fuller and Earley *et al* (1997) believe that there is potential for improvement through preparation and implementing the post-inspection action plan; nearly three-quarters of their sample of secondary schools saw inspection as having a positive effect.

However, there is the view that inspection can have negative effects on school development. Field *et al* (1998) considered that the language of inspection reports was stylized and restrictive and, although generally 'positive' was open to interpretation. This can make inspection reports less useful to schools than they might be. When action recommended by Ofsted was already in school development plans (SDPs), then reports did not offer anything new and the impact on development was consequently diminished. This aspect is also discussed in Ouston, Fidler and Earley (1996) and Maychell and Pathak (1997).

As well as contributing to school development, inspection can have beneficial effects on staff morale; enhancing staff morale is important both in itself and for school development. Matthews and Smith (1995) have written about the potential benefit of documenting a school's achievements and strengths; there is also a potential benefit in the growth in confidence which comes from the affirmation of a school's quality and its sense of direction. A clear example of this is shown by Carpenter and Stoneham (1994); they described a secondary school with a special needs unit which found inspection rewarding particularly in relation to demonstrating how a policy for special needs can translate into practice.

But staff morale can also be adversely affected by inspection. The stress of inspection (both before and after) can be so demoralizing that teachers can become seriously deprofessionalized, even in a school which is not failing and has strong leadership (Jeffrey and Woods, 1996). Russell (1994) questions whether inspection is for accountability purposes (including to parents and the community through the publication of inspection reports) or for evaluation leading to improvement. She states that many schools hope to 'survive' the experience but the overload of preparation is bound to lead to anxiety, exhaustion and anticlimax. An area where there is the potential for adverse effects on morale is in Ofsted's teacher gradings; in secondary schools, there were discrepancies between inspectors' gradings of 'very poor' and the schools' judgements which were likely to be divisive and damaging (Fidler *et al*, 1998). Wragg *et al* (1999) found that 15 per cent of cases of teacher 'incompetence' had been identified by an Ofsted inspection and a great deal of time and energy were spent by head-teachers (who were not always successful) on trying to help individual teachers improve.

HEAD-TEACHERS' EVALUATIONS OF OFSTED'S IMPACT

Now we turn to a study of primary school head-teachers' views on Ofsted inspections. Their responses concerned whether the inspection process, as they experienced it, can help schools to develop, how it helps and whether there are detrimental effects of inspection.

The research team had questionnaire returns on recent applications (autumn 1996) from 124 primary school head-teachers. Documentation on SDPs, Ofsted's KIs and post–Ofsted inspection action plans was then collected from 47 of the head-teachers and telephone interviews were undertaken with them. The main purpose of the study was to investigate compatibility between KIs and targets in existing SDPs (Cuckle, Hodgson and Broadhead 1998). Information was also gathered on how inspections contributed to school development and how inspection affected staff morale. This data came from three sources as follows:

- The *questionnaires* asked a general question about the 'worthwhileness' of inspection. This was an open-ended question and responses addressed aspects of staff morale, the process of the inspection in general, views on inspection teams, the contribution to school development, using the report for school management and value for money.
- In *telephone interviews*, head-teachers were asked about the perceived usefulness of the KIs new to them, that is, not already in the SDPs. Head-teachers also expressed their views on the impact of the inspection on a range of issues such as the process of inspection in general, issues concerning implementing KIs, the role of governors, the effect on staff morale and how they could use the inspection for school management. The interviews covered some of the same ground as the questionnaires but provided a level of detail and feeling which was not available in the questionnaires.
- *Post-inspection action plans* sent by the head-teachers who were inter-

viewed and we could see how KIs were translated into action, some of the complexity involved in the process of implementing KIs and who was involved in the process. Head-teachers commented on aspects of school development and school management in relation to what was in the action plans.

AN OVERVIEW OF INSPECTION

An overview was provided from responses in the 124 questionnaires to the general question on the 'worthwhileness' of their own inspections; head-teachers' responses were categorized with the following results. Seventeen per cent thought inspection 'very worth while'; the main reason for this was a confirmation of the school's aims in the post-inspection report plus a contribution to further school development through the KIs. Sixty one per cent thought inspection 'acceptable' or had 'some reservations' about it. In this category were many head-teachers who acknowledged some contribution to school development but questioned the expense of inspection and the stressful process it involved. Twenty-two per cent thought inspection was 'not at all worth while'. These head-teachers generally considered that very little had been contributed to the school's development and thought that inspection was a faulty process. Head-teachers thought that so much stress had been caused that this greatly outweighed any contribution to school development.

Combining the detailed data from the above questionnaire responses and the other two sources (telephone interviews and reference to documentation), we were able to group it into four categories related to positive and negative contributions to school development and staff morale. These categories are shown in the framework in Table 10.1

There are two points to bear in mind before going on to the discussion of the four categories. A first glance at this framework might suggest that the positive and negative effects of Ofsted inspections were balanced, but further consideration reveals that some aspects are likely to have deeper and longer lasting impacts than others. This is discussed in more detail later in the chapter. In the discussion to follow, it should be remembered that some of the head-teachers' comments came from open-ended questions which invited a variety of responses or arose incidentally in the course of the interviews. Consequently, some of the categories to be discussed contain only a few examples, but are sufficiently interesting and relevant to be worthy of comment.

Table 10.1   *Head-teachers' views of positive and negative aspects of Ofsted inspections*

Positive	Negative
School development	
Objective view from outside	Plans already made for most KIs
Confirmation of plans for development	Expertise of inspectors questioned
Preparation helps development	Verbal reports unlike written report
Tool by which head can make changes	KIs caused controversy with governors
Report used to change staff attitudes	Complex KIs very difficult to implement
KIs form basis of new SDP	Difficult to create success criteria
Increased governor involvement	Cost of inspection could be better spent
	Preparation time consuming
Staff morale	
Favourable report boosts confidence	Report can be demoralizing
Confirmation of school's self-image	Inspection is very stressful procedure

OFSTED'S CONTRIBUTION TO SCHOOL DEVELOPMENT

The time when Ofsted inspection had the most potential for contributing to school development was when there was perceived to be a reasonable amount of agreement between the Ofsted inspection team (as reflected in their KIs) and the school (reflected in their SDP) regarding areas for development. This potential for school development existed in 52 per cent of schools where head-teachers said there was a 'reasonable' amount of agreement. Confirmation of the school's view of itself was reassuring but needed to be balanced with an objective, positive and evident contribution from the inspection team to agreement. Confirmation of the school's view of itself was reassuring but needed to be balanced with an objective, positive and evident contribution from the inspection team to future development. Such circumstances are likely to lead to more positive attitudes to and more progress in development (Ouston, Fidler and Earley, 1996; Maychell and Pathak, 1997).

The inspection process was said by 20 per cent of head-teachers to have provided a useful, objective view or a focus for development. A small number of head-teachers (4 per cent) thought that the preparation for inspection had helped school development more than the actual inspection. This, they claimed, was because it provided the opportunity to review some areas of development and provided an incentive for staff to complete targets or generally set policies and documents in order; head-teachers said that preparation helped to focus schools' thinking.

Eight per cent of head–teachers mentioned that they 'exploited' the inspections and post–inspection reports by using them as tools to bring about change in relation to staff; head–teachers saw this as a positive effect in terms of school management. They said that they could use the reports as objective views of the school without overtly imposing their own (sometimes unpopular) view on the staff to help development. These included a small number of head–teachers who considered that they had 'reactionary' members of staff, had taken up an appointment just before inspection and had inherited 'weak' members of staff or had inherited virtually non–existent development plans. In one extreme case the newly appointed head–teacher said during interview that she had told her staff that changes had to be made because Ofsted said so; she remarked that the staff 'prided themselves on not delivering the National Curriculum because they didn't think it was necessary'. A small proportion of head–teachers (about 8 per cent) said that rather than incorporating KIs into revised versions of development plans (as Ofsted recommended), they would 'exploit' the inspection by making the post–Ofsted action plan their development plan where existing ones did not fit in with their visions of development for the schools to which they had recently been appointed.

Another positive aspect of inspection was increased governor involvement in school development. Only a few head–teachers (2 per cent) mentioned it, but governor involvement was very evident when the researchers studied post–inspection actions plans. In every one of the 47 action plans received at least one governor was named who had been allocated some responsibility in implementing the action plan. As one head–teacher explained, since the governing body had legal responsibility for drawing up, presenting and implementing the action plan it made sense to document their responsibilities; another head–teacher said that he welcomed the inspection report's direction to involve the governing body in development planning. Apparently, head–teachers nearly always did the bulk of the work of drawing up the action plans, but acknowledged their governors' responsibilities by including them in the action and documentation. This level of governor involvement in post–inspection action plans had been found elsewhere (Pathak and Maychell, 1997) and is in sharp contrast to governor involvement in development planning which has previously been fairly minimal (Earley, 1994; Cuckle *et al*, 1998a).

WHEN OFSTED DOES NOT HELP DEVELOPMENT

We have seen that it is desirable for there to be an optimum amount of agreement between KIs and SDPs if school development is to be promoted. There are, however, circumstances where inspectors might be considered to contribute little to school development, eg when there was too much overlap between KIs and SDPs. There was the potential for this situation in 39 per cent of schools where head-teachers reported 'very close' or 'complete' overlap between KIs and SDPs. Nine per cent of head-teachers made such remarks as 'Ofsted only told us what we already knew', 'didn't tell us anything we didn't know' and 'no real surprises'.

But difficulties can also arise where a serious mismatch exists between SDP priorities and KIs. The situation may occur if a school is not effective in identifying its weaknesses or if a school and an inspection team's assumptions about the features of an effective school differ. This was potentially the case for another 9 per cent of head-teachers who indicated that there was 'hardly any' or 'no match' between their KIs and SDP priorities. Eleven per cent of KIs were thought to be unsuitable as KIs either because they were trivial, the staff disagreed that they needed attention, they were the concern of the Local Education Authority (LEA) or governors, they were outside the school's control or they referred to an isolated incident. In these cases head-teachers dismissed the KIs saying that they contributed nothing to school development.

The perceived lack of experience or expertise of inspectors sometimes caused head-teachers to be cynical of individual KIs or the inspection report as a whole and this was seen as a potential hindrance to development. While 5 per cent of head-teachers (and their staff) thought that inspection teams were 'professional' and 'courteous', 8 per cent made negative comments about inspectors, one said that 'privateers' (but not LEA inspectors) created problems. Other head-teachers were doubtful of teams' or individual inspectors' credibility, especially their knowledge of the primary school curriculum. In such cases head-teachers expressed 'little confidence in the team'. Another factor which caused 2 per cent of head-teachers to doubt the usefulness of the inspection was the disparity that was occasionally reported between the verbal report they received and the subsequent written report.

References to involvement of governing bodies in inspection reports could have negative effects. While some head-teachers welcomed more involvement of governing bodies, two found that increased governor involvement was a likely hindrance to school development by potentially giving their governors too much power to force their own priorities – a worry noted in earlier work on development planning (Cuckle *et al*, 1998a).

Some head-teachers remarked that KIs were difficult to interpret because they could not see an obvious way to improve, eg one head-teacher queried how the school was to improve teaching across Key Stage 1 when all lessons observed were proclaimed at least 'sound'. Three per cent of head-teachers said that the inspection team struggled or 'scraped around' to find KIs for improvement. Other head-teachers thought that the language and meaning of KIs were unclear or thought that some KIs were so complex that they would either not be able to implement them successfully or were such that staff were demoralized by them and had lost interest in development. With this important point in mind, the research team studied the KIs from the documentation received. Fifteen per cent of KIs were judged by the research team to be very complex; examples of these were: 'Develop a scheme of work in each subject that maps continuity and progression across the whole school'; and 'Evaluate the effect of school development initiatives on the quality of educational provision and standards of attainment'. KIs such as these require a great deal of 'unpacking'. When a smaller sample of Ofsted KIs (from inspections in 1998) were studied there seemed to be more clarity in the way KIs were being framed and were, therefore, potentially more helpful to schools (Broadhead, Cuckle and Hodgson, in press). However they are framed, it is clear that such KIs as these would take a great deal of interpretation and involvement of the whole staff in planning and implementation. Measuring their progress and success would be difficult, especially as post-Ofsted action plans like earlier SDPs were lacking in precise success criteria (Matthews and Smith, 1995; Ofsted 1995; Broadhead *et al*, 1996; Broadhead *et al*, 1998; Cuckle *et al*, 1998b; Cuckle, Hodgson and Broadhead, 1998c). Whether schools could hope to make substantial progress on such KIs before the next inspection remains to be seen. As schools have started to be reinspected there is evidence that some KIs are recommended a second time; it is unclear as yet to what extent Ofsted are taking into consideration any evident progress on previous KIs (Fidler and Davies, 1998).

While it was stated earlier that the preparation for Ofsted inspection was felt to be useful for ongoing development by some head-teachers, others (7 per cent) felt that preparation was stressful (with too much 'lead-up time') or was time consuming and the time could have been better spent on working on some of their own priorities for development. Sixteen per cent of head-teachers thought inspection an excessively expensive process for the amount of improvement it was likely to bring about and made such comments as 'could have spent £10,000 better supporting children' and 'the money could have been better spent directly on the school'. Head-teachers, especially of small schools with tiny budgets, pointed out that they spent substantial amounts of money on preparing for inspection (eg photocopying, preparation courses and consultations). This money, they said, could have been spent directly on the school for making improvements.

PROMOTION OF STAFF MORALE

Whatever the contribution of inspection to school development there was no doubt that a favourable or 'good' report boosted the head-teacher and staff morale; the importance of this contribution to the well-being of staff and to future development was acknowledged by a number of head-teachers. Nineteen per cent of head-teachers thought the inspection confirmed their professionalism in a general sense, or felt that a 'good' report congratulated them for their hard work, confirmed their self-image and indicated that they were going in the right direction. A 'good' report also enhanced a school's image in the eyes and minds of governors, parents and the wider community. This was a very important aspect particularly for schools which had falling rolls, where head-teachers were anxious to form better links with the whole school community or where relatively new head-teachers thought that they and their staff had made much progress in improving their schools in a short time.

NEGATIVE EFFECTS ON STAFF MORALE

Conversely, an unexpectedly 'bad' or highly critical report inevitably had the opposite effect on morale. Some of the most strongly stated views about how staff morale had been adversely affected came from head-teachers whose schools had had highly critical reports. Head-teachers said that some staff were so demoralized by the inspections and reports and overwhelmed by the amount that had to be done that they did not know where to begin and did not know where the energy to start to move forward was to come from. This was especially the case in schools in particularly difficult social circumstances. Twenty-six per cent of head-teachers mentioned high levels of stress that had been felt by themselves and their staff saying that there was 'too much hype' or 'too much nervous energy expended'. A few head-teachers took the view that inspection had been 'damaging' or 'destructive to staff morale'. A substantial amount of absence due to illness was reported throughout the process of inspection. In some cases head-teachers and staff were taking early retirement as a result of inspection; two acting head-teachers reported that head-teachers had already done so at the time a date for inspection was announced. In two extreme cases acting head-teachers reported that a head-teacher and a teacher suffered 'nervous breakdowns'. Stress was reported to be felt during the period of preparation and anticipation, during the inspection week, immediately after the inspection and when the report was received and KIs had to be turned into an action plan. This stress was regardless of how well the inspection went or whether the report was good or not so good. One head-teacher, three months after inspection, was so over-wrought by the whole process that he spent considerable time during the telephone interview drawing the researcher's attention to the spelling mistakes, poor grammar and perceived inconsistencies in his Ofsted report and describing in detail the letters of complaint he had sent to Ofsted and the LEA.

A few head-teachers pointed out that inspection was 'bound to be' stressful but should not detract too much from the positive aspects of it; in any case, said some, the effects of inspection soon faded as the staff got on with the daily job of teaching. While a few head-teachers mentioned that the school had celebrated with staff parties immediately the inspection was over, others reported a huge feeling of anticlimax and such complete exhaustion that they 'just wanted to go home'. Again, these feelings seemed irrespective of how well or badly the inspection had gone.

As mentioned earlier, it may seem on the surface that positive and negative effects of Ofsted inspections are balanced, but this is difficult to measure overall in quantitative terms. An Ofsted inspection obviously has a meaning and an impact for an individual school which cannot be balanced against the different impact on another school. For instance, if a head-teacher believes that staff morale and health (and subsequent school development) have been detrimentally affected by inspection he or she is unlikely to be able to console the staff by urging them to remember what a neighbouring school has gained by developing and having the staff's confidence boosted.

SO CAN OFSTED CONTRIBUTE TO SCHOOL AND STAFF DEVELOPMENT?

Head-teachers perceived that inspection could bring about development and subsequent improvement by recommending sound issues for action and by enhancing morale which could inspire schools to develop and improve. The most positive comments concerned the contribution to a school's development and confirmation that schools were, in the head-teachers' views, achieving their aims. The most negative comments concerned damage to staff morale and the perceived ineffectiveness of the inspection process in achieving development and improvement.

The extent to which head-teachers valued inspection seemed to be related to a combination of the following factors:

● the perceived value of the pre-inspection preparation process in terms of how much time was invested and what was achieved during this period;
● the conduct of inspectors and the perceived quality of inspection teams in terms of their professionalism and ability to demonstrate relevant knowledge;

- the expense of the inspection in relation to its contribution to school development;
- the extent to which inspection provided a new focus or a starting point for further school development;
- the extent to which inspection provided a tool either for school management or relationships with the wider school community;
- the residual effect on the morale or sense of professionalism of the school staff;
- the extent to which schools thought it possible to implement the more complex of Ofsted's KIs.

It remains to be seen whether schools improve after inspection. As the first round of inspections of primary schools has finished and re-inspection has begun, data on improvement will no doubt emerge. It remains to be seen how many KIs (including the very complex ones) have been implemented, their effect and whether schools have been given the same KIs again. There are views that inspection alone cannot bring about improvement because it does not take sufficient account of local circumstances (Faruqi, 1996; Lockhart, 1996; Broadhead, Cuckle and Hodgson, in press). There is a considerable body of opinion that different approaches to development (other than Ofsted inspection) may be more useful; these are discussed in Earley, Fidler and Ouston (1996). Whatever the approach taken, a commitment to change must come from *within* the school (Fidler, Earley and Ouston, 1996). This commitment may come about with Ofsted inspection as a catalyst if the process and resulting reports are such that they are valued by schools, if reports are useful to them, if they offer explicit starting points and if they acknowledge ongoing development.

REFERENCES

Bennett, PL (1994) Many happy returns, *Education*, **184**, p 195

Brimblecombe, N, Shaw, M and Ormston, M (1996) Teachers' intention to change practice as a result of Ofsted school inspections, *Educational Management and Administration*, **24**, pp 339–54.

Broadhead, P, Cuckle, P, Hodgson, J and Dunford, J (1996) Improving primary schools through school development planning: building a vision, exploring the reality, *Educational Management and Administration*, **24**, p 277

Broadhead, P, Hodgson, J, Cuckle, P and Dunford, J (1998) Development planning – moving from the amorphous to the dimensional and making it your own, *Research Papers in Education*, **13**, pp 3–17

Broadhead, P, Cuckle, P and Hodgson, J (in press) Promoting pupil learning within a school development framework, *Research Papers in Education*

Carpenter, B and Stoneham, C (1994) Inspection effectiveness: an analysis of an Ofsted inspection, *British Journal of Special Education*, **21**, pp 70–72

Cuckle, P, Dunford, J, Hodgson, J and Broadhead, P (1998a) Governor involvement in development planning; from tea parties to working parties, *School Leadership and Management*, **18**, pp 19–33

Cuckle, P, Broadhead, P, Hodgson, J and Dunford, J (1998b) Development planning in primary schools – a positive influence on management and culture, *Educational Management and Administration*, **26**, pp 185–283

Cuckle, P, Hodgson, J and Broadhead, P (1998) Investigating the relationship between Ofsted inspections and school development planning, *School Leadership and Management*, **18**, pp 271–83

Earley, P (1994) *School Governing Bodies – Making Progress?* NFER, Slough

Earley, P (1995) Secondary heads fear 'planning blight' from early starts, *Times Educational Supplement*, 4097, January 6, p 10.

Earley, P, Fidler, B and Ouston, J (eds) (1996) *Improvement Through Inspection? Complementary Approaches to School Development*, David Fulton, London

Faruqi, S (1996) A culture of despondency, *Education*, **187**, pp 10–11

Fidler, B and Davies, J (1998) The inspector calls again: the reinspection of schools, in *School Improvement after Inspection? School and LEA Responses*, ed P. Earley, Paul Chapman Publishing, London, pp 153–67

Fidler, B, Earley, P and Ouston, J (1996) School development, school inspection and managing change, in eds P Earley, B Fidler and J Ouston, *Improvement Through Inspection? Complementary Approaches to School Development*, David Fulton, London, pp 186–90

Fidler, B, Earley, P, Ouston, J and Davies, J (1998) Teacher gradings and Ofsted inspections: help or hindrance as a management tool? *School Leadership and Management*, **18**, pp 257–70

Field, C, Greenstreet, D, Kusel, P and Parsons, C (1998) Ofsted inspection reports and the language of educational improvement, *Evaluation and Research in Education*, **12**, p 125–39

Gray, J and Wilcox B, (1995) In the aftermath of inspection: the nature and fate of inspection report recommendations, *Research Papers in Education*, **10**, pp 1–18

Jeffrey, B and Woods, P (1996) Feeling deprofessionalised: the social construction of emotions during an Ofsted inspection, *Cambridge Journal of Education*, **26**, pp 325–344.

Lockhart, A (1996) Week by week, *Education*, **87**, (5), pp 7, 12

Matthews, P and Smith, G (1995) Ofsted: inspecting schools and improvement through inspection, *Cambridge Journal of Education*, **25**, pp 23–34

Maychell, K and Pathak, S (1997) *Planning for action. Part 1: A Survey of Schools' Post-inspection Action Planning*, NFER, Slough

Ofsted (1994) *Improving Schools*, HMSO, London

Ofsted (1995) *Planning Improvement: Schools' Post-inspection Action Plans*, HMSO, London

Ouston, J, Fidler, B and Earley, P (1996) Secondary schools responses to Ofsted: improvement through inspection in *Ofsted Inspections: The Early Experience*, eds J Ouston, P Earley and B Fidler, David Fulton Publishers, London, pp 110–25

Ouston, J, Fidler, B and Earley, P (1997) What do schools do after Ofsted inspections – or before? *School Leadership and Management*, **17**, pp 95–104

Pathak, S and Maychell, K (1997) *Planning for Action. Part 2: A Guide to Post-inspection Action Planning*, NFER, Slough

Peatfield, J (1995) Coping or managing: Assisting primary schools to prepare for, manage and exploit the potential of the Ofsted inspection system for internal development through in-service, *Journal of Teacher Development*, **4**, pp 48–52

Russell, S (1994) The 'ah-ha' factor, *Education*, **184**, pp 311, 313

Sharon, H (1996) Back from the brink, *Managing Schools Today*, **5**, pp 12–14

Wragg, E, Haynes, G, Wragg, C and Chamberlin, P (1999) The role of the headteacher (School Principal) in addressing the problem of incompetent teachers. Paper presented to the American Educational Research Association Annual Conference, 19–23 April

Chapter Eleven _____

Ofsted, the Teacher Training Agency and initial teacher education: a case study

Vivienne Griffiths and Angela Jacklin

The authors wish to point out that they are writing here in a personal capacity and do not necessarily represent the views of their institution.

INTRODUCTION

This paper documents one institution's experience of the regime which affected all higher education institutes (HEIs) in the 1990s – Ofsted inspections and the Teacher Training Agency (TTA). In one sense it is an account of one HEI's experience of being 'inspected to death', a term coined rather aptly by Ted Wragg (1997) in relation to the inspection of initial teacher education (ITE).[1] But in another sense it is much more than this, because in addition to the inspections, there is another force for HEIs to contend with: the TTA. Because of the link between assessment of quality and funding allocations, one unsatisfactory grade in an inspection led to a downward spiral and eventual closure of the course.

What happened to Sussex University's Primary Postgraduate Certification in Education (PGCE) course could arguably be seen as a critical case study and will be presented here in that way. A number of factors, in combination, led to the University's eventual withdrawal from primary

ITE. The culture in which initial teacher education is increasingly operating is a punitive, threatened one where individuals and individual institutions, especially those who may be smaller or in a more vulnerable position, do not wish to speak out. Evidence for this may be found in the Universities Council for the Education of Teachers (UCET) documentation where there are frequent requests for anonymity (eg Graham, 1997a). Additionally, as Graham (1998: 26) points out, 'critical debate is dismissed as 'whingeing' disloyalty to a well-intentioned government with fine-sounding principles'.

Throughout this chapter, we will argue firstly that the combination of multiple/constant inspections together with the increasing control and prescription of the TTA, and secondly, the way in which the TTA use inspection findings in their funding formulation, are counter-productive to developing practice and 'raising standards'. We will draw mainly on data from the experiences of the Sussex course to raise questions and issues about what is happening in initial teacher education today. By so doing, we hope that lessons may be learnt and that our experiences may prove helpful to others, especially HEIs. However, we do not claim to present a complete analysis of the current culture in which ITE operates, but to provide evidence in the form of a case study which will contribute to the debate. While arguing in this way, we would also like to stress that at all times individual Ofsted inspectors/Her Majesty's Inspectors (HMIs) were extremely professional: they consistently showed integrity and were helpful and positive. We especially welcomed the restoration of the link HMI role. Our critique is aimed at the current regime, and those responsible for it, not at individual inspectors.

SO WHERE ARE WE NOW IN ITE?

Despite being part of on-going change, far-reaching initiatives in schools, higher education and local education authorities introduced under the Thatcher and Major Governments came to be seen as a 'revolution' in education. Many of these were later taken on and consolidated by the New Left (Maclure, 1998). As changes in initial teacher education were introduced in the 1980s and 1990s, research and critical debates grew (eg Menter and Pollard, 1989; Rudduck, 1989; Welsh, 1992; Miles *et al*, 1993; Furlong *et al*, 1994). Larger-scale projects began to be reported (eg Furlong *et al*'s (1996) Modes of Teacher Education (MOTE) project). By the beginning of the 1990s, the initial teacher education world was used to change, but in the next few years with the creation of Ofsted and the TTA, it was to see something arguably more profound.

The Teacher Training Agency (TTA)

Since its inception in September 1994, the TTA has generated an ever-widening network of initiatives. Starting with initial teacher training, which was generally initially assumed to be its predominant concern (Mahony and Hextall, 1997a), the TTA has moved into almost all spheres of teacher education.

> From recruitment, course accreditation, allocation of student numbers, funding and quality criteria, through to curriculum content, appraisal, national professional qualifications (NPQs) and research, there is no aspect of the occupational and professional lives of teachers which is not affected by the Agency (Mahony and Hextall, 1998: 547).

In addition to this gradually widening net, a further feature of the TTA's mode of operation began to emerge. Many of the initiatives did not appear to be open to professional debate or consultation. Notably Graham (1996a, 1996b, 1997c, 1998) and Kane (1997a, 1997b) strongly critiqued the prescriptive and over-regulatory nature of the TTA. The voice of providers tended to be relayed through fora such as the National Primary Teacher Education Conference (NAPTEC), the Standing Committee for the Education and Training of Teachers (SCETT) and the UCET, because often providers felt unable or unwilling to make individual representations. Graham argued that the TTA's influence in both teaching content and methodology, as well as its control of national teaching qualification structures, was having a deprofessionalizing effect on teachers and creating crises of both teacher morale and recruitment.

The deprofessionalizing effects of the TTA have been taken up by others, specifically in relation to the National Curriculum for Initial Teacher Training (NCITT). For example, Blackledge (1998) strongly critiques the NCITT for both exacerbating and institutionalizing inequality (in relation to literacy acquisition) while Hartley (1998) questions its legitimation and structure, drawing similarities with the National Curriculum in schools. Pointing to the 'technicist' approach which was emerging through this, Richards, Harding and Watt (1997: 6) describe the Initial Teacher Training (ITT) curriculum as having 'the makings of a very useful detailed training manual for would-be-technicians'.

For many people working in the field of teacher education, there are a number of very worrying problems associated with this growing control and prescription. Firstly, its stealth and speed: within five years there is little in teacher education which remains outside the control of the TTA, and its effects have perhaps yet to be fully appreciated or evaluated. Secondly, the degree of centralization and control, and the amount and detail being prescribed: for example, there seems to be little room for manoeuvre or for such things as European schemes like ERASMUS or SOCRATES (Owen, 1997; Graham, 1998). Thirdly, the subtle 'reshaping' of views of 'teachers' and 'teaching' within a culture which has little tolerance for a critically reflective dialogue and lacks transparency of procedure (eg see Mahony and Hextall, 1997a, 1998; Graham 1998). However, there is another part to the equation: Ofsted.

Ofsted

The creation of Ofsted (in 1992), two years before the TTA, brought enormous changes to the nature of education inspections and with this there also came many concerns. Many of these, such as methodological problems and costs, have been well documented (eg Gilroy and Wilcox, 1997; Gray, 1997). Other writers such as Jeffrey and Woods (1996), Woods *et al* (1997) and Ouston, Earley and Fidler (1996) have highlighted the stress on schools caused by inspections. This stress is evident, albeit in different forms, before, during and after the inspection period. It is interesting to consider this stress in relation to the four-stage model of inspections endured by HEIs during the 1996–98 'Primary Follow-up Survey' (PFUS).[2] As the four stages of the inspection were so tightly packed together, periods of 'after' merged instantly into periods of 'before' with little time for relaxation, reflection or action after one stage finished, before preparations for the next stage were begun. Indeed, even during the stages of the inspection themselves, those inspected were often preoccupied with previous and subsequent stages. It is not difficult to appreciate how HEIs felt the inspections actually lasted a whole year.

As well as the constant and concentrated nature of inspections, an important concern for this chapter is that which is also highlighted by Mortimore and Mortimore (1998) – the changing culture of inspections. They argue that the inspection culture is now 'strident and punitive' as opposed to the 'rigorous yet supportive' approach previously adopted by HMI (Mortimore and Mortimore, 1998: 209). This is an important point as we do not wish to argue here against rigorous inspection but feel strongly that this should not be within a punitive culture. As Williams (1997) also advocates, we would argue for a modified return to the former 'improvement through inspection' model.

In a wider critique of the changed role of HMI following the 'Thatcher years', Bolton (1998) highlights subtle yet significant differences in HMI's role and the role of the initial inspections of ITT in the 1980s. In 1984, the Council for the Accreditation of Teacher Education's (CATE) task was to review all ITT courses using criteria put forward by the Secretary of State (generated partly politically and partly by HMI) and make recommendations about accreditation. HMI had firstly to judge the effectiveness of each course as a preparation of new teachers and secondly, once judgements were agreed, to assess courses against the criteria. This meant that judgements could be made on the effectiveness of courses *and* on the degree of usefulness of the criteria (Bolton, 1998: 49–50). Where now are judgements made about the usefulness of criteria?

In relation to schools, Ball (1997) argues against the use of simple labels such as 'good'/'bad', 'successful'/'failing' on the grounds that institutions are inherently complex and paradoxical in nature. The argument is one which could clearly be applied to HEIs. Williams (1997), arguing specifically in relation to ITE, makes the point that different interest groups define quality in different ways. More specifically, fundamental questions have been raised about the methodology applied in recent Ofsted inspections (Tymms, 1997; Wragg, 1997) as well as concerns about the way in which inspections have been carried out (Graham, 1997a; Sutherland, 1997) and their use in the creation of league tables (Williams, 1997; Gilroy, 1998).

We need a professional debate leading to clarity about the purpose of inspections and the use to which data will be put. We believe that it should lead to improvements, the sharing of successes and the celebration of achievements. As Hegarty (1998) has pointed out in relation to schools, there is potential for the collection of valuable information about effectiveness.

We now move to the case study itself to see how these factors were worked out in the Sussex context.

THE CASE STUDY

This section details the experiences of the Sussex PGCE course and provides a summary of the Ofsted inspections carried out from 1995. The data on which it is based come from a wide range of sources in addition to our own experiences. We drew on documentary evidence from the inspections including letters and faxes, as well as records of discussions, meetings and phone calls – detailed notes and records had been kept throughout. In addition, we drew on published material such as circulars and letters from the TTA, Government and Ofsted, as well as, for example UCET publications. We also sought the perspectives of members of the Sussex Consortium: staff from partnership schools and the university teams. Our own attendance at meetings by bodies such as UCET and NAPTEC also provided a forum in which to seek and hear views and experiences of colleagues in other HEIs. Thus, although in no way wishing or attempting to represent the views and perspectives of other HEIS, we feel confident that what we present here will not be unfamiliar to others.

The value and limitations of case study approaches have been well documented. Not only does strength lie in the possibility of richness and detail, but also, important to this chapter, the case study approach allows a focus on a specific situation in order to attempt to uncover and understand processes which brought it about. A corresponding weakness of the approach is the issue of generalizability. We do not attempt to generalize from our experiences, but as indicated above we do hope the findings and issues raised are relatable (Bassey, 1981), and that others will find the opportunity to analyse, record and evaluate their experiences.

The Sussex Experience

The PGCE at Sussex University pioneered school-based teacher education in the late 1960s, and it was the focus of two major research projects in the 1970s and 1980s (Lacey, Hoard and Horton, 1973; Furlong *et al*, 1988). Research about aspects of the course by Sussex PGCE tutors has resulted in numerous publications, from its early years (Lamont, 1972; Lacey, 1977) to more recent developments (Drake and Dart, 1997; Griffiths, Robinson and Willson, 1997). Partnership with local schools has always been a strong feature of the course (Lacey and Lamont, 1975; Griffiths and Owen, 1995), and this was formalized in February 1995 by the launch of the Sussex Consortium for Teacher Education and Research, with Anthea Millett, recently appointed to the TTA, as keynote speaker.

In March 1995, the Sussex Primary PGCE course was one of the first to be inspected by Ofsted as part of what was called the Primary 'sweep' (UCET, 1995). At this point, the course was operating under DES (1989) Circular 24/89, and working towards implementation of DfE (1993) Circular 14/93. By May 1995, the earliest sweep completion date, Ofsted reported that training at Sussex in English, mathematics and assessment was 'sound',[3] but quality assurance (QA) was considered unsatisfactory. The main weaknesses in QA cited by Ofsted were that the university did not audit the school experience closely enough, and that experienced mentors had not been retrained to meet new requirements. Although the Sussex Consortium had been set up earlier that year, new procedures were not yet fully in place. Circular 14/93 was not due to be fully implemented until September 1996. Being inspected in transition between circulars was a key issue for the Sussex course.

A leak to the press about Sussex being 'an unsatisfactory course' appeared in November 1995 (Scott-Clark, 1995). Following this, HMI stressed verbally on several occasions that Ofsted had passed on their grades confidentially to the TTA and had not leaked the information to the press. They also assured the Sussex team that the four areas inspected were assessed as separate elements and that an overall judgement on the course was not being made. Although HMI had also stressed that the training was sound, in December 1995 the TTA notified the University

Vice-Chancellor that withdrawal procedures might be started if the unsat-isfactory QA had a non-compliant element. The week after this letter, the draft inspection report was received from Ofsted.

Receipt of the draft report, which included the first mention of non-compliance by Ofsted, started a process of lengthy negotiations about the wording of the final report. This was mainly because the aspect of QA cited as non-compliant (mentor training) was also praised as good else-where in the draft report. The outcome of the negotiations led to the clar-ification of non-compliance: the eventual wording referred only to the need for the retraining of experienced mentors (Ofsted, 1996a). Immediately after publication of the final report in May 1996, the TTA started the first stages of withdrawal of accreditation procedures.[4] The withdrawal process carried on until August 1996 when the TTA finally accepted a detailed action plan for the Sussex Primary PGCE.

In November–December 1996, QA at Sussex was reinspected by Ofsted and awarded 'good' grades in all five areas covering overall training, management and QA (Ofsted, 1997a). This moved Sussex from an overall 'E' grade (unsatisfactory and non-compliant) into a grade 'C' category. These categories had been introduced by the TTA as part of their funding mechanism. The week after the reinspection, the Vice-Chancellor was informed by the TTA that primary student numbers were to be halved, based on the original sweep inspection results. In spite of protestations in writing and in person by senior members of the University, this decision was upheld. The cut in numbers was implemented in September 1997, two and a half years after the start of the sweep inspection, and nearly a year after the reinspection (see Table 11.1).

The Primary team continued to make substantial improvements to the course, and after the next round of Ofsted inspections, the 'Primary Follow-up Survey' (PFUS) of literacy and numeracy in 1997/8, the Sussex course received seven grade ones and seven grade twos (Ofsted, 1998), and moved into TTA category 'B'. However, direct enquiries to the TTA

Table 11.1   *Target and actual numbers on the Sussex Primary PGCE, 1994–99*

Year	Target	Actual (home)	Overseas	Total
1994/5	55	55	14	69
1995/6	50	49	11	60
1996/7	44	47	4	51
1997/8	22	25	–	25
1998/9	27	25	–	25

suggested that the most the course could hope for was 5 per cent growth in the next round of allocations, rather than the full restoration of pre-1997/8 numbers which had been anticipated.

The course had been under review by the University since the initial cut in numbers was confirmed, and the course team fought hard to retain it. University accountants had calculated that the course would not be viable with fewer than 50 trainees. The course team had already been considerably reduced (from eight staff to four) because of the halved trainee numbers, and from 1997/8 was run predominantly by two members of faculty. In December 1998, the University decided that the cost of running such a small course was too high, given the resourcing of new requirements (DfEE, 1998), and the prospect of four further Primary inspections between 1999–2002. It was decided that the course should close in July 1999.

ISSUES ARISING FROM THE SUSSEX EXPERIENCE

Many factors which face other ITE providers are brought together in the case study of the Sussex Primary PGCE. The issues discussed below have also been raised in fora such as UCET and NAPTEC, and discussed in published articles and papers.

1. Requirements for ITT and the scope for inspections

The constant change in requirements for initial teacher training over the last seven years has led to a major problem for ITE providers, especially when it comes to being inspected (UCET, 1997). The first round of Primary sweep inspections took place in 1995, when Primary courses were operating under DES 24/89 and working towards DfE 14/93. Courses were expected to show how they were working towards partnership criteria, which did not have to be fully in place until September 1996, more than a year after the earliest inspections.

Similarly, on the PFUS, courses were being inspected under circular 14/93, working towards DfEE (1997) circular 10/97 and the introduction of the National Curriculum for ITT. Institutions were concerned about being inadvertently non-compliant (UCET, 1998a) because of the change from competences to standards, and lack of clarity about subject knowledge requirements (Ofsted, 1996b). These concerns were widely voiced at UCET meetings, and at Ofsted/TTA dissemination conferences for Circular 4/98, particularly by BEd providers who were operating under three different circulars: one for each year of the course. ITE providers also raised concerns about how the inspection criteria related to the DfEE circulars (UCET, 1998b).

This inadvertent and seemingly unavoidable non-compliance, because of the change from one circular to the next, was a key issue in relation to the Sussex Primary PGCE sweep inspection. On the one hand, the clause cited in the Ofsted report as the non-compliance issue (re mentor training) came from circular 24/89 (Ofsted, 1996a), yet the course was criticized for not having *re*trained experienced mentors 'to meet their changing roles' (ibid, para 9). The changing role of mentors referred to 'their responsibilities within school-based initial training' (ibid, para. 53) – a circular 14/93 requirement. On the other hand, developments towards circular 14/93 which Sussex was already piloting – a partnership agreement, trainee entitlement and profiling – were acknowledged in the report, but were not judged enough to move the QA grade from unsatisfactory to 'sound' ('shortcomings, if any, balanced by positive features').

The continual change in requirements and the effect this had on courses undergoing almost constant inspections is cited as a major criticism in the UCET evidence on Ofsted to the House of Commons' Select Committee:

> Planning for new curriculum requirements and standards that must be achieved takes place simultaneously as the old requirements are inspected ... Nothing is evaluated before it is changed ... Provision is generally reinspected during the first year of implementing a change under a new framework (UCET, 1998b: 3).

2. Timing of inspections and inspection criteria

The constant changes in criteria for ITT have been paralleled by continuous changes in inspection criteria. The timing of publication of inspection frameworks has almost always been later than the start of the earliest inspections of that particular round (UCET, 1998b), raising questions of equity in relation to judgements made about the first courses to be inspected under a new round. For instance, on the Sussex Primary sweep, the course team were working under draft inspection papers for phase 1, and were handed the final working papers (Ofsted, 1995) at the feedback meeting, a week *after* the end of phase 1. Similarly, the final criteria for institutional self-assessment were not available until after the Sussex sweep inspection had been completed. Although providers inspected early in the Primary sweep were allowed to submit their self-assessments retrospectively, it is questionable whether or how far these were taken into account in the final reports, since the grades had already been awarded. On the Sussex reinspection, the new inspection criteria (Ofsted/TTA, 1996), were published only three days before the first inspection visits, and were faxed to Sussex by the reporting inspector.

The timing of the inspections themselves has also been problematic. Sir Stewart Sutherland, a former HMCI, raises concerns that the 'sweeps' were 'poorly planned and hurriedly performed' (Sutherland, 1997, para

77–80). In the case of Sussex, the two phases of the Primary sweep were very close together (March and May), leaving only two weeks to contact schools once the Easter holiday was excluded. Another provider who had a similarly small gap between phases (UCET, 1995) also received unsatisfactory QA (Ofsted, 1997b). Although it is impossible to substantiate a direct causal link between the two factors, what is clear is that courses with a small gap between phases had little opportunity to make or demonstrate improvements, or adequately to brief schools. The timing of gradings on the PFUS has also been criticized as unduly penalizing some institutions, and an example of faulty methodology (Graham, 1997a).

The difference in timing of sweep inspections for the 67 providers involved (February 1995–July 1996) also meant that some institutions could learn and benefit from the perceived shortcomings of the first courses inspected. This was certainly true for Sussex, where, for example, the findings from the sweep inspection were directly disseminated to other southern region providers through a local network. In turn, the first courses inspected under the PFUS (1996/7) informed HEIs through fora such as UCET/Ofsted seminars about their experiences and concerns, and this could assist those HEIs being inspected in the second round (Graham, 1997a). On this occasion, the Sussex course benefited from the later timing. As Graham asserts:

> This raises the question of fair and consistent treatment between those who have had the advantage of some exemplification in the current round, and those who were working 'in the dark' in the previous inspection (Graham, 1997a: 8).

The timing of the PFUS directly following the sweep inspections has also been widely criticized (eg CVCP, 1996). In their report on the sweep findings, Furlong and Kane (1996) record how the first reference to some 'reinspections' was made in the press as early as June 1996, before the last sweep inspections were complete. Although the draft Ofsted report on the sweep reached 'generally encouraging' conclusions (Kane, 1997a: 3), the views of the Chief Inspector of Schools, Chris Woodhead, prevailed, and the 'reinspection' of a few HEIs was expanded into the PFUS of all Primary PGCE courses. A brief, fairly general, final Ofsted report on the sweep was not published until February 1997, and contained a justification for the PFUS which was already under way (Ofsted, 1997b).

3. Inspection procedures

Criticisms by HEIs of inconsistency, lack of expertise, and confusion between inspectors has been widespread, particularly in relation to the Additional Inspectors (AIs) used in the PFUS (Graham, 1997a; UCET, 1998b). In relation to the sweep, Sir Stewart Sutherland expresses concern that 'some comments [from providers] suggest that HMI inspectors were not familiar with the Framework and consequently, may have allocated gradings on uncertain evidence' (Sutherland, 1997, para 77–80).

In the case of the Sussex sweep, HMI were constructive and helpful; however, some procedures were unhelpful, and questionable in the light of what has later been proposed as good practice (Ofsted/CVCP, 1998). For example, after phase 1, indicative grades were given on all areas except QA. Although weaknesses in QA were mentioned, there was no indication at this stage that there would, or could, be an unsatisfactory grade, especially as all other areas were considered sound. After phase 2, although QA was given an unsatisfactory grade, non-compliance was not mentioned at the feedback, and the first time this appeared was in the draft report. However, by this stage there was no possibility of producing supporting evidence before the final grade was confirmed. This goes directly against current proposed procedures (Ofsted/CVCP, 1998; TTA/Ofsted, 1999).

It must be stressed, as earlier, that this chapter is not intended as a criticism of any individual HMI or additional inspectors (AIs) involved in the Sussex primary inspections. However, because of the timing of the first sweep inspections, procedures and good practice were still being clarified and established. Another crucial factor was that the sweep inspection results were the first to be used by the TTA for funding purposes. The implications of this link for ITE courses were not known and could not have been anticipated by HEIs when HMI reached their first judgements. Even so, questions of equity must be raised when the subsequent application of a rigid funding methodology used by the TTA has had such a drastic effect on the future of some courses.

4. Ofsted/TTA axis

The Ofsted/TTA 'axis of control' (UCET, 1998b: 5), is widely criticized as having a detrimental effect on the quality of teacher education (Mahony and Hextall, 1997b; Sutherland, 1997; UCET 1997; Graham, 1997a). In the summary of findings from an Economic and Social Research Council (ESRC) funded project on the impact of the TTA, Pat Mahony and Ian Hextall point out that 'HEI respondents ... were specifically exercised over the relationships between the TTA and Ofsted and their respective roles and jurisdictions' (Mahony and Hextall, 1997b, p. 7).

Two main areas of concern are cited in published critiques: firstly and centrally, the link between assessment of quality in ITE and funding allocations. As Newby stresses:

> a government policy which links quality judgements to the allocation of numbers and the funding of institutions ... sets in train an entirely different set of resonances about punitive measures, about working not to train and

educate teachers but to make sure we get through the latest set of hurdles (Newby in UCET, 1997, 15).

UCET's evidence to the House of Commons' Select Committee on Ofsted also cites the 'fear of failure' (UCET, 1998b: 4) associated with the possible withdrawal of accreditation from an institution as a whole resulting from *one* unsatisfactory element of an inspection of *one* particular course. This was the situation faced by Sussex and other HEIs after the sweep and by other institutions after the PFUS. UCET argues that there should be a return to the former HMI model of improvement through inspection rather than such a punitive model. The Sussex experience shows that it is also because the TTA have applied their funding methodology both retrospectively and inflexibly that a 'downward spiral' (Ofsted/UCET, 1998) can result.

A second area of concern is the apparent lack of communication between Ofsted and TTA, which can be experienced as a major problem by providers. It can sometimes seem to HEIs that each agency is playing one off against the other. As UCET (1998b) stresses, HEIs feel that they are caught in the middle of this tension or pincer movement. During the sweep inspections, the tension probably resulted from a genuine lack of knowledge on Ofsted's part as to how the TTA would use their results.

In Sussex's case, lack of communication and contradictions between the two agencies were manifest in several different ways. Firstly, the leak of information to the press about unsatisfactory provision after the sweep caused considerable concern among HMI, who stressed verbally that Ofsted had passed on inspection results confidentially to the TTA. In turn, the TTA vehemently denied in writing that the leak could have come from them.

Secondly, contradictory messages were given during the withdrawal of accreditation process. On the one hand, communications with senior members of Ofsted's teacher training division were reassuring. HMI asserted that weaknesses in QA at Sussex were mainly procedural, not endemic to the training, and also stressed their confidence that improvements would be in place before the full implementation of 14/93, and that the reinspection would only need to be a light touch. On the other hand, communications with the TTA were at the other extreme, with hints that the unsatisfactory provision might be much deeper ('the tip of the iceberg') and that a full reinspection might, therefore, be needed. The stress and confusion that these contradictions caused were considerable, and exacerbated further by a lack of clear information, for example no jointly agreed Ofsted/TTA guidelines for drawing up an action plan.

Thirdly, tensions and poor communication between Ofsted and the TTA were also apparent before the reinspection of QA at Sussex. In the run up to the reinspection, the possible requirements ranged from HMI inspecting only overall training and QA and visiting a minimum of two schools, to a full reinspection over six months on a similar scale to the original sweep. It was clear that pressure for a more wide-ranging inspection was coming from the TTA. In the end, HMI confirmed that the TTA required the grades for Sussex before Christmas 1996, and a compromise was reached about the scope of the inspection, with two concentrated phases over two weeks and visits to six schools. The assumption that the TTA would use the good reinspection results positively was dashed when student numbers were halved the following week. Contacts with other HEIs also undergoing reinspection confirmed similar mixed messages and confusion.

5. Costs

As well as criticisms of the model itself, the costs associated with Ofsted/TTA's assessment of quality and changing requirements for ITT are extremely high (Kane, 1997a). UCET's report to the House of Commons' Select Committee (UCET, 1998b) estimates the average cost per institution of the PFUS at £35,000. A log of time spent on the PFUS at Sussex showed an average of two days a week each throughout the year for the director of PGCE and Primary co-ordinator, with full weeks during the actual inspection visits which amounted to 30 inspector days. With Secondary PGCE inspections added in, the total time when the Sussex PGCE programme was being inspected during 1997/8 was 15 weeks out of 38; the average cited for HEIs was 13 weeks (UCET, 1998b).

The costs of inspections fall particularly heavily on small courses (Graham, 1997b; UCET, 1997b), which have to meet the same requirements whether there are 25 trainees or 250. Graham stresses that the core team bear the main brunt of the inspection pressures, time involved in writing policy documents and meeting new requirements. He also asserts that 'significant management costs are triggered by the extent and unnecessarily compressed rate of change. These are compounded by the problems of implementation across complex partnership arrangements' (Graham, 1997b: 19). Graham argues that there should be a fundamental review of inspections in the light of costs incurred, that additional demands for QA should be matched by additional funding, and that inspection frequency should be reduced (ibid).

6. Damage to reputation and morale

As well as financial costs, the personal costs of the inspection load are high and the pressures involved in constant inspections have led to stress and ill health (Graham, 1997b; UCET, 1998b). The punitive results of even one unsatisfactory element in an inspection have led to low morale among ITE course teams. This was confirmed by contact with other HEIs facing possible withdrawal procedures after the sweep and the first round of the PFUS, who reported the devastating effect that such a situation could have on morale. As Tim Brighouse (1999) outlined at a recent NAPTEC conference, in a compliance culture low self-esteem can give rise to lowered expectations, which can lead to further failure. At Sussex, it was difficult to sustain motivation in the face of possible closure, but support from partnership schools and from our link HMI raised the team's self-confidence and made us even more determined to succeed.

Damage to course reputations through media coverage, equivalent to the 'naming and shaming' of schools, also exacerbated the pressure. At Sussex, this started with the *Sunday Times* article (Scott-Clark, 1995) which contained leaked and incomplete information about certain courses and led to a single 'unsatisfactory' label which was then perpetuated in other subsequent articles. Press coverage of the Primary sweep was widespread and uncritical in its presentation of information about inspection results and the possible withdrawal of accreditation or closure of courses. It is interesting to note that more recent newspaper reports about the PFUS results have taken a rather different tone, containing critical reactions from HEIs, and the mention of possible legal action against Ofsted and the TTA (eg Gardiner, 1997).

At Sussex, repercussion from the press coverage, and also from information leaked through the local network of HEIs, led to rumours abounding in partnership schools about possible closure of the Primary PGCE from the time of the sweep inspection (1995) onwards. This was not helpful to students on school placements, and was most upsetting to course tutors. Much time had to be spent in countering the rumours and disseminating subsequent successful Ofsted inspection results to schools. Now that the course is actually to close, more time is having to be spent in ensuring that schools know that the closure is for financial reasons resulting from the TTA methodology, despite our recent Ofsted successes.

A further aspect of the current climate is its competitiveness, exemplified by the TTA performance tables and competition between providers for scarce student numbers. In some respects, the effects of this have paralleled what has happened in schools in relation to competition and league tables. One result for HEIs is that in some cases, those who were formerly open with each other have become more wary and mistrustful, rather than being able to work together for mutual improvement. This undermining of professional relationships may take a long time to repair.

CONCLUSION

In the above account we have identified a number of issues which are exemplified in the Sussex case study, but which have also been experienced by other ITE providers. Paramount among these are the problems caused by the coupling of judgements about quality with funding allocations, and the Ofsted/TTA axis of control.

If positive lessons are to be drawn from the Sussex experience, then recommendations for change need to be put forward. Firstly, there is a need for ministers, the DfEE and the leaders of the TTA and Ofsted to take responsibility, rather than attribute blame, for the culture pervading initial teacher education at present. In addition, they need to work towards creating a culture of co-operation and genuine consultation with colleagues in HEIs, rather than the coercive and punitive one which pervades at present. It is to be hoped that the proposed General Teaching Council may be able to provide what the TTA does not currently seem able to do.

Secondly, there is also a need for a learning culture based on rigorous and informative inspection evidence, coupled with institutional self-evaluation, rather than the flawed system which operated with the recent inspections of initial teacher education. We would share the call (Graham, 1997b; UCET, 1998b) for an inspection cycle of reduced frequency to allow HEIs time for consolidation and review, and along similar lines to that for the rest of higher education.

Thirdly, we would like to build on the suggestions for ministers that Mortimore and Mortimore (1998) put forward in their argument that conflict between 'the political and the professional' need not exist in education. They make three suggestions: that there be a focus on teachers' achievements; that ways are found of consulting with professionals and allowing some flexibility; and that trust in professionals is restored and initiatives encouraged. We believe this must also happen in initial teacher education. The recent moves made by Ofsted and the Committee of Vice-Chancellors in holding joint meetings and drawing up working papers in consultation with ITE providers, (Ofsted/CVCP, 1998) are encouraging for the future.

ACKNOWLEDGEMENTS

In addition to those contributors who wish or need to remain anonymous, the authors would like to extend particular thanks to Professors Colin Lacey and Colin Richards for their helpful comments on an earlier draft of this paper.

NOTES

1. We believe in the term 'initial teacher education' (ITE) and will use it in this chapter unless referring to government/TTA directives where the term 'initial teacher training' (ITT) is used.
2. The PFUS was the second round of inspections of Primary ITT. It focused on the inspection of training in literacy and numeracy. The first round of inspections occurred in 1994/6 and was known as the 'primary sweep'. That focused on English, mathematics, assessment and quality assurance.
3. Grades awarded in the Sweep inspections were on a four-point scale: very good; good; sound and unsatisfactory.
4. All providers of ITT are statutorily required to be accredited. Withdrawal of accreditation refers to the institution as a whole, not just to a single course, ie in Sussex University's case, accreditation for the Secondary PGCE as well as the Primary course, could have been withdrawn (TTA, 1995).

REFERENCES

Ball, S (1997) Good school bad school: paradox and fabrication, *British Journal of Sociology of Education*, **18**, pp 317–336.

Bassey, M (1981) Pedagogic research: on the relative merits of search for generalization and study of single events, *Oxford Review of Education*, **7**, pp 73–93.

Blackledge, A (1998) The institutionalisation of inequality: the Initial Teacher Training National Curriculum for Primary English as cultural hegemony, *Educational Review*, **50**, pp 55–64.

Bolton, E (1998) HMI – the Thatcher Years, *Oxford Review of Education*, **24**, pp 45–55

Brighouse, T (1999) The future of teacher education, paper presented to NAPTEC Annual Conference, St Hugh's College, Oxford, March

CVCP (1996) Letter to Chris Woodhead, 30 October

Drake, P and Dart, L (1997) Different perceptions of teacher competence: trainees and their mentors, in eds A Hudson and D Lambert, *Exploring Futures in Initial Teacher Education*, Bedford Way Papers, Institute of Education, University of London, 333–46

DES (1989) *Initial Teacher Training: Approval of Courses, Circular 24/89*, HMSO, London

DfE (1993) *The Initial Training of Primary School Teachers: New Criteria for Schools, Circular 14/93*, HMSO, London

DfEE (1997) *Teaching: High Quality. High Standards, Circular 10/97*, HMSO, London

DfEE (1998) *Teaching: High Quality, High Standards, Circular 4/98*, HMSO, London

Furlong, VJ, Hirst, PH, Pocklington, K and Miles, S (1988) *Initial Teacher Training and the Role of the School*, Open University Press, Milton Keynes

Furlong, J, Whitty, G, Barrett, E, Barton, L and Miles, S (1994) Integration and partnership in initial teacher education – dilemmas and possibilities, *Research Papers in Education*, **9**, pp 281–301.

Furlong, H, Whitty, G, Whiting, C, Miles, S, Barton, L and Barrett, E (1996) Redefining partnership: revolution or reform in initial teacher education? *Journal of Education for Teaching*, **22**, pp 39–55

Furlong, J and Kane, I (1996) Recognising quality in Primary initial teacher education: findings from the 1995/6 Ofsted Primary 'Sweep', UCET occasional paper no. 6.

Gardiner, J (1997) Second wave of inspectors claim their first casualty, *TES*, 12 December

Gilroy, P (1998) New Labour and teacher education in England and Wales: the first 500 days, *Journal of Education for Teaching*, **24**, pp 221–30

Gilroy, P and Wilcox, B (1997) Ofsted, criteria and the nature of social understanding: a Wittgensteinian critique of the practice of educational judgement, *British Journal of Educational Studies*, **45**, pp 22–38

Graham, J (1996a) The Teacher Training Agency, continuing professional development policy and the definition of competences for serving teachers, *British Journal of In-service Education*, **22**, pp 121–32

Graham, J (1996b) Closing the circle: research, critical reflection and the National Curriculum for teaching training, *Higher Education Review*, **29**, pp 33–56.

Graham, J (1997a) Initial Teacher Education: *TTA/Ofsted quality framework – a critique*, UCET occasional paper no. 9

Graham, J (1997b) Initial Teacher Education: *TTA/Ofsted quality framework – the costs*, UCET occasional paper no 9

Graham, J (1997c) The National Curriculum for teacher training: playing politics or promoting professionalism? *British Journal of In-service Education*, **23**, pp 163–77

Graham, J (1998) From New Right to New Deal: nationalism, globalisation and the regulation of teacher professionalism, *British Journal of In-service Education*, **24**, pp 9–29

Gray, J (1997) A bit of a curate's egg? Three decades of official thinking about the quality of schools, *British Journal of Educational Studies*, **45**, pp 4–21.

Griffiths, V and Owen, P (eds) (1995) *Schools in Partnership: Current Initiatives in School-Based Teacher Education*, Paul Chapman, London

Griffiths, V, Robinson, C and Willson, M (1997) Evaluation of a developmental profile in initial teacher education: towards a common entitlement, in *Exploring Futures in Initial Teacher Education*, eds A Hudson and D Lambert, Bedford Way Papers, Institute of Education, University of London, 378–90

Hartley, D (1998) Repeat prescription: the National Curriculum for initial teacher training, *British Journal of Educational Studies*, **46**, pp 68–83

Hegarty, S (1998) Research and Inspection: untidy bedfellows, *Journal of Education for Teaching*, **24**, pp 259–60

Jeffrey, B and Woods, P (1996) Feeling deprofessionalised: the social construction of emotions during Ofsted inspection, *Cambridge Journal of Education*, **26**, pp 325–44

Kane, I (1997a) The future of teacher education, paper presented to NAPTEC Annual Conference, St Hugh's College, Oxford, April

Kane, I (1997b) The TTA and teacher training: a retrospective and prospective critique, paper presented at SCETT Seminar, London, 12 June

Lacey, C (1977) *The Socialization of Teachers*, Methuen, London

Lacey, C, Hoard, P and Horton, M (1973) *The Tutorial Schools Research Project 1964–73*, Social Science Research Council

Lacey, C and Lamont, W (1975) Partnership with Schools: An Experiment in Teacher Education, occasional paper no 5, University of Sussex Education Area

Lamont, W (ed) (1972) *The Realities of Teaching History: Beginnings*, Chatto & Windus/Sussex University Press

Maclure, S (1998) Through the revolution and out the other side, *Oxford Review of Education*, **24**, pp 5–24

Mahony, P and Hextall, I (1997a) Problems of accountability in reinvented Government: a case study of the Teacher Training Agency, *Journal of Education Policy*, **12**, pp 267–83

Mahony, P and Hextall I (1997b) *The Policy Context and Impact of the Teacher Training Agency, Summary of ESRC Project Findings*, Roehampton Institute

Mahony, P and Hextall, I (1998) Social justice and the reconstruction of teaching, *Journal of Education Policy*, **13**, pp 545–58

Menter, I and Pollard, A (1989) The implications of the National Curriculum for reflective practice in initial teaching education, *Westminster Studies in Education*, **12**, pp 31–42.

Miles, S, Barrett, E, Barton, L, Furlong, J and Whitty, G (1993) Initial teacher education in England and Wales: a topography, *Research Papers in Education*, **8**, pp 275–304

Mortimore, P and Mortimore, J (1998) The political and professional in education: an unnecessary conflict? *Journal of Education for Teaching*, **24**, pp 205–19

Ofsted (1995) *Working Papers for the Inspection of Primary Initial Teacher Training*, Ofsted, London

Ofsted (1996a) *University of Sussex Primary Initial Teacher Training*, ref 35/96/ITTP, Ofsted, London

Ofsted (1996b) Action points arising from meeting between Ofsted and representatives from the Teaching Training Sectors on 17 December, Ofsted, London

Ofsted (1997a) *University of Sussex Primary Initial Teacher Training*, ref 34/97/ITTP, Ofsted, London

Ofsted (1997b) *Primary Initial Teacher Training 1995/6*, Ofsted, London

Ofsted (1998) *Primary Initial Teacher Training Partnership based on University of Sussex: Initial Training of Primary School Teachers to Teach Number and Reading*, ref 185/98/ITTP, Ofsted, London

Ofsted/TTA (1996) *Framework for the Assessment of Quality and Standards in Initial Teacher Training 1996/7*, Ofsted, London

Ofsted/CVCP (1998) *Working together in initial teacher education and training: making inspection work*, draft paper, Ofsted/CVCP

Ofsted/UCET (1998) Minutes of joint meeting between Ofsted and UCET, 1 January

Ouston, J, Earley, P and Fidler, B (eds) (1996) *Ofsted Inspections: The Early Experience*, David Fulton, London

Owen, P (1997) Looking beyond a 'National' Curriculum: some thoughts on ways to develop an international component in Initial Teacher Training, paper for the International Day Conference on Teacher Professionalism and the State: some key questions in framing a National Curriculum for Teacher Training. London, 8 October

Richards, C, Harding, P and Webb, D (1997) *A Key Stage 6 Core Curriculum? A Critique of the National Curriculum for Initial Teacher Training*, Association of Teachers and Lecturers, London

Rudduck, J (1989) Practitioner research and programmes of initial teacher education, *Westminster Studies in Education*, **12**, pp 61–72

Scott-Clark, C (1995) Grading scheme will weed out failing teachers, *Sunday Times*, 19 November

Sutherland, S (1997) National Committee of Inquiry into Higher Education, *Higher Education in the Learning Society*, (The Dearing Report) Report 10, Teacher Education and Training: A Study, HMSO, London

TTA (1995) *Procedures for the Withdrawal of Institutional Accreditation and Mechanisms for a Request for Reconsideration*, TTA, London

TTA/Ofsted (1999) *Procedures to be followed in cases where non-compliance is found in the 1998/99 inspection programme*, April, TTA, London

Tymms, P (1997) The security of inspection of Initial Teacher Training, Education-line site http://www.leeds.ac.uk/educol

UCET (1995) Primary Sweep, UCET, London

UCET (1997) The role of universities in the education and training of teachers, Seminar, Institute of Education, London, February, UCET occasional paper no. 8, p 15

UCET (1998a) *Annual Report 1998*, UCET, London

UCET (1998b) *UCET Evidence to the House of Commons' Select Committee*, UCET, London

Welsh, GF (1992) When will they ever learn? Trends and issues in initial teacher education in the United Kingdom, *Teacher Educator*, **27**, pp 33–46

Williams, A (1997) Quality assessment in initial teacher education: lessons from the 1993/94 Ofsted experience, *Higher Education Quarterly*, **51**, pp 189–200

Woods, P, Jeffrey, B, Troman, G and Boyle, M (1997) *Restructuring Schools, Restructuring Teachers*, Open University Press, Buckingham

Wragg, T (1997) View From Here, *The Independent*, 4 December

Chapter Twelve _____

Conclusion – a modest proposal for the improvement of the school inspection system in England and Wales

Cedric Cullingford

The Government's laudable intention to raise standards in schools rests on clear measurable targets. It is widely recognized what all schools and all teachers are required to achieve. The targets are very clear and the timetable for success emphatically laid down. It is, of course, imperative for the Department for Education and Employment (DfEE) to state what is to be learnt and how all subjects are to be taught, to put forward clear guidelines for initial teaching training and for every detail of the delivery of the curriculum, but the success of these policies needs to be carefully measured. This is why inspection is such an important part of the Government's strategy.

An inspection system ensures that all people operating within the public sector, or in regulated industries, are fully accountable. Any failure to meet the set targets or to carry out the Governments intentions should be fully and publicly exposed.

The policy of naming and shaming schools and teachers depends on clear and constant scrutiny, not just of results but of the daily practices, of all that takes place in schools. The Office for Standards in Education (Ofsted) is the most vital element in the Government's education policy.

The remit for Ofsted is perfectly clear. It inspects, in detail, all State schools. It reports all its findings, exposing schools that are failing and teachers who are no longer performing as well as they should. With far more detail than league tables, Ofsted scrutinizes exactly what takes place in schools. It has a clear system that is rigid and controlled, treating each school in the same way. It reports its findings not only to the central Government, amassing a wealth of detail about how it sees schools perform, but makes most of these findings public. Governors and parents and the local community are in no doubt about the performance of the schools.

There are many indications of the success of this policy. Schools which are failing are exposed. Weak local authorities are unearthed. The possibility of them being taken over is promoted. Poor head-teachers are forced to resign. Teams of specialists are appointed to knock underachieving schools back into shape. Above all, no one is in doubt of the concern for higher standards and the failure of teachers to meet them.

And yet we constantly hear criticism of the efficacy of such a system. The Chief Inspector of Schools feels that Ofsted is being 'demonized', fearing that there is a conspiracy to undermine the system by those who are exposed by it or who are threatened by it. Naturally, not all people wish to be held to account, to be deservedly criticized in the press and by inspectors. The exposure of failure is not always welcome. Perhaps it is a natural reaction for people to blame the very agency that makes the accusation, as if there could be any excuse for failure.

Despite its laudable intentions there are possible reasons why there should be doubts about the Ofsted system. It is open and public. It warns schools well in advance that a team of inspectors will be coming. It demands a very comprehensive and detailed set of documentation. It ensures that all teachers concentrate for months on the coming inspection. It makes sure that the lessons seen will be carefully planned and that all the necessary policy decisions are clearly made and exposed.

Those who criticize Ofsted do so because the system seems overformal and unnatural. They argue that what is being measured is artificial and not a true reflection on the more intimate daily realities of learning. The teachers are all seen to perform to the publicly stated targets that Ofsted provides. The curriculum and the teaching styles conform to the government's demands at least during the inspection. But what happens when the inspectors are not there?

The great problem for Ofsted is that its inspections are not constant. The schools are forewarned. They can prepare themselves every four years. They learn how to gear themselves to what Ofsted demands. They become experienced with coping with inspection. One could argue that this is a sign of Ofsted's success, that schools are adapting to the targets.

While the number of schools blamed and shamed is increasing rather than diminishing this is because its targets and its standards are constantly rising. The possibility of extending this exposure of failure should never be eschewed.

But there are still lingering doubts about what schools are doing between inspection. Are they then reverting to bad habits? Are they acquiring presentational skills to cope with the inspectors? Are they allowing children to learn matters outside the National Curriculum? Do their teaching styles not conform to guidelines? Do they not follow the literacy hour to the minute?

While it may be desirable for Ofsted inspections to be constant, so that every school can be monitored on a daily basis, this would be impossible, on purely financial terms. That there should be a constant supply of inspectors, especially lay inspectors, eager to be involved, and that this would be a most perfect outcome, might be true but the Treasury would no doubt baulk at the idea. After all, for every inspector there needs to be someone to whom he or she is accountable. The system of collecting and collating information centrally is as important as its gathering, so an expansion in the number of inspectors would lead to an equal need for a larger and more powerful DfEE and all its many agencies. While it is tempting for the Department to fulfil its own title by massive recruitment this would not be feasible in the Treasury's eyes.

If Ofsted inspections cannot be constant and if they are too open and formal in their operation what could be done to help? The beleaguered Chief Inspectors need as much clear and accurate information as they can get. They need to know exactly what goes on in schools and exactly how each individual teacher is adhering to the National Curriculum. It is only by a constant exposure to every part of every lesson that they will know when targets are not being met, and the timetables for the delivery of the curriculum are slipping. The question is how they can gather this vital information?

I have learnt from some of the highest authorities in other countries that there is a clear and cost-effective solution to this problem. In certain well-ordered countries the education system is not only clearly laid out but is also properly controlled.

A successful inspection system needs to cover the full range of methods of assessment. While the results of tests are the most important factor, the means of recovering these results should also be constantly evaluated. This implies that all teachers should not only be reflecting on their practice but be under observation. Nothing is more useful than the sharing of best practice. The government's laudable intention is that the best practice should be manifested everywhere in a consistent and effective manner. Schools should be always accountable for their efficiency.

So, in order to achieve the necessary standards teachers need to be monitored on a daily basis. How can this be done?

Having a known inspector on a visit to a school can make a temporary difference to the performance of a teacher, but how can inspectors be sure that the performance adheres to the guidelines when the inspector is not there? What is really going on in the teacher's mind? Is he or she fully committed to the achievement of the latest targets?

The only way to detect and evaluate the actual performance of schools and teachers is to do so when they are not aware of it. Much of the information that Ofsted gathers could well be contaminated by the fact that it depends on only a moment in time; a 'snapshot' of it is gathered in conditions where the teacher is consciously performing to expectation. It is far more revealing to know what is actually happening when the teacher is unaware that he or she is being inspected.

The most valuable information that Ofsted can gather is that which explores individual teachers, and even individual lessons. How else can standards be improved? This means that every school should have their own inspectors, monitoring and reporting on all that is going on. It is, of course, crucial that the inspectors should not be known. How else can they carry out their role objectively? The confidential nature of the role would not only have the advantage of the evidence being objective, but it will improve the daily performance of all teachers, since they would not know when they are being inspected. The inspectors would need to keep an eye on all the teachers, all the time, just in case.

The authorities who have made such a system of inspection work would suggest that a proportion of between 10 per cent and 20 per cent of all staff in an institution should be such State inspectors.

Confidentiality is vital so it is necessary to have just such a proportion that makes it possible for any colleague to be an inspector, while not having too many for fear than they may be tempted to talk to each other. It is vital that all communication must be with Ofsted itself.

The communications between its state inspectors and the central office are very important. Information should be passed on a weekly basis, not just waiting for an unfortunate lapse to be exposed, but making sure the individual files are constantly kept up to date. It is impossible to anticipate failure. It could come at any time.

The result of information gathered in this way would greatly strengthen the power of Ofsted. The Chief Inspector would be able to call on detailed evidence, far wider and deeper than that on which he now relies on. His statements about the proportions of poor teachers should have all the credibility of the constant monitoring, of every teacher in the land. His pronouncements about failing schools would carry even more weight. There could be no more doubt about the importance of his message.

The inspectors themselves would find this constant reporting rewarding and interesting. Without exposing themselves to the reactions of their colleagues they would be directly helping the State in its fulfilment of its mission. The would help raise standards by exposing those who fail to meet targets. They would be able to keep Ofsted fully aware of all that is going on.

Such a delicate role would, of course, need careful training. One of the prime functions of Ofsted would demonstrate how information can be gathered without colleagues being aware of it, how to note down conversations not meant for the public, how to detect what teachers really think and what they are telling their pupils. It is not an easy matter to learn how to be an undercover inspector. It is a matter of great delicacy. But it can be learnt and has been learnt by other societies in the recent past. It is, of course, essential that none of the inspectors know which of their colleagues are carrying out the same important task.

Such a system of inspection would also meet the requirements of equal opportunities. All kinds of people in a school, not only teachers, could be inspectors. The system could easily be extended to parents as well as governors. Keeping the proportion of those involved at about 10 per cent to 20 per cent would ensure that there would be plenty of choice to pick out the most suitable and dedicated to fulfil this secretly prestigious task.

Such a system of inspection would meet all the requirements of the Government, without an undue demand on the public purse. It is recommended to Ofsted in its praiseworthy desire to raise standards by setting targets and making sure those targets are met. The sooner such a system of inspection is introduced the better.

After the careful, measured tone of this book, such satire might come as a surprise. Worse still, it might not even be noticed as satire. Satire depends on being plausible enough to be almost taken seriously. Such an account of the intentions and motivations Ofsted has, after all, at least a veneer of the actuality of its circumstances. Even the first paragraph makes bland assertions of the kind that on closer scrutiny are very questionable. Does raising standards really depend on targets? Is it imperative for the Government to say exactly what is to be learnt and how? Are teachers really 'rude mechanicals' imposing the official will?

Ofsted is at one level a world, a system in itself. One might question the motivations of those who join such a system, but not all motivations are bad. Inspectors learn about schools and the more sensitive feel they can at least mitigate the excesses by joining the party rather than helplessly criticizing from outside.

Ofsted is, however, also a small part of a far greater cultural system, of assessment and control. It is a symbol of what has become a general governmental strategy towards education, with central directives which go into immense detail and with a clear idea of exactly what should take place. The education system is not the only area in which outcomes are carefully measured. The question remains which is of more importance;

the measurement, with the impact on outcomes, or the outcomes themselves?

One of the conclusions one must reach is whether the idea of target setting coupled with inspection is the only way to improve standards. We know all the research evidence that demonstrates that a climate of fear and stress reduces performance. We also know that standards of achievement are not rising, and that exclusions and truancies multiply. The question is whether the two are connected.

Another conclusion must be the question of the costs of such a system. In the 'modest proposal' one of the ostensible arguments for secret inspections, as in Communist Europe, was that of cost. The present system is very expensive. If all those agencies of educational control and inspection, from the Teacher Training Agency (TTA) to Ofsted were abolished, the savings would be such that thousands of extra teachers could be employed. Whether they would be recruited is another matter. The impression given to the public about teaching is such that it is increasingly difficult to find people willing to enter a profession so constantly vilified. To be fair to the Government agencies every negative remark about teachers has a commensurate advertisement attempting to attract would-be recruits. But the money spent on the positive is such a small proportion to that spent on the negative, one has to question whether it is worth doing it all.

The question of cost effectiveness does, however, raise other issues. The harassment and damage done to teachers and, therefore, pupils is pursued relentlessly and with relish in the mass media. News is by most definitions 'bad'. It is shocking. It goes against the expected norms but the enthusiams with which the negative messages of Ofsted are passed on are quite astonishing. While parents might have their own experience and perception of what is happening one must question the effects of such a quantity of bad publicity. Is there something in our society that is so deeply biased against education that any disparagement is to be pursued? The impression, based on carefully contrived anecdotes, is powerful. The imagery used is telling and mechanistic. What is conveyed in the general press is the sense of the lazy and incompetent, rather than the hard-working and dedicated teacher. This could either be a deliberate, deprofessionalizing process turning teachers into craftspeople fulfilling instructions, or an unfortunate and accidental by-product of the constant presentation of the kind of sensational headlines that the press seek out.

Schools were once assessed as being secret gardens, of doing things their own way, without accountability. Teachers taught what they knew best, and in their own way. There was a sense that not all children received the same treatment, that not all schools were alike: indeed some schools (and teachers) were better than others. Now we have, instead, a world of secret judgements rather than secret gardens. All is observed and accounted for. The inspectors pass on information, schools and departments are praised or dammed, sometimes accidentally and sometimes arbitrarily. While the system depends on accountability, inspection itself is rarely under scrutiny. In the past, for all the enclosures of classrooms, teachers were, in fact, accountable, to their pupils first and foremost and to their peers and parents. Strengths and limitations were well known. But it sometimes seems that the accountability has been turned away from pupils. Limitations are exposed. Strengths are no longer permitted.

The question that underlies all others in the book is whether Ofsted is successful, within its own terms. The Commons Select Committee and the National Audit Office have their doubts. The evidence presented here suggests that the answer is clear. Ofsted lowers standards. Indeed, the possibility of long-term damage to the pupils' academic and social abilities is immense. But Ofsted is part of an outlook. No one would disagree with the discrete raising of standards. But the very language used to describe the means of doing so reminds us of the medieval torture chamber. Look up the terms used and in the literature and they could be read as a design manual for the Rack.

Whilst there are questions about personalities and personal styles, these are ephemeral. The real underlying question in these studies is how a society goes about the business of education. Some directives might seem plausible and some attractive. But what really works is more complex than a directive. The system within which Ofsted operates is one that is premised on the notion that orders results in sections as people must be made to be obedient to those orders and that if they fulfill what is expected, then all will be better. It is this outlook, that is of the *apparatchik*, that needs to be questioned.

Index

Visit Kogan Page on-line

Comprehensive information on
Kogan Page titles

Features include

- complete catalogue listings,
  including book reviews and
  descriptions

- on-line discounts on a variety
  of titles

- special monthly promotions

- information and discounts on
  NEW titles and BESTSELLING titles

- a secure shopping basket facility
  for on-line ordering

- infoZones, with links and
  information on specific areas of
  interest

PLUS everything you need to know
about KOGAN PAGE

http://www.kogan-page.co.uk